CAMBRIDGE UNIVERSITY PRESS

CAMBRIDGE ENG
Language Assessment
Part of the University of Cambridge

CW00722117

Cambridge English

OFFICIAL
PREPARATION MATERIAL

Louis Rogers
Series Editor: Annette Capel

Prepare!
TEACHER'S BOOK
Level 7

Cambridge University Press
www.cambridge.org/elt

Cambridge English Language Assessment
www.cambridgeenglish.org

Information on this title: www.cambridge.org/9780521180399
© Cambridge University Press and UCLES 2015

First published 2015

Printed in Poland by Opolgraf

A catalogue record for this publication is available from the British Library

ISBN 978-0-521-8036-8 Student's Book
ISBN 978-1-107-49801-3 Student's Book and Online Workbook
ISBN 978-1-107-49800-6 Student's Book and Online Workbook with Testbank
ISBN 978-0-521-18038-2 Workbook with Audio
ISBN 978-0-521-18039-9 Teacher's Book with DVD and Teacher's Resources Online
ISBN 978-0-521-18042-9 Class Audio CDs
ISBN 978-1-107-49798-6 Presentation Plus DVD-ROM

Teacher's resources, including progress and achievement tests, worksheets for the
video and additional teaching activities at www.cambridge.org/prepareresources

Contents

Introduction to *Prepare!*

Where English meets Exams

Prepare! is a lively new seven-level English course for teenagers. It takes learners from A1 to B2 and has comprehensive Cambridge English exam preparation throughout. So whether you're teaching general English or preparing students for an exam, *Prepare!* has a wealth of material to help you do both.

Produced and endorsed by Cambridge English Language Assessment, using cutting edge language learning research from English Vocabulary Profile and the Cambridge Learner Corpus, *Prepare!* is a course you can rely on and trust.

Prepare! is written by a team of writers with extensive experience and knowledge of secondary school students as well as in-depth knowledge of the Cambridge exams.

The Student's Book

The Student's Book includes 20 short units, covering a wider variety of teen-related topics than other courses. After every two units, there is either a culture or cross-curricular lesson which encourages students to learn about the world around them or about other subject areas through English. After every four units, there is a review section which revises and consolidates the language from the previous four units through further practice of key language and skills.

There are ten videos of authentic interviews with teenagers which are included with this Teacher's Book and worksheets to go with them are provided online.

At the back of the book, students will find a grammar reference section, with further practice activities to be used in class or as self-study. Vocabulary lists provide useful lists of all the key vocabulary taught in each unit, together with its pronunciation and definition.

● Exam preparation

CEFR	Cambridge English Scale	Level	Cambridge English Exam
B2	160–179	7	Cambridge English: First for Schools
		6	
B1	140–159	5	Cambridge English: Preliminary for Schools
		4	
A2	120–139	3	Cambridge English: Key for Schools
		2	
A1	100–119	1	

Level 1 covers A1. The remaining six levels are split into pairs – Levels 2 and 3 cover A2, Levels 4 and 5 cover B1 and levels 6 and 7 cover B2. The first book in each pair gradually exposes students to typical exam tasks and techniques, while the second book in each pair makes exam tasks more explicit, thereby preparing students more thoroughly for the relevant exam. All exam tasks in Levels 2–7 are clearly referenced in the Teacher's Book.

In addition to regular practice of each exam task in the main units, Level 3, Level 5 and Level 7 have five additional *Exam profile* sections, which are located at the back of the Student's Book. These pages focus on each part of each paper, giving detailed information about the exam task, as well as practical guidance on how to approach each task, with useful tips and training to familiarise students with the whole exam and prepare them thoroughly for examination day.

The *Exam profiles* can be used as focused training after first exposure to an exam task in the main units, or alternatively towards the end of the year when students require more intensive exam practice.

The Cambridge English Scale

The Cambridge English Scale is used to report candidates' results across the range of Cambridge English exams. This single range of scores covers all levels of the Common European Framework of Reference for Languages (CEFR). The total marks for each of the four skills (Reading, Writing, Listening and Speaking) and for Use of English (where relevant) are converted into scores on the Cambridge English Scale. These individual scores are averaged to reach the overall Cambridge English Scale score for the exam. Results clearly show where the exams overlap and how performance on one exam relates to performance on another.

EP English Vocabulary Profile

The English Vocabulary Profile (EVP) is an online resource providing detailed information about the words, phrases, phrasal verbs and idioms that learners of English know and use at each of the six levels of the CEFR. The vocabulary syllabus of *Prepare!* has been informed by using EVP to ensure that students at each CEFR level are presented with high-frequency words and phrases that are suitable for their language level and relevant to each unit topic. Many of the most common words in English have a great number of different meanings and a thorough knowledge of these words helps students to operate successfully even with limited language. The special Word profile feature in Levels 4–7 deals with these powerful words in detail. Furthermore, the main vocabulary sections regularly focus on aspects other than 'concrete' topic nouns and verbs, such as adjectives and adverbs, prepositions, phrasal verbs, word families and phrases. All of these aspects are important if the syllabus is to provide true breadth and depth.

Systematic vocabulary development is crucial to real progress across the CEFR levels. Great care has been taken to organise the vocabulary syllabus in a logical way both within and across the seven levels of *Prepare!* The course offers regular recycling of vocabulary and builds on what students already know, to guarantee successful language learning from A1 to B2.

For more information on EVP, including information on how it was compiled, how you can access it, as well as ways to get involved in the English Profile programme, visit **www.englishprofile.org**

The Cambridge Learner Corpus

The Cambridge Learner Corpus (CLC) has been used to inform exercises in both the Student's Books and Workbooks of *Prepare!* This ensures that exercises target the language that students need most, as they focus on the areas that students at each level find most difficult, and where errors commonly occur.

Cambridge English Resources

Help your students make friends with other English learners around the world through our fun, international Cambridge English Penfriends activity, where students design and share cards with learners at a school in another country. Cambridge English Penfriends is practical, fun and communicative, offering students an opportunity to practise what they have learned.

Through Cambridge English Penfriends, we will connect your school with a school in another country so you can exchange cards designed by your students. If your school hasn't joined Cambridge English Penfriends yet, what are you waiting for?

Register at **www.cambridgeenglish.org/penfriends**

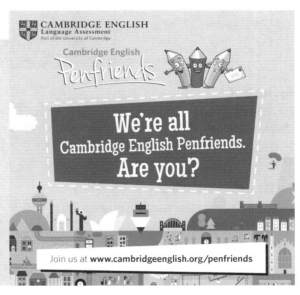

For more teacher support, including thousands of free downloadable resources, lesson plans, classroom activities, advice, teaching tips and discussion forums, please visit **www.cambridgeenglish.org/teachers**

Component line up

Workbook with audio

The Workbook gives further practice of all the language from the Student's Book and provides students with comprehensive work on skills development, which can be used either in class or for homework. In Levels 3, 5 and 7 exam tips provide students with advice on how to prepare for and do the exam as well as further exam tasks which provide further practice of the exam tasks encountered in the Student's Book. The accompanying audio is provided as downloadable MP3 files and is available from **www.cambridge.org/PrepareAudio**.

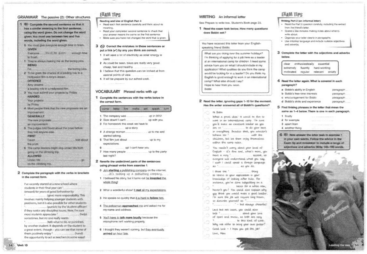

Online workbook

The *Prepare!* online Workbooks are accessed via activation codes packaged within the Student's Books. These easy-to-use workbooks provide interactive exercises, tasks and further practice of the language and skills from the Student's Books.

Teacher's Book with DVD

The Teacher's Book contains clear teaching notes on all of the Student's Book tasks as well as keys and audioscripts. The audioscripts include underlined answers.

The teacher's books provide plenty of lesson ideas through warmers, coolers, extension ideas and projects, as well as ideas for fast finishers and mixed ability classes. Each unit also directs you to where additional resources can be found. **Workbook answer keys** and **audioscripts** are also included.

Exam descriptions, exam tips, explanatory keys, model answers and underlined scripts provide guidance to the teacher and students on how to excel at the exam.

The **DVD** includes 10 video extra films and two First for Schools speaking test videos.

Class Audio CDs

The **Class Audio CDs** contain all of the audio material from the Student's Book.

▶ The audio icon in the Student's Book clearly shows the CD number and the track number.

Teacher's resources online – Downloadable materials

Complete suite of downloadable teacher's resources to use in class including:

- First for Schools speaking test video worksheets
- Video extra worksheets
- Progress tests
- Achievement tests
- Corpus tasks
- Pronunciation

These are available from **www.cambridge.org/prepareresources**

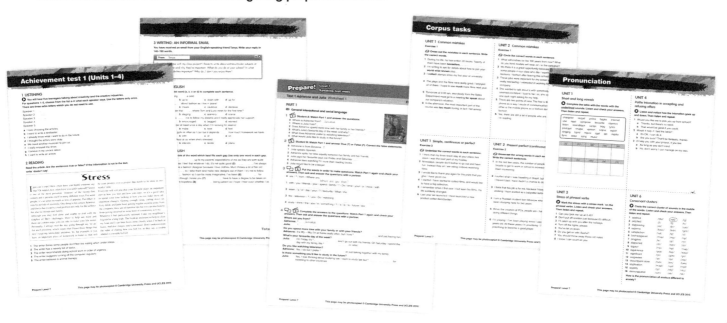

Presentation Plus

Presentation Plus is the next generation planning and presentation tool for teachers.
Perfect for creating engaging lessons, it includes:

- Interactive whiteboard tools
- Student's Book and Workbook with interactive exercises
- Access to teachers' resources

Ideal to use with a computer and a projector or with an interactive whiteboard.

Cambridge English Practice Testbank

Prepare! Level 7 Student's Book with Online Workbook and Testbank contains an access code to four individual practice tests in **Testbank** Cambridge English: First for Schools. **Testbank** provides authentic exam practice in an online simulation of the Cambridge English test environment.

How **Testbank** works:

- 'Practice mode' allows up to three attempts at each answer
- 'Test mode' provides timed test practice and only one attempt
- Teacher can set students a whole test or by part
- Instant marking and comprehensive gradebook

Student's Book overview

Vocabulary sets informed by English Vocabulary Profile to ensure they are appropriate for the level

Each unit starts with *Your profile*. This gives students the opportunity to discuss the topic area through a personalised speaking task

Motivating, topic-based **texts** specifically chosen to engage and inform students

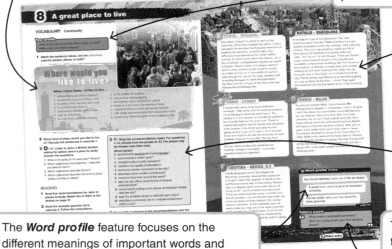

The full range of **Exam tasks** are introduced and practised in the Student's book and are easily identifiable

The *Word profile* feature focuses on the different meanings of important words and phrases and are specifically chosen to be relevant to your students' level

The *Talking points* feature after the reading text gives students the opportunity to give their opinion on the text

Common mistakes relevant to your students' level are identified and practised in the **Corpus challenge** to ensure meaningful learning

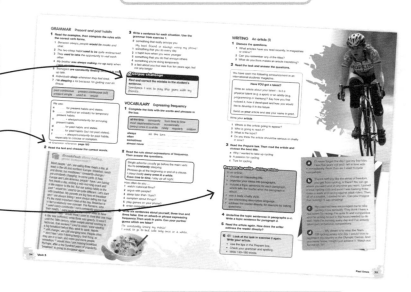

Clear **grammar presentation** and **practice** is extended in the Grammar reference section at the back of the book

The stages in *Prepare to write* give students helpful advice to help them plan and check their writing

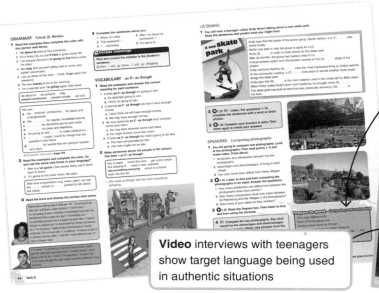

The stages in *Prepare to speak* provide students with useful words and phrases for effective communication

Video interviews with teenagers show target language being used in authentic situations

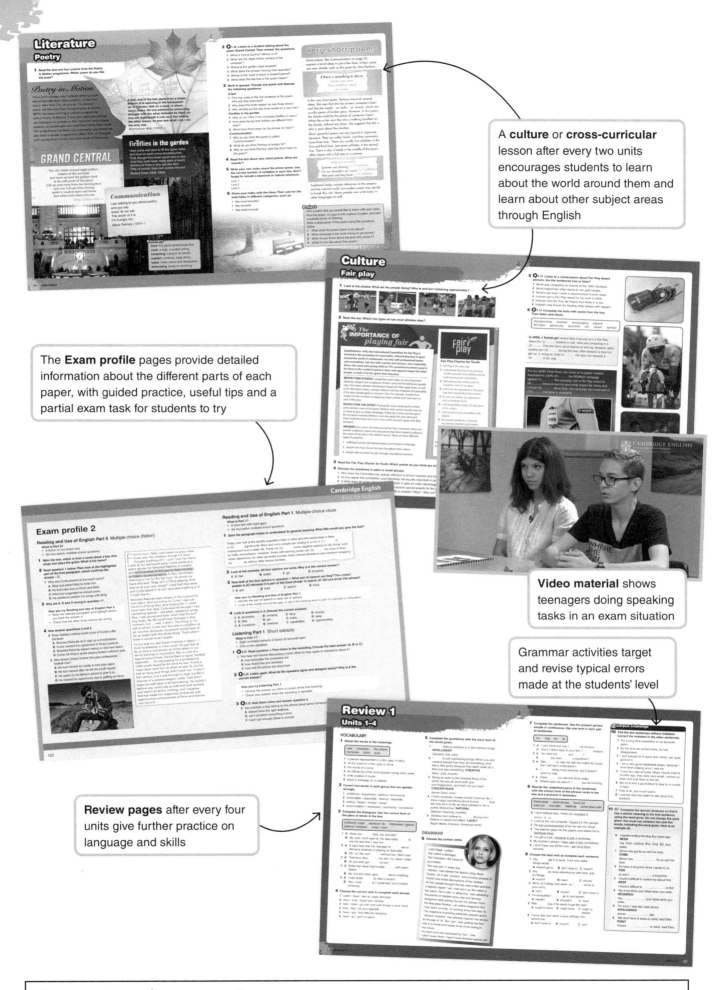

A **culture** or **cross-curricular** lesson after every two units encourages students to learn about the world around them and learn about other subject areas through English

The **Exam profile** pages provide detailed information about the different parts of each paper, with guided practice, useful tips and a partial exam task for students to try

Video material shows teenagers doing speaking tasks in an exam situation

Grammar activities target and revise typical errors made at the students' level

Review pages after every four units give further practice on language and skills

Answers to quiz on page 9

1 Stress 2 Unit 19 3 Unit 15 4 CLIL 1 – page 29 5 Shakira – page 63

VOCABULARY 2	WRITING	LISTENING AND SPEAKING	EXAM TASKS	VIDEO
Spelling	An essay (1) Organising essays		Reading and Use of English part 7 Writing part 1	Creative minds
Verb + preposition, e.g. *apologise for, cope with, laugh at*		**Listening** The boy who wore a skirt to school **Speaking** Interviews Introducing an opinion	Speaking part 1	Fashion
Verb + *to* infinitive, e.g. *agree to do something, advise someone to do something*	An informal letter or email		Reading and Use of English part 6 Writing part 2	
Phrasal verbs: Health, e.g. *cut down on, get over*		**Listening** Talking about stress **Speaking** Offering help	Reading and Use of English part 4 Listening part 3	
Expressing frequency, e.g. *from time to time, rarely*	An article (1)		Reading and Use of English part 2 Writing part 2	
Adverbs: Type and position		**Listening** Everyday situations 🅮 **Word profile** *thing* **Speaking** Favourite things Generalising	Reading and Use of English part 1 Listening part 1	
Time phrases, e.g. *before long, in no time*	A story		Reading and Use of English part 5 Writing part 2	Stories
as if / as though		**Listening** A new skate park **Speaking** Comparing photographs Comparing and contrasting	Reading and Use of English part 7 Listening part 2 Speaking part 2	Where we live
Adjective and noun suffixes	An essay (2) Comparing and contrasting		Reading and Use of English part 3 Writing part 1	
Extended meanings of words		**Listening** A radio phone-in **Speaking** Surprising news Expressing surprise 🅮 **Word profile** *expect*	Reading and Use of English part 6 Reading and Use of English part 4 Listening part 4	Surprises!

VOCABULARY 2	WRITING	LISTENING AND SPEAKING	EXAM TASKS	VIDEO
Compound adjectives, e.g. *long-distance, well-built*	An article (2) Varying sentence structure		Reading and Use of English part 2 Writing part 2	Families
both, either, neither		**Listening** The violinist in the Underground **Speaking** Discussing options Keeping talking	Listening part 2 Speaking part 3	
Phrasal verbs with *up*, e.g. *keep up, speak up*	A review (1)		Reading and Use of English part 7 Writing part 2	
Reporting verbs, e.g. *confess, insist*		**Listening** Travel problems **Speaking** Making decisions **EP** **Word profile** *break*	Reading and Use of English part 4 Listening part 3	Travelling
Phrases with *in*, e.g. *in general, in secret*	An essay (3) Linking words (1)		Writing part 1	The big picture
Adverb + adjective collocations, e.g. *environmentally friendly, well-balanced*		**Listening** Advertising **Speaking** Expressing opinions	Reading and Use of English part 2 Speaking part 2 Speaking part 3	
Phrasal verbs, e.g. *bring up, leave out*	A review (2) Language for reviews		Reading and Use of English part 3 Writing part 2	The news
Word pairs, e.g. *now and then, sooner or later*		**Listening** Unique Tees **Speaking** Agreeing and disagreeing	Reading and Use of English part 5 Listening part 4	Jobs
Plural nouns	An essay (4) Linking words (2)		Reading and Use of English part 6 Writing part 1	
Commonly confused words		**Listening** Eight everyday situations **Speaking** Taking turns and negotiating	Listening part 1	

Pairwork page 130   **Word profiles** page 132   **Vocabulary list** page 139   **Grammar reference** page 148

1 Creative minds

Unit profile

Vocabulary: Online, films, music, media; Spelling
Reading: Four profile texts
Grammar: Simple, continuous or perfect
Writing: An essay (1)

Warmer

1 Read these questions aloud. Ask students to note down their guess for each question.

1 How many hours a day do you think teenagers spend watching TV, listening to music, surfing the Web, social networking and playing video games?
2 How many hours per weekday do you think teenagers spend on sport and exercise?
3 How much TV do you think a teenager watches per day and how much does a person over 75 watch?
4 How much time each day do you think teenagers spend reading books, including schoolbooks?

2 Write these numbers on the board: *7.5, 1, 2, 4, 0.5.* Tell students these refer to hours spent, and ask them to match each one to a question with a partner. Then give students the answers and find out how similar or different these were to their own guesses before discussing which piece of information they found most surprising.

Answers
1 7 ½   2 1   3 2 and 4   4 0.5

Your profile

Ask students to discuss the questions in small groups. Do their results match the results from the Warmer? How do most students in the class spend their free time?

VOCABULARY   Online, films, music, media

1 Read through the questions as a whole class. To check students understand, read each question aloud, asking for volunteers to answer and to provide a definition of the word in pink. Then give students time to answer the other questions individually. Monitor and deal with any difficult vocabulary, adding definitions of these words to the board, as they could be useful to other students in the class too (e.g. *blog*: a record of your thoughts that you put on the internet for other people to read; *cast*: all the actors in a film or play; *lyrics*: the words of a song; *charts*: official list of the most popular songs each week). Model and drill the pronunciation of *lyrics* /'lɪr.ɪks/.

Fast finishers

Ask fast finishers to add one more question to the questionnaire and to ask their extra question in exercise 2.

2 Before students discuss the questions, ask them to underline the verbs in the example and identify the tense being used (*present perfect and present simple*). Then give students time to discuss the question in pairs. Nominate one or two pairs to give their answers to the whole class.

3 Write the names of a TV presenter, novelist and director (e.g. Steven Spielberg) the students are likely to know on the board. Ask students to describe what they do. Then ask them to complete the exercise individually before checking answers. With weaker students do this as a whole-class activity.

Answers
1 critic   2 editor   3 director   4 novelist   5 TV presenter

4 ▶1.02 Tell students that they will hear five people talking about their jobs. Play the recording once for students to match the people to the jobs in exercise 3. If necessary, with weaker students, pause the recording after each speaker. Then ask students to check their answers with a partner. In feedback, ask students *How do you know?* for each speaker, so that they explain what they heard.

Answers
1 novelist   2 critic   3 director   4 editor   5 TV presenter

5 ▶1.02 Play the recording again, pausing after each speaker to give students time to write, and ask students to take notes. In feedback, bring the students' notes together on the board. Students can then use this information in their discussion. In pairs, students discuss the questions. Monitor and help with vocabulary and pronunciation as necessary. Encourage students to add details. Give positive feedback for interesting ideas. After a few minutes, select two pairs to tell you their responses in front of the whole class.

Audioscript

Speaker 1: I aim to do at least four thousand words every day. It might not sound like a lot but that's about six hours' work. The first draft of anything takes me at least two months. I haven't had any bestsellers yet, but there is a film version of one of my short stories.

Speaker 2: Most of my work is related to TV, rather than films. So most days I receive DVDs of new shows – sometimes months before they're going to appear on TV. I watch them, take notes on key scenes and the characters and then write my review. Most of my stuff is published online but the odd thing is printed in newspapers.

Speaker 3: You might imagine I'm always behind a camera, telling the cast members what to do, and shouting 'Cut!' In fact, my day-to-day work's not half as exciting as people think. A lot of my time is spent in an office, phoning people, making plans. Boring stuff like that. When we're actually filming, I often work more than 12 hours a day. It can be exhausting.

Speaker 4: I work very closely with the author of a book to get it ready for publication. A lot of people think we just correct spelling and grammar mistakes, but it's a lot more than that. I'm responsible for everything, from the very first idea of a story until the book is finally on the shelves, and hopefully a bestseller!

Speaker 5: People think I have the easiest job in the world but it's not true. The show I'm doing at the moment is live from seven in the morning. That means I have to be up at four, ready to leave home by four thirty and at the studio by five, not to mention being in bed by eight the previous evening to make sure I get enough sleep! Then it's meetings, rehearsals and, of course, make-up. You have to look good if millions of people are watching!

READING

1 Ask students if they know of any teenage writers or singers. Give them a few minutes to read the questions and check they understand words and phrases, such as *famous, talent, in order to, private, well received* (reacted in a positive way), *confident, unsupportive* (not giving help or encouragement) and *benefitted from* (was given an advantage). Then give students five to ten minutes to complete the exercise.

Answer
Text A:
2 revealed a surprisingly mature singing voice
4 her mum started uploading Jackie's performances to the web … Jackie used the clips to enter an audition for the TV show

Prepare for First for Schools
Reading and Use of English Part 7

Task description
Reading and Use of English Part 7 requires students to match ten options to different parts of a text. The text can be one long text or, as in this example, a number of short texts. This part tests students' understanding of opinion, detail, specific information and implication.

Tip
Where there are multiple short texts, tell students to read quickly through each one to understand the gist before they attempt the specific matching task.

→ See Exam Profile 1, Student's Book page 120.

2 Remind students that the people can be chosen more than once. They will need between five and ten minutes to complete this exercise. Monitor and give help with vocabulary if needed. If they found exercise 1 challenging, break the exercise down by asking them to read paragraph B and write *B* next to two questions. Then read paragraphs C and D, to make it more manageable. If your class is preparing for the First for Schools exam, set them a time limit of ten minutes for this task.

Answers
Text B:
1 While Emerson was reading the first novel in the Harry Potter series, he came up with the idea of Mugglenet
8 Emerson persuaded his parents to let him leave school and teach himself at home … it quickly proved successful for him.
Text C:
3 Nancy even trained in martial arts in order to write the fight scenes more accurately.
6 Nancy believed in her ability to succeed.
Text D:
5 But just as popular as Tom's comments on the game itself were the details he gave about what he was up to personally.
7 At first, Tom's father wasn't convinced the project would be successful.

3 Stronger students can try to complete the sentences first without looking back at the text. With weaker students, encourage them to complete the sentences from context, but allow them to use a dictionary for any difficult words. Give students a few minutes to complete the task, monitoring, and giving help where necessary. Then check answers as a class.

Extension activity
Ask students to discuss these questions in groups: *Who inspires you in life? How would you like to make a living? What do you have the potential to excel at in life?* Monitor and join in conversations. Encourage students to add details. Share the most interesting ideas as a class.

Talking points
In pairs, students discuss these questions. For the first question, tell them to provide reasons to support their opinion. For the second question, tell students to think of at least five other qualities. Monitor and comment on interesting ideas. Ask for volunteers to share ideas with the class.

EP Word profile

When students have read the phrases with *not*, put them into pairs to take turns saying a new sentence with each phrase. Then set the exercise on page 132.

Cooler

Ask students to work in small groups and to discuss whether they would prefer to work in music, writing or video gaming. Ask one or two groups to feed back their discussion to the class.

GRAMMAR   Simple, continuous or perfect

1 Ask students to find and underline sentences 1–6 in the text. Read the meanings aloud and go through the exercise together as a class. Ask for volunteers to give another example for each meaning and write these on the board. Give students a few minutes to do the matching exercise in pairs. Check answers.

2 Give students a few minutes to complete the rules, using the example sentences in the book and those on the board to help them. Focus on sentence 1 and ask about the form of the present perfect (have + past participle). Ask *Does the sentence link the past and the present?* (Yes). Ask students to look at sentence 2 and ask about the form of the past perfect (had + past participle). Check answers.

→ Grammar reference Student's Book **page 148**

3 Do the first sentence as a class and explain the reason why *b* is correct (see Answers). Then give students a few minutes to complete the rest of the exercise in mixed ability pairs. Monitor, and give additional help if needed. Nominate students to give answers and ask the class to say if they are correct before giving feedback.

Corpus challenge

Ask students to correct the sentence and to explain the error. We need to put the second verb (*have lost*) in the past simple to show that it was a single event at a fixed point in the past.

Answer

My worst experience was when I lost my house key.

4 Tell students to read the text once, setting a time limit of just a few minutes. Then read out these questions for students to answer: *How did Kishan get the idea for the story he wrote? What does Kishan do for a job? What does he hope to achieve in the future?* Reading the whole text first should help students to make better choices when considering which verb is correct. Ask students to complete the exercise individually, and to check their answers in pairs. Monitor and give help where necessary.

Fast finishers

Ask fast finishers to look back at each answer and to think about the reason for their choice. Once all students have finished exercise 4, ask some of the fast finishers to explain their reasons.

Extension activity

In pairs, ask students to discuss these questions: *What do you think is Kishan's biggest achievement? What qualities do you think he has? Do you think he will achieve his dream in the future? Why / Why not?* Feed back as a class.

VOCABULARY   Spelling

1 Tell students to write down these words (don't spell them!):

   a definitely
   b efficient
   c wonderful
   d travelled

Ask volunteers to spell the words aloud and check them as a whole class. Then give students two minutes to complete exercise 1.

2 Give students a few minutes to complete this task. Then ask them to look at the words you read out in exercise 1 again and to decide what kind of spelling mistakes they made, if any.

Answers
b especially c believed d surprisingly e although

Extension activity

In small groups, students write an example of a misspelt word for each category a–e. They can use a dictionary if necessary. Give them no more than five minutes for this. They then swap their list with another group, who has to spell each word correctly. Groups swap back and mark each other's words. They show scores by raising their hands. Groups can report those words which were not spelt correctly by the other group.

---

3 Set this as an individual task with a time limit of just a few minutes, before students check their answers in pairs. Then check answers as a whole class.

Answers
1 choice – b
2 necessary – a
3 until – e
4 receive – c
5 environment – d
6 whether – d

WRITING   An essay (1)

1 Write *creative subjects* and *academic subjects* on the board. Ask students to come up with examples for each (e.g. *art and music are creative subjects; biology and spanish are academic subjects*). Put students into pairs to discuss the questions. Extend the discussion by asking students which subjects they think are most important and why. Monitor and report interesting ideas back to the class.

2 Ask the students to do this task individually and then check answers as a whole class. Highlight the structure of these types of questions, which are divided into three sections. The first section tells them what they are writing and for whom (an essay for their English teacher). The second section is the actual essay question, written in bold type (Subjects such as drama and music...). The third section (Write about) tells them the three things that their answer *must* include. Ask students to discuss their ideas, and how they might organise them, in mixed ability pairs. Monitor and join in discussions, helping with ideas if necessary.

Answer
Subjects such as drama and music are just as important as maths and languages. Do you agree?

3 Books closed. Write *Paragraph 1*, *Paragraph 2*, *Paragraph 3* and *Paragraph 4* on the board. Invite students to give ideas for what each paragraph should contain for the task in exercise 2. Books open. Ask them to compare what you have written on the board with the paragraph plan in the *Prepare* box. Give students time to do the matching exercise on their own before checking answers as a whole class. When checking, you could ask students to highlight the parts in each paragraph that helped them make their decisions.

Answers
Paragraph 1: B
Paragraph 2: D
Paragraph 3: C
Paragraph 4: A

4 Once students have found the highlighted expressions, ask them to work with a partner to think of one extra word or phrase that performs each function (e.g. *Finally, In addition, For example, It is generally thought that, However*).

Answers
1 Most people agree that (The majority of people agree that)
2 Furthermore (Moreover, In addition)
3 In contrast (Conversely)
4 For instance (For example, such as)
5 To sum up (In conclusion, In summary)

---

5 Give students 15 to 20 minutes to answer questions 1–4. Monitor and help students with ideas and organisation. If appropriate for your class, put students in mixed ability pairs so that weaker students are supported more. Once students have completed the task, ask them to compare their answers with a partner or another pair if they have been working in pairs.

Mixed ability

You could suggest these ideas if some students are struggling to generate ideas:
For: Not all students are academic. School should teach practical life skills, e.g. budgeting and CV writing. Students often have no experience of applying for a job and need to learn how to.
Against: These life skills should be taught by parents. There is not time to teach such things in school. Teachers do not necessarily know about managing money or how to apply for a job.

● Prepare for First for Schools

Writing Part 1

Task description

This part is a compulsory task. Students are required to write an essay giving their opinion on the essay title using the ideas given and providing an idea of their own. Students should write 140–190 words.

Tip

Before attempting to write the essay, encourage students to brainstorm their ideas and organise them in a logical way. They can use the ideas in the *Prepare* box to decide where each idea fits best.

→ See Exam Profile 3, Student's Book page 125.

6 ● Ask students to write the essay. If students are working towards an exam, set a strict time limit of 40 minutes to encourage them to get used to exam conditions.

Sample answer

This is a complex issue, and the balance of subjects will depend on the type of school and the aims of its students. However, it is certainly true that most teenagers would benefit from learning some practical skills.

Academic subjects such as science, maths and history are clearly important for any students intending to study at university, and there may not be much free time left for other aspects of education.

On the other hand, students do need basic skills to survive in the wider world. For instance, they should be able to set a spending budget and save money. Furthermore, when young people leave home, they will need to know how to change a plug or a light bulb!

Another thing to consider, in my opinion, is the continuing need for creative subjects in school, such as art and drama. Even if a student is not planning to have a career in these areas, they are enjoyable subjects and will make that individual a more interesting person.

To sum up, having a wider choice of subjects is good in theory. However, it may not always be achievable.

Cooler

Ask students to make brief notes on the main points of their essay. Then tell them to use these notes to present their essay's main ideas in groups of four. Ask them to decide who has the most convincing arguments and why. Discuss some ideas as a class.

Project

Tell students they are going to write a questionnaire to find out an older person's (e.g. a parent) opinions on education. Brainstorm some possible questions on the board e.g. *What was your favourite subject at school?* Then in pairs, ask students to write their questionnaires. Their questionnaires should have at least six questions. To recycle the tenses you could suggest these ideas:

- subjects their parents studied
- their opinion on creative and academic subjects
- any courses or training they are doing now
- jobs they have done
- who they think should teach young people about life skills

Ask students to write up their findings in a short paragraph. Give them some useful expressions to help, e.g. *Everyone agreed that …, Almost half the respondents stated that …, No one thought that …, The most common opinion was …*

Students can present their findings in the following class, using PowerPoint if you have access to it. They could also publish their results on the class blog.

Teacher's resources

Student's Book
Grammar reference and practice page 148
Vocabulary list page 139
Video
Creative minds
Workbook
Unit 1, pages 4–7
Go online for
- Pronunciation
- Video extra worksheet
- Corpus tasks

2 Addicted to fashion

Unit profile

Vocabulary: Adjective + preposition; Verb + preposition
Reading: An article about fashion
Grammar: Present perfect (simple and continuous)
Listening: A TV chat show
Speaking: Interviews

Warmer

1 Write these sentences on the board. Divide the class into groups of four to six students and ask them to correct the mistakes in their teams. The fastest team wins.

1 I have been shopping in town yesterday.
2 While I read a magazine I was seeing a dress I want to buy.
3 He was launching his own fashion company when he was a student.
4 The company is having over 2000 stores across the world.
5 What are you doing? I shop in town.
6 I worked in fashion for two years now.

Answers
1 went 2 was reading; saw 3 launched 4 has
5 am shopping 6 have worked

2 Students should give their corrected sentences to another group for checking. Go through the answers as a whole class and give each team one point for a correct answer and minus one for a wrong answer. Use the sentences to review the rules for the tense uses from Unit 1 if necessary.

Your profile

Ask students to rank the four options from most to least important and to explain their choice to a partner.

VOCABULARY Adjective + preposition

1 1.03 Do the first sentence as a whole class and then set the rest of the exercise as individual work. Play the recording for students to check their answers. You could make a note of the answers on the board. Ask students to tell their partner which person best reflects their own views.

Answers
1 c 2 b 3 a 4 b 5 c 6 a 7 b 8 c 9 a
10 c 11 b 12 a

2 ▶1.03 Ask students to do this task with a partner and then play the recording again to check answers.

Audioscript

Narrator: Emma
Emma: I'm aware of what's in fashion because I read blogs like models.com and Fab Sugar. I never buy any of the stuff they feature, though! I admit it, I'm easily impressed by designer labels – my favourite is Prada. I love looking at the window displays in their city centre shop, but I've never had the courage to go in. I couldn't afford any of it, for one thing. <u>I get most of my stuff from department stores or online</u>. You can usually get quite good versions of the 'real thing' for a fraction of the price. Even so, I think I dress really well. I'm pretty adventurous with my taste in clothes, but I'd never wear fur.

Narrator: Ahmed
Ahmed: I'm addicted to clothes shopping! I just can't stop. It's a bit of an obsession of mine. I do need to be cautious about spending too much, though. Once I accidentally spent £200 on clothes. I'd been given some money for my birthday, and I went shopping with one of my friends. I'm absolutely hopeless at making decisions about clothes, so I bought loads. When I got home and added up how much they all cost, I couldn't believe it! It was a bit of a disaster really and <u>I had to return a lot of stuff</u>.

Narrator: Dan
Dan: I'm not all that bothered about what others think of my dress sense. I just wear whatever I like, mainly jeans and football shirts. You could say it's a bit conventional, but <u>I believe in keeping things simple</u>. Anyway, you shouldn't be critical of the way others dress. It's up to individuals to choose how they want to look. I've never been mean about a friend's dress sense. People can be very sensitive about their appearance.

Narrator: Sara
Sara: People are obsessed with brands, I think. <u>There's no point in being loyal to a particular brand</u>. You should feel free to wear anything that looks good. And you should enjoy it for what it is, not for the label it's got on it. I certainly wouldn't be jealous of a friend just because they had an expensive brand of trainers or something like that. You're paying for the label most of the time, not the actual quality of the clothing. I know what clothes suit me and I'm fairly decisive about what to buy. I don't waste time worrying about what else might be available, worrying that there might be something slightly better in the next shop.

Answers
1 In department stores or online
2 He had to return a lot of clothes.
3 He believes in keeping things simple.
4 She thinks there's no point being loyal to brands.

3 Give students a few minutes to decide which statements are true and false, before comparing answers with a partner.

READING

Cultural background

The photo shows Camden Lock Market, which is an extremely popular tourist attraction in London with about 100,000 shoppers each weekend. The market sells crafts, clothing, bric-a-brac and fast food, and attracts a young, trendy and alternative crowd.

1 Give students the Cultural background to Camden Lock Market and ask them to look at the photo on page 15. Ask students if they have ever been to Camden Lock Market or if their country has anything similar. Ask them if they would like to visit this market and why.

2 Give students a time limit of one minute to skim through the article and decide which one is the correct answer. Tell students to ignore words they do not understand and to concentrate on the general meaning of the text. Check answers.

Answer
2 Does fashion actually matter?

3 Give students five to ten minutes for this task. Ask students to compare their answers with a partner before checking answers as a whole class.

Answers
1 False. The traditional colours associated with boys and girls were the opposite 100 years ago.
2 False. Cheaper ones are no different.
3 False. They may try to steal them.
4 True 5 True 6 True 7 True

4 After students have matched the words, ask them to write five example sentences using each of the target words. Ask for volunteers to read out their sentences to the class.

Fast finishers

Ask fast finishers to select three or four new words from the text. Tell them to give a definition of the word and write an example sentence using it. They can use their dictionaries to help. Ask one or two of the students to present their words to the class once everyone has finished.

Answers
1 stunning 2 alternative 3 conventional 4 functional
5 classic

EP Word profile

Before doing this task, write *point* on the board, and ask students how many meanings they can think of, e.g. *idea*, a point in sport, *to show*, *to aim*. Tell students to read the Word profile and compare the meanings with those on the board. Set the exercise on page 132.

Answers
1 There's no point in   4 You made a good point
2 get to the point   5 The point is
3 up to a point   6 You've missed the point of

Talking points

In pairs, students discuss the questions. If your students are preparing for the First For Schools exam, ask them to speak for at least one minute as a monologue for each question. Monitor and help with ideas if necessary. Ask two or three students to tell the class about their partner's views.

Cooler

Play Bingo! with new words from this lesson, including those from exercise 4. Write ten words on the board, and tell students to choose five of these words and write them down. Read the words aloud in any order. If students have written down one of the words they hear, they cross it out. The first person to cross out all five words shouts *Bingo!*, and wins the game.

GRAMMAR   Present perfect (simple and continuous)

1 Books closed. Write sentences 1–4 on the board, and ask students to work in pairs to identify the tenses used (*present perfect simple and present perfect continuous*). Books open. Ask students to match the sentences to the rules individually. Check answers, and go through any difficult points.

→ Grammar reference Student's Book page 149

2 After students have completed this exercise individually, ask them to explain their choices to their partner. Ask them to work together to match the uses to the rules in exercise 1.

Answers
1 a 2 b 3 b 4 a 5 a 6 b

3 Ask students to complete the sentences with a partner. In whole-class feedback, ask stronger students to explain the reason for their choice.

Answers

1 have been sitting	4 have bought
2 has produced	5 have been reading
3 has been raining	6 have been waiting

4 Give students five minutes to write their sentences. Monitor as students complete this task. Elicit an example sentence for each word in the box and write it on the board, e.g. *I've been learning English for five years*.

Corpus challenge

Ask students to correct the sentence and to explain the error (we use the present perfect continuous as the action started in the past and is still continuing).

Answer
I have been thinking of you since I arrived in Athens.

VOCABULARY Verb + preposition

1 Ask students if they have heard of *onesies* and tell them to look at the photo on page 16. Highlight the pattern of verb (*heard*) + preposition (*of*). Check students understand all of the words in the box; *do without* and *cope with* might be new to some students. Then ask them to do this exercise in pairs. Remind students to record both the verb and preposition when making notes of such new words.

Answers
1 apologised for
2 laugh at
3 compared with
4 depending on
5 cope with
6 do without

2 Give students five minutes to write as many questions as possible using the verb + preposition phrases. Then ask students to work with a partner to ask and answer the questions. Ask some students to report back to the class about their partner.

Mixed ability

Weaker students may find it difficult to form the questions and hold a conversation. Put strong and weak students into pairs to write the questions, and then form groups of four for the conversation part of the activity.

LISTENING

1 Ask the class if any of them watch chat shows. If they do, find out which chat shows they prefer. Tell the students to look at the picture and discuss in pairs what they might hear. Ask some students to tell the class their ideas.

2 ▶1.04 Play the recording and ask students to check their answer. Ask students what they think about the situation. Would any of the boys make a similar protest?

Audioscript

Speaker 1: A schoolboy from a small town in the south west of the country has been in the news this week and you'll never guess why …

Speaker 2: He's …!

Speaker 1: He's wearing a skirt, yes.

Speaker 2: But why?

Speaker 1: Good question. I've been reading quite a lot about this guy. His name's Chris Bennett and he's 17. He's a student at the local high school in his town.

Speaker 2: And the skirt?

Speaker 1: Let me explain. A year ago, the school changed its rules about what students could wear in different weather conditions. So the new rules stated that most of the time, everyone had to wear trousers. It was felt that trousers were the right kind of clothing to encourage students to behave well and to create an atmosphere in which they would want to study hard. When it was hot – and believe me, it does get hot there in summer, temperatures reach 40 degrees and more – so, when it was hot, girls at the school could wear skirts instead of long trousers. However, boys weren't allowed to wear shorts – they had to wear long trousers whatever the weather. The school felt that wearing shorts would have a bad effect on pupils' concentration.

Speaker 2: I can't see their point, really. Why would anyone be bothered about boys wearing shorts?

Speaker 1: That's exactly what Chris Bennett and his classmates thought. They complained about the new rules and explained that in 40-degree heat, trousers were just too hot. But it seems that the school didn't like anyone being critical of the rules, and they refused to make any changes. So Chris and some of his classmates planned a protest. The college's new rules stated that girls could wear trousers or skirts, but that boys couldn't wear shorts. However, the rules didn't say that boys weren't allowed to wear skirts! So one day, Chris borrowed a skirt from his sister and he arrived at school wearing a skirt.

Speaker 2: Wow. What a great idea! I am vaguely aware of this story in fact. It was mentioned on a documentary a few months ago. Some of the male presenters even wore skirts to support Chris and his classmates.

Speaker 1: That's right.

Speaker 2: I saw a clip online; I was really impressed, actually. And it really makes you think about dress and gender, and why is it that society says men shouldn't wear skirts? <u>There are plenty of African and Asian countries where clothes that look like skirts are completely normal for men.</u>

Speaker 1: Yes, it doesn't make sense when you think about it. Anyway, <u>the school sent Chris home</u> and told him not to come back unless he was prepared to abide by the rules. There was a lot of press coverage of the story and the Skirt Case, as it became known, was featured in a documentary that was broadcast internationally. Finally, <u>about a year later</u>, the school governors agreed to ask the students and parents what they wanted. A debate was organised at the school and at the end there was a vote.

Speaker 2: That's great!

Speaker 1: Yeah!

Speaker 2: What happened in the debate? Who won?

Speaker 1: The students made the point that long trousers make it harder to concentrate in hot weather because they're uncomfortable. The parents were fairly loyal to their kids and supported the idea of shorts for boys, and <u>the school's point was simple – they just wanted to make sure everybody was smart.</u> The majority of those at the debate voted in favour of shorts, and <u>the revised school uniform policy allows boys to wear shorts during the summer term.</u>

Answer

They are discussing what happened when a boy wore a skirt to school.

3 ▶1.04 Play the recording again. Ask students to check their answers with a partner before whole-class feedback.

Answers

1 Everyone had to wear trousers, although in hot weather girls could wear skirts.
2 to encourage good behaviour and an academic atmosphere
3 boys wearing skirts
4 in parts of Africa and Asia
5 They sent him home.
6 one year later
7 They wanted everyone to be smart.
8 Boys are allowed to wear shorts.

4 Ask students to talk about their school for question 1 and discuss any clothing that has been banned. Bring together students' ideas for question 2, and then take a class poll to decide whether school uniforms are positive or negative overall.

SPEAKING   Interviews

1 ▶1.05 Tell students that they are listening to find out which information is *not* included. Give the students a few minutes to read the interviewer's questions and then play the recording. Check answers.

Answer

4 What do you do after school?

Audioscript

Interviewer: What's your name and where are you from?

Sophia: My name's Sophia. I'm from Milan, in Italy.

Interviewer: How long have you lived there?

Sophia: I was born in Milan and I've lived there all my life.

Interviewer: What do you like most about your school?

Sophia: I find it a really positive place to be. The atmosphere's quite relaxed and I think the teachers are really good at motivating us to do our best. They manage to keep a balance, though, and they don't put too much pressure on us. I think I'm lucky really. <u>I would say</u> one of the best things about the school is the extracurricular programme. That includes things like sailing and climbing. They're the kind of thing I wouldn't think of doing myself, outside of school I mean, but when it's organised and lots of people you know are doing it, it's a lot of fun. For me, having a lot of activities outside school is really important because it helps me deal with all the stress of exams.

Interviewer: Do you like shopping?

Sophia: I absolutely love shopping, especially for clothes and shoes! <u>To tell the truth</u>, I probably spend too much time shopping! I go into town every weekend, and probably spend two or three hours walking around the shops. I don't buy stuff all the time, but I am always reading fashion blogs and window shopping.

Interviewer: What else do you like doing in your free time?

Sophia: Let me think. Well, <u>I guess</u> I spend quite a lot of time online, chatting and using social media, that kind of thing. I have a tablet at home and I tend to have it with me wherever I go. I spend a lot of time with friends, too. We don't always go out, but we maybe just hang out together and chat about things.

Interviewer: Thank you, Sophia.

Interviewer: What's your name and where are you from?

Pavel: My name's Pavel. I'm from Moscow in Russia. But I'm living in Birmingham at the moment.

Interviewer: How long have you lived here?

Pavel: I've been living here for three months. My dad's got a one-year contract at Birmingham International.

Interviewer: At the airport?

Pavel: Yes. He's an engineer.

Interviewer: I see. How long have you been at your school?

Pavel: I've just started. I've been studying here for about two weeks, so it's all quite new to me.

Interviewer:	What do you like most about your school?
Pavel:	I've found it very friendly so far. People have been talking to me quite a lot and I've made a couple of friends already. It seems to be very sociable and there's lots to do after classes, which is really nice for someone who's new, like me. The classes are interesting, too. I'm quite interested in science, and there's a very good science department here. The teachers know a fantastic amount, and they're good at explaining things to the students.
Interviewer:	Do you like shopping?
Pavel:	That's an interesting question. I've just been talking about that. I do sort of like hanging out and going in computer and game shops, but, frankly, I'm not that bothered about clothes shopping. If I want something, I tend to buy it online rather than going into town. It's quicker that way, and often cheaper, too.
Interviewer:	What else do you like doing in your free time?
Pavel:	Let me think … Well, I do spend a lot of time playing games, and the brilliant thing about online games is that I can still play with my friends back home in Russia. To be honest, I probably spend too much time sitting in front of my computer … Apart from games, I guess movies are a big interest of mine. I always went to the cinema once a week on Sundays when I was back home, and it's something I still do now, though a bit less than before. I like having movie nights in with friends too. You know, watch a movie together and have a pizza or something. That's cool.
Interviewer:	Thank you, Pavel.

2 ▶ **1.05** Before they listen, ask students to write answers to any they can remember from the first listening. They then complete the task to find out if they were right. If necessary, explain the meaning of *frankly* (honestly). Check answers as a class.

Answers
Sophia: I would say, To tell the truth, I guess
Pavel: frankly, To be honest

3 Give students five to ten minutes to prepare their ideas individually. Monitor and assist as needed.

Fast finishers
Ask fast finishers to prepare one or two additional questions to ask and answer in exercise 4, encouraging them to add extra detail. If necessary, help with vocabulary and pronunciation.

◖◗ Prepare for First for Schools
Speaking Part 1

Task description
Part 1 is a two-minute conversation between the interlocutor and each student. The focus is on general interactional and social English.

Tip
Tell students to focus on giving full and developed answers. Encourage them to give more information as well as answering the questions they are asked.

4 ◖◗ Ask students to interview each other in pairs. Encourage them to add as many questions to the interview as they can and to use the expressions in the *Prepare* box. Afterwards, ask students to tell you any questions they added and write them on the board. Ask the rest of the class what tenses might be needed to answer each question.

Extension activity
Ask students to spend a few minutes writing a summary of their partner's answers. Students then compare their summary with a new partner to see if they have discussed the same main points.

Cooler
Ask students to write eight new words from this lesson onto separate pieces of paper. On the back they should write the definitions. Monitor and help as necessary. Students should then work with a partner and take it in turns to read their definitions. Their partner should guess the word being defined. Share any challenging ones as a class.

Project
Tell students that they are going to create a fashion poster for homework. They can either focus on styles they like, or styles they find ridiculous. Ask them to include photos or drawings of clothes. In the following class, students can present their poster and explain how it represents their view of fashion.

Teacher's resources
Student's Book
Grammar reference and practice page 149
Vocabulary list page 139
Video
Fashion
Speaking Part 1
Workbook
Unit 2, pages 8–11
Go online for
• Progress test
• Video extra worksheet
• Speaking test video worksheets
• Corpus tasks

Culture
Fashion design

Learning objectives

- The students learn about different fashion awards and designers around the world.
- In the project stage, students write a profile of a famous fashion designer.

Warmer

1 Ask students to work with a partner to brainstorm the names of fashion designers and brands.

2 Tell students to work in small groups to compare their lists and to discuss what they like about their favourite designers and brands. Share some ideas as a class.

1 Ask students to look at the pictures and describe what they see. They then match the words to the pictures. Make sure that they understand the word *slogan* (a short phrase that is easy to remember and is used to make people notice something). Then ask students to read the text. Give them only a few minutes to do this. Check answers as a whole class.

Cultural background

The British Fashion awards were established in 1989 by the British Fashion Council to showcase the talents of British designers. As a result of the the work of the British Fashion Council, including the establishment of London Fashion Week in 1984, London is now considered one of the four most important fashion capitals, alongside Paris, Milan and New York.

Answers
a high heels **b** slogan **c** menswear **d** miniskirt

2 Ask students to read the text again and answer questions 1–5. Check understanding of *lifetime, achievement, talent, outstanding* and *accessories*. Ask students to correct any false sentences with their partner. Check answers as a class.

Fast finishers

Tell fast finishers to underline the people mentioned in the text and to write down anything they know about them. Ask students to share this information after checking answers to exercise 2. Open up the discussion to find out if anyone knows anything else about the people mentioned.

Answers
1 True
2 False. They were in 1984.
3 False. There are also awards for best accessories, best menswear, best brand, best fashion model, outstanding achievement and emerging talent.
4 True.
5 False. She entered the BFA Hall of Fame in 1990.

3 Give students one minute to read the text again. Tell them to close their books. Read the questions in exercise 3 aloud, and see if students can answer them from memory. Books open. Give students one minute to find the answers in the text and check answers as a class. Afterwards, ask stronger students what strategy they used. Elicit that all the questions use key words, such as *new designer*, which are repeated in the text, allowing quick navigation around the text. This is a good skill to practise for a number of different exam question types.

Answers
1 One 2 Victoria Beckham 3 Emerging Talent awards
4 Best fashion model 5 Alexander McQueen 6 Kim Jones

Extension activity

Ask students to work in pairs and brainstorm as many different clothing items as they can in two minutes. Then put two pairs together to form a group of four. Ask students to compare their lists and to add up how many different words their group has. Find out which group has the longest list and ask them to read it aloud. Tell the other groups to listen and tick off things on their own list. Once the group has read out their whole list, ask the other groups if they have any different words left.

4 Ask students if they recognise the people in the photos. They should quickly read the whole of each text first, ignoring the gaps for the moment, so they have a general understanding of what each text is about. Then tell them to complete the texts with words from the box. Check answers as a whole class.

Answers
Text A
1 British 2 simple 3 animal 4 own 5 brand
6 uniforms
Text B
7 bright 8 comfortable 9 customers 10 furniture
11 founded 12 house

5 Ask students to discuss these questions in small groups. Monitor, giving positive feedback for interesting ideas. After students have discussed the questions, give each group a question number. Tell them this is the question they will report back on in feedback. Listen to each group's ideas, and ask the rest of the class if their opinions were the same.

Extension activity

Put students into groups of six to eight. Tell each group to divide itself into two halves and to decide which half is A and which is B. Tell the A groups that they must argue in favour of using animal products, such as fur and leather, in fashion design and tell the B groups that they must argue against. Give the groups a few minutes to think of their arguments and how they might counter the other group's arguments. Then allow a few minutes for the debate. Afterwards ask one student from each group to summarise the main points both teams made.

6 ▶1.06 Tell students that they are going to listen to a podcast about Christopher Raeburn, a British designer. Ask them to make notes about what they hear. Play the recording. Then tell students to compare their notes in small groups, adding any information they missed. In feedback, get each group to tell you one thing they learnt about the designer.

7 ▶1.06 Ask students to read through the questions, and check understanding of any potentially difficult words, e.g. *artificial* (not natural), *military* (relating to the army) and *extravagant* (extreme or unusual). Tell students to look at their notes from exercise 6 and circle the correct answer. Play the recording for students to check their answers.

Audioscript

Presenter: Good afternoon, everyone. Today on *Fashion Focus*, we're talking about a talented young designer on the fashion scene, named Christopher Raeburn. Have you heard of him, Susan?

Susan: Yes, I have, Alan. In fact, I saw his menswear collection in London this year, and I love what he does with recycled fabric. It's quite amazing, really.

Presenter: Yeah, I've heard that. It seems he only works with recycled clothing and sustainable materials? Everything very ecological, right?

Susan: Exactly, and he also reuses a lot of old military clothing, for menswear and for women's wear, which is a bit more unusual, I think. He buys old uniforms from various countries around the world.

Presenter: And how long has he been in the fashion business?

Susan: Well, he graduated from the Royal College of Art in 2006, and started his own brand company straight away. In 2008, he presented his first collection during London Design Week.

Presenter: That's quite a fast start for a new designer, isn't it?

Susan: Yeah, it is, and only four years after that he won a British Fashion Award for Emerging Talent in menswear design, though he started off designing clothes for women. He also does some beautiful accessories.

Presenter: And what caught your attention most about his collection? What stood out for you?

Susan: Well, at first glance, it was the simplicity of his designs. They're very practical and easy to wear. Nothing too extravagant, so I think they appeal to a very wide audience of customers. I remember reading an interview where he said that his four basic rules are 'desirability, detail, function and fun'.

Presenter: Really? That sounds like a good strategy these days. And he also produces most of his clothing right here in the UK, doesn't he?

Susan: Yes, in fact his company's slogan is 'Remade in England'. It can be more expensive to produce the clothing here, but it's good for the local economy, with more jobs for people here in England.

Presenter: Well, you can't argue with that, can you? With that, we'll take a short break for advertising. When we come back, Susan and I will be discussing other designers who work with recycled materials. Stay tuned for more …

Answers

1 recycled 2 reusing 3 2006 4 has 5 men and women 6 simple 7 the UK

Cooler

Ask students to discuss these questions with a partner:
1 Is fashion more important to boys or girls?
2 What's the most important thing about clothes for boys?
3 What are the most important things about clothes for girls?

Discuss some ideas as a class.

Project

Ask students to write a short paragraph about a designer they admire, using the questions on page 19 for guidance. They can do this for homework, using the internet, and add pictures of the designer and their work. Their texts can be displayed around the classroom.

3 All in the mind

Unit profile

Vocabulary: Abstract nouns; Verb + *to* infinitive
Reading: Humans: The smartest species?
Grammar: The grammar of phrasal verbs
Writing: An informal letter or email

Warmer

1 Write these 12 adjectives on the board: *aware, adventurous, impressed, bothered, critical, mean, addicted, cautious, hopeless, loyal, jealous, decisive.* Ask students to work in pairs and to write each adjective on a separate piece of paper.

2 Tell them to write the correct preposition for each adjective onto a separate piece of paper, without looking at their books.

3 Put students into small groups. Each group places two sets of cards face down on the table. They should turn them over to find a matching pair. Once they find a matching pair they should give a sentence using the word. If they can, they keep the pair. If they can't, the pair is returned to the table. This continues until all the cards have gone and the winner is the one with the most pairs.

Your profile

Ask students to list one or two things they are naturally good at and something that they have learnt to be good at. Then ask them to explain to a partner why they think they are naturally good at some things and how they learnt to be good at others. Ask one or two students to tell the class about their partner.

VOCABULARY Abstract nouns

1 ▶ 1.07 Before setting this task, brainstorm some common noun endings on the board with the class (e.g. *-ment*, *-ion*). Check understanding of the words in the box. Then tell students to listen to the recording and circle the correct abstract noun. Check answers.

Audioscript

Speaker: *THE Debate.* Is there finally <u>agreement</u> in the debate over <u>nature</u> versus nurture? Are we born with a personality that never changes, and with a fixed amount of <u>intelligence</u>? In other words, is our <u>fortune</u> in life dictated by our genes – the 'nature' argument? Or do we start life as a blank sheet? Does our social and intellectual <u>development</u> come from our life experiences – the 'nurture' view? New research appears to suggest that both sides in the debate might be right.

Answers
1 agreement   2 nature   3 intelligence   4 fortune
5 development

2 ▶ 1.08 Ask for a show of hands from students as to whether they think nature or nurture has more impact on developing personalities, but don't enter into a discussion about this yet. Give students time to read the sentences and clarify some words such as *podcast* and *professional* by asking volunteers to explain the words. Play the recording, and then allow students to check their answers with a partner before whole-class feedback.

Audioscript

Sara: <u>Have you listened to *THE Debate* yet this week</u>?
Ahmed: <u>No.</u> I haven't downloaded the podcast. Was it any good?
Sara: Yeah, fascinating, actually. It was all about your genes and your environment – nature versus nurture – and they discussed what you need to achieve <u>success</u> in life.
Ahmed: Sounds interesting. So, what do you need?
Sara: Well, first you need the right genes! <u>If you're going to be a great footballer or a brilliant scientist, you need the luck to be born with the right genes</u>.
Ahmed: So, it's all down to nature then?
Sara: Well, not exactly. That was a common belief in the past, but it seems it's only part of it. <u>As well as the right genes, you also need the right environment</u>. Basically, the genes you have will only become active if you're brought up in the right environment.
Ahmed: So, you mean you could be born naturally athletic, or with the <u>creativity</u> to be a great artist. But if you're brought up in the wrong environment, you'll never achieve greatness?
Sara: That's right.
Ahmed: Hmm, so it seems you need more than just ambition to become a professional footballer or a brilliant scientist, then? I guess I'll probably have to accept that those things aren't for me.
Sara: Well, it seems there might be a bit of hope, when it comes to being a scientist anyway.
Ahmed: Really?
Sara: Yeah. <u>The presenter said that students who have the determination to study hard, can actually become more intelligent – more academic, as they get older</u>.
Ahmed: Really?
Sara: Yeah. It seems that if you really try to improve your <u>concentration</u>, really push yourself, you can actually develop different parts of your brain that could then allow you to be more successful.
Ahmed: Great! So, if it's true that you can improve your intelligence, maybe the same is true for your sporting ability. So maybe there is still hope that I could be the next Cristiano Ronaldo!

Answers
1 False   2 False   3 True   4 True

3 ▶1.08 Ask students to explain the meaning of each word in the box to their partner. Then elicit a definition for each word from different pairs. Students can complete the exercise in pairs, before listening to check their answers.

Answers
1 success 2 luck 3 belief 4 creativity 5 determination
6 concentration

4 Give students a few minutes to complete these sentences. Check answers as a class.

Fast finishers

Ask fast finishers to write two or three more sentences about themselves using nouns from exercises 1 and 3. They can share their answers during feedback to exercise 4.

Extension activity

To practise word formation and sentence transformation, ask students to rewrite the sentences from exercise 4 using a verb or adjective formed from the noun. Model the first one on the board, e.g. *Sleeping more helps me to concentrate.* Check answers.

Answers
1 determination 2 luck 3 intelligence 4 concentration
5 nature

5 Ask students to discuss the questions in small groups, helping with ideas where necessary. Do any of them know about twin case studies, where identical twins are separated at a young age and brought up in different environments? Ask one or two groups to feed back on their discussion to the whole class. To extend the discussion you could also ask students to consider different areas in the nature/nurture debate, e.g. crime, sport and education.

READING

1 Ask students to look at the photos and to tell their partner what they can see. Then ask pairs to make a list of as many things as possible that show humans are more intelligent than animals. Give students one minute to read the text and check their answers.

2 Ask students to read the sentences and underline the pronouns. Then tell students to discuss with a partner what they think each pronoun refers to. Why do they think this?

Answers
A dog B parrots C tropical fish D human E chimpanzee
F elephants G empathy

3 Direct students' attention to the pronouns in the example answer. Point out that pronouns generally refer to nouns in the previous sentence or within the same sentence.

● Prepare for First for Schools
Reading and Use of English Part 6

Task description
Part 6 is a text from which six sentences have been removed and placed in jumbled order, together with an additional sentence, after the text. Students must decide from which part of the text the sentences have been removed. In this part, there is an emphasis on cohesion, coherence, and text structure.

Tip
Tell students to pay particular attention to the sentences before and after the gaps. Synonyms or pronouns will often refer forwards or backwards to different ideas.

→ See Exam Profile 4, Student's Book page 126.

4 ● Look at the first sentence as a class, and read the example together. Then give students five minutes to complete the exercise. They should work through the text first and then try out each remaining sentence to see if it fits. They should cross out each sentence as they use it. Ask students to check their answers with a partner before checking as a whole class.

Answers
2 C – *It* refers to the tropical fish in the previous sentence and the rock mentioned in that sentence is an example of a tool.
3 A – The content of the missing sentence relates to *understand commands* before the gap, and *one* refers to the *It* of the next sentence.
4 B – The paragraph makes the contrast between animals and humans, and the final sentence *Only humans can use complex language with grammar* after the gap ties in with *can't put individual words together to form sentences.*
5 D – The sentence before the gap mentions the *mirror stage*, which matches *an image in a reflection is actually of themselves.*
6 F – The content of the paragraph before the gap refers to elephants in groups, so the mention of *whether or not they are in the same family* fits with this idea.

5 Make this exercise into a competitive game by giving students just 30 seconds to find as many of the animals as possible. Then check answers as a whole class. Ask students how intelligent they think each species is. You could get them to rank the three most intelligent and the three least intelligent creatures in small groups.

Answers
1 whales	5 chimpanzees	9 parrots
2 dolphins	6 bears	10 elephants
3 octopus	7 fish	11 gorillas
4 humans	8 dogs	12 orang-utans

6 Give students two minutes to complete the exercise in pairs before checking as a class. Elicit an example sentence for each word from the class.

Extension activity

Ask students to write sentences using three of the nouns from exercise 5. They should write two sentences that are true and one that is false. Then ask students to work with a partner. They should read their sentences aloud and guess which ones are true.

Answers

determination   thought   ability   empathy   commands
self-awareness   intelligence

EP Word profile

Books closed. Write the word *smart* on the board and elicit some example sentences using this word. Books open. Ask students to look at the Word profile and compare the meanings of the word *smart* on the board with those in the book. Are there any meanings which are different? Ask students to write down one more example sentence for each meaning in the box on page 21. Set the exercises on page 132. Discuss their responses to exercise 2 as a class.

Answers

1 technology   2 stylish   3 clever

Talking points

Ask students to discuss the questions with a partner. Ask one pair to summarise their discussion and then ask the rest of the class if they covered any other points. With weaker classes, you could introduce this activity with a class brainstorm to include things like other species having more developed senses, humans' ability to survive in the wild compared with animals', the length of time humans take to become adult/independent, use of animals to support humans in their work, exploitation of animals by humans for food and in experiments, etc.

Cooler

Ask students to work in groups of three and to draw a noughts and crosses board. Write the phrasal verbs from the article on page 21 on the board. One student is crosses (X), another is noughts (0) and the third is the judge. Students take it in turns to make sentences using the phrasal verbs, using each phrasal verb on the board once only. Tell them they have a limit of 20 seconds to create a sentence. If the judge is happy with the sentence then they can put their nought or cross on the board. The winner is the first student to get a line of three noughts or crosses.

GRAMMAR   The grammar of phrasal verbs

1 Students have seen these phrasal verbs on page 21, so this should be quite a quick checking activity which can be done as a whole class. As an alternative, you could write the sentences on the board with the phrasal verbs missing. Students then offer the missing words from what they remember from the text. If there are any the class can't complete, they open books and check them in the Grammar section.

Answers

1 live up to   2 showing off   3 care for   4 adding up
5 pick it up

---

2 Tell students to read the rules and to match them to the phrasal verbs from exercise 1. Do the first one together as an example. Once students have matched all the rules, double check their understanding by writing these phrasal verbs on the board: *get up (a), turn down (b), care for (c), fall out with (d)*. Ask students to discuss which category these belong to (answers are given in brackets).

Answers

1 d   2 a   3 c   4 b   5 d

→ Grammar reference Student's Book **page 150**

3 Do the first one as an example with the class and then set the exercise as individual work. Ask students to compare their answers with a partner before checking answers as a whole class.

Answers

1 put it off   2 get out of it   3 looking forward to it
4 let you down   5 throw them away   6 show me around
7 book us in   8 pass on my thanks

---

4 Remind students that if there is no object then the verb and particle cannot usually be separated (e.g. *sit down, turn round*). Give students five minutes to complete the exercise individually. Check answers.

Fast finishers

Ask fast finishers to write additional questions using the phrasal verbs. For example, *Have you ever put off visiting your grandma?* Ask students to ask their questions after checking answers to exercise 4.

Answers

1 Have you ever put off revising for an exam?
2 Do you get on with everyone in your family?
3 Do you clear up at home?
4 Do you ever join in with team sports?
5 Are you looking forward to the summer holidays?

---

5 Ask students to discuss the questions in pairs. Once students have answered the questions, ask one or two people to tell you about their partner.

VOCABULARY   Verb + *to* infinitive

1 Ask students to look at the first example and identify the object (*my friends*). Ask students what they notice about the structure in each example (the first is always used with an object, the second is sometimes used with an object, and the third is never used with an object).

Fast finishers
Ask fast finishers to write true sentences for them using the verbs and structures in exercise 1.

Answer
tend

2 You could do this exercise as a whole-class activity. Ask a student to give you a sentence with *agree,* another with *ask* and another with *advise.* If students cannot identify the pattern with these three examples, then repeat the process with the next three words in the table. If necessary, show students how to find the information in a dictionary which tells them whether a verb is never/sometimes/always followed by an object.

Extension activity
Put students into groups of three or four. Tell them to take it in turns to make a sentence using the verbs from the table. Students have a maximum of 20 seconds to think of a sentence. If they can't, it's the next person's turn. Students continue until there are no verbs left. The winner is the one who has used the most verbs. While students are doing this, monitor and check their use. In feedback, ask each group to give you four example sentences.

Answers
Never with an object	intend
hope	refuse
plan	want
pretend	**Always with an object**
tend	advise
Sometimes with an object	encourage
ask	force
beg	persuade
expect	remind
help	warn

3 Start by modelling a sentence saying when you last refused to do something. Then ask students to discuss the questions with a partner and monitor, listening for any mistakes with the verb patterns. Write any mistakes on the board and correct them as a class.

WRITING   An informal letter or email

1 Tell students about a new skill that you have learned (e.g. I've recently learned to play golf). Ask students to work in pairs to discuss the questions. Elicit four or five new skills (e.g. *playing the guitar*) from different students and different tips on how to learn them (e.g. *with a teacher, with online tutorials*). Ask for a show of hands to vote on the best way to learn a new skill.

2 Give students five minutes to read the questions and Dan's email. Ask them to underline Raj's questions and any parts in Dan's answer that helped them make their decision.

Answer
No, not his final question (Would you recommend other teenagers to take up the same skill?)

3 Set this exercise as individual work, then ask students to compare their answers with a partner. Encourage them to underline the relevant language in Dan's email.

Answers
a It's great to hear from you.
b Keep in touch
c Possible answers: get into, pick up, rely on, let down
d Possible answers: down at the beach, pretty scary, right, Anyway, reckon, stuff, loads, good shape, The thing is, abbreviations (e.g. can't)

4 Do the first one as an example with the whole class. Answer any questions students have about register, making sure they understand which are the formal and which are the informal expressions. Then set this as an individual task before checking answers together.

Suggested answers
1 It's great to hear from you.
2 We're there to help swimmers and surfers who get into difficulties.
3 … this could be pretty scary without any training, right?
4 Plus you must be in good shape.

5 Ask the class to identify the question Dan has not answered. Give students a few minutes to discuss their ideas with a partner. Monitor and help whilst they write their paragraph.

Mixed ability
To support weaker students, you could do the planning stage as a whole class and write notes on the board for students to use in exercise 6. Encourage stronger students to volunteer their ideas.

6 Set this as an individual task with stronger groups or follow the mixed ability notes with weaker students.

● Prepare for First for Schools

Writing Part 2

Task description

In Part 2, students have a choice of task. They may be asked to write an article, an email or letter, a review or a story. They are given a clear context, topic, purpose and target reader. Students should write 140–190 words.

Tip

Remind students to read the prompt letter or email carefully and make sure they respond to all of the questions. When they finish writing, advise them to cross-check their reply against the original letter or email.

→ See Exam Profiles 3 and 5, Student's Book pages 124 and 128.

7 ● If you have students preparing for the First for Schools exam then set a strict time limit of 40 minutes for this task. Put students into pairs and ask them to comment on their partner's answer. Do they think their partner has given enough detail? Have they used the right register?

Sample answer

Hi Niki

Of course I can help you with your project. Thanks for asking me!

I suppose my earliest childhood memory is thinking I had lost my parents at the city zoo. I guess I must have been about three years old at the time. I remember I was sitting on a low wall and I looked everywhere for them. Actually, they were taking my photo and I hadn't realised! Why has that memory stayed with me? Probably because it was the first time I really felt frightened, even though it can only have been for a few seconds.

Another thing I remember to this day is my fourth birthday party. My Dad did some magic tricks and all my friends thought he was great.

Your final question is a difficult one to answer. I'd like to say 'the World Cup in 2014', because we had some great times on Copacabana beach, watching the matches on the big screen and hanging out with friends. But I don't want to remember Brazil's massive defeat in the semi finals! It was a nightmare. I hope my ideas have helped you.

Love Federica

Extension activity

Ask students to write a plan for how they would approach this writing task in an exam. Encourage them to have at least five stages to their plan, e.g.

1 Analyse the question – what exactly is it asking you to do and how many questions need answering?
2 How long should the answer be?
3 What informal expressions can I use?
4 How will I structure my answer?
5 What will I check in my answer afterwards?

Cooler

Ask students to swap books, and to write a short reply to their partner's email. They should include two questions. Students swap books and write a response. For feedback, ask pairs to swap with another pair and to comment on the details of the answer and the register.

Project

Allocate one animal from the reading text to each student or allow them to choose one. Tell students to research their animal online for homework and to find some examples of their animal demonstrating any of the signs of intelligence listed in the article. In the next class ask students to talk in small groups about their research. Ask groups to tell the class which of the animals they researched is the most intelligent. Discuss as a whole class which is the most intelligent animal overall.

Teacher's resources

Student's Book
Grammar reference and practice page 150
Vocabulary list page 140
Workbook
Unit 3, pages 12–15
Go online for
• Pronunciation
• Corpus tasks

4 Take a deep breath

Unit profile

Vocabulary: Stress; Phrasal verbs: health
Reading: Under pressure?
Grammar: Modals (1): Necessity and obligation
Listening: People talking about stress
Speaking: Offering help

Warmer

1 Write these adjectives on the board: *successful, lucky, creative, determined, intelligent*.

2 Ask students to work in pairs and to write the related abstract nouns for each adjective.

3 Tell students to write two questions to ask and answer, using the nouns. Monitor and help where necessary. Share interesting questions and answers with the class.

Your profile

Tell students to think of three more examples of stress. Then ask them to work with a partner and to rank the stresses from the biggest cause to the smallest cause of stress. Put pairs together into groups of four to compare their lists and agree their top three causes of stress. Then ask students to report back to the class.

VOCABULARY Stress

1 **1.09** Students should describe what is happening in each cartoon to a partner. Tell students at this stage that there is no right or wrong answer and encourage them to use their imagination. Ask different pairs to describe one of the cartoons to the class. Play the recording and pause it after the first extract. Ask the class which picture it matches. Do the same after the second extract and then play the final six extracts in one go if you feel your class can continue with the matching unaided. Alternatively, continue to pause the recording after each extract and agree answers as a class before proceeding. Students can check answers in pairs before whole-class feedback.

Audioscript

Narrator: One
Speaker: Where's my red pen? Mum! My red pen? Have you borrowed it? I don't believe it. I put it down for a few minutes and someone takes it. So annoying.
Narrator: Two
Speaker: I had a sandwich for lunch at school but I just don't feel like anything. Maybe it's because I'm a bit worried about tomorrow. I'll be ok, though. I'll probably feel like something later but I'll make it myself. Don't worry.

Narrator: Three
Speaker: I don't think it's anything serious. I think I just stood up too quickly. I don't remember anything else, until I woke up lying on the floor. It didn't last for long, did it?
Narrator: Four
Speaker: The film starts at seven thirty and it'll take over half an hour to get there. It's after seven, already! We're definitely going to be late. Oh no! Where's Cassie? I hope she gets here soon.
Narrator: Five
Speaker: It's been like this since very early this morning. I'm quite hungry but I think I should avoid food until later. Perhaps it was something I had last night. But I don't remember eating anything different from anyone else.
Narrator: Six
Speaker: Oh, my head feels funny. I think I need to sit down. I don't feel very well. Can you do me a favour and get me a glass of water? Thanks.
Narrator: Seven
Speaker: I don't know what to do. I've tried reading, listening to music, everything. I've been lying here since eleven and it's now after midnight. I have to get up at seven, too.
Narrator: Eight
Speaker: I keep thinking about my driving lesson. It was so scary. I almost lost control of the car. I saw the corner but I didn't slow down in time. The instructor had to use his controls to stop the car – and he grabbed the steering wheel! We only just avoided hitting a wall.

Answers

1 b **2** d **3** g **4** h **5** f **6** c **7** a **8** e

2 Before setting this task, check that students understand *faint* (feel very weak and as if you might fall down), *dizzy* (feeling like everything is turning round, so that you feel sick or as if you might fall), *upset stomach* (pain in your stomach) and *temper* (be *bad-tempered* means *feel angry*). Then ask students to work in pairs, before checking answers together.

Answers

a have difficulty sleeping
b lose your temper / get bad-tempered
c feel dizzy
d lose your appetite
e go over and over something in your mind
f have an upset stomach
g faint
h get in a panic

3 Model the first answer by describing when you last lost your temper. Ask students to ask and answer the questions in pairs and then elicit some ideas for each question from different pairs.

READING

1 Books closed. Write *Stress is for adults, not people my age* on the board. Elicit responses from the class. Then give students a few minutes to read the rest of the headings and think about their answers. They should then compare their ideas with a partner. Ask for one or two volunteers to share their answers with the class.

Fast finishers

Ask fast finishers to write one or two more sentences that show their feelings about stress, and to compare these with their partner.

2 Read out the first bold sentence and ask: *What do you think the topic of the next paragraph will be?* Elicit answers, then ask students to choose the heading that matches their ideas. Tell them to read the next paragraph to see if it fits. Students then complete the exercise individually. They can check answers with a partner before whole-class feedback.

Answers

2 e 3 b 4 c 5 d

3 Emphasise the strict word limit, as this can be common in exam tasks, and then give students five minutes to complete the task. Monitor and give help where necessary. Ask students to compare their answers with a partner before checking answers together.

Fast finishers

Tell fast finishers to underline sentences that they agree with in the text. After checking answers to exercise 3, ask one or two fast finishers which sentences they underlined and why they agree with them.

Answers

1 to feel stressed **2** than meeting **3** increase and decrease
4 to have fun **5** positive opportunities in

EP Word profile

Ask students to identify which use of *control* is a verb (*control*)? Which use is a noun (*his controls*)? Which expressions mean that you can't control something (*beyond our control, lost control*)? Then set the exercise on page 133.

Answers

1 d **2** a **3** f **4** c **5** g **6** h **7** b **8** e

Talking points

Students can discuss these questions in small groups. Encourage them to use the vocabulary they have already learnt in this unit. When discussing the second question, make a note of students' ideas on the board for them to use in the project at the end of this unit.

Extension activity

Ask students to write two sentences: one beginning *I get stressed when …* and the other beginning *I deal with stress by …* Collect the sentences in and redistribute them. Ask students to try to guess who they think wrote the sentences.

Cooler

Give students a few minutes to make a note of a new word they have learnt in this lesson, and its definition in English. In pairs or small groups, get students to teach each other their new words. Ask one or two students to share their new words and definitions with the class.

GRAMMAR Modals (1): Necessity and obligation

1 Books closed. Write *You should … , You don't have to …* and *You need to …* on the board. Ask students how to combat stress, trying to elicit an example for advice (e.g. *You should go to bed early*), lack of obligation (e.g. *You don't have to run every day, but some exercise is good*) and necessity (e.g. *You need to find a way to relax*). Books open. Students can work in pairs to complete the rules, before checking answers as a whole class.

Answers

1 should **2** need to **3** don't have to

→ Grammar reference Student's Book **page 151**

⬤ Prepare for First for Schools
Reading and Use of English Part 4

Task description
Reading and Use of English Part 4 is a key word transformation task that tests vocabulary, grammar and collocation. It consists of six questions, each with a lead-in sentence and a gapped sentence. Students must complete the gapped sentence in two to five words, including the given 'key' word.

Tip
Tell students to read the entire sentence to look for clues about the type of word that might be needed to complete the gap. There might be clues that help students to decide on, for example, which modal verb to use, or which tense is needed to keep the same meaning as the first sentence.

→ See Exam Profile 1, Student's Book page 121.

2 ⬤ Look at the example together and then work through number two as a whole class. Give students a few minutes to complete the exercise, before checking answers together.

Answers

1 it was necessary   2 I need to attend more / need more
3 didn't have to   4 have to wear

3 Books closed. Write *You must do your homework* and *You mustn't be late* on the board. Ask students which sentence means something is prohibited and which means something is an obligation. Ask students for a synonym for *must* and *mustn't* in these examples (*have to* and *can't*). Books open. Ask students to complete the rules individually.

Answers

a have to; must   b mustn't; can't   c must; mustn't
d have to; can't

4 ● Remind students that in some cases, both *must* and *have to* are possible. Give students a few minutes to complete the task. When checking answers, make sure students are clear on the difference in meaning (see Answers below).

Answers

1 must   2 mustn't   3 mustn't
4 both: must = often when the feeling of stress expresses an internal obligation (i.e. imposed by the speaker)
has to = often when the feeling of stress expresses an external obligation (i.e. imposed by a rule, convention or someone else).
5 both: must = the speaker personally feels it's necessary to do some exercise
have to = the speaker personally feels the pressure comes from elsewhere, e.g. for a school sports team.

◎ Corpus challenge

Ask students to correct the sentence and explain the error. We use *needn't* or *don't have to* to show that something isn't necessary. *Mustn't* indicates that it is forbidden.

Answer

The bicycle is cheaper than the car, and you needn't / don't have to spend any money on petrol.

5 Set the exercise for students to complete individually. Give positive feedback for interesting ideas. Then tell students to read their sentences to a partner and to ask each other questions to find out more about each statement.

Mixed ability

Set stronger students the challenge of joining all of the sentences together into one paragraph. The paragraph must make sense and be focused on one topic only.

Fast finishers

Fast finishers should add a further example for each sentence in exercise 5.

Extension activity

Tell students to write four sentences about themselves using *have to* and *must*. One must be false and three must be true. They should then show their sentences to a partner who must guess which one is false.

VOCABULARY   Phrasal verbs: health

1 Encourage students to look at exercise 4, number 4 again, and to focus on the phrasal verb *deal with* (take action in order to achieve something or to solve a problem). Ask for a volunteer to explain its meaning. Then ask students to do the matching exercise individually before checking answers as a whole class.

Answers

1 f   2 c   3 b   4 a   5 e   6 d

2 Ask students to complete the gaps without looking back at exercise 1 if possible. Then put them into pairs to complete any that are missing, checking against exercise 1 if necessary. They then ask and answer the questions. For feedback, ask different pairs to report back on each question.

Answers

1 stay up   2 get over   3 passes out   4 come down with
5 cut down on

LISTENING

1 ▶1.10 Tell students that they are going to listen to someone talking about stress. Ask them to read the sentences first, and clarify any words students might not know such as *suffer* and *technique* (a particular or special way of doing something). Then play the recording. Ask students to compare their answer with a partner. Then play the recording again, if necessary, before checking as a class.

Audioscript

Narrator: One
Emma: It's not a big deal but I do get stressed – almost always for exams. The first thing that happens is I lose my appetite and partly because of that, I reckon, I get a bit bad-tempered. I do a variety of things to keep the stress under control. I talk to my parents about whatever's worrying me, I avoid staying up late, I even do a bit of sport. And all these things help. Within a day I've usually got over whatever it is, or I've moved on to something else. I try not to let things get me down in general.

Answer
C

2 Ask the students to underline key words in sentence C, e.g. *range of ways, deal with stress*. When you check answers, point out how these key words match key ideas in the text (*range of ways = variety of things*; *deal with stress = keep stress under control*). Point out to students that this use of synonyms is common in many listening and reading exam questions, and encourage them to record synonyms in their vocabulary notebooks.

Answer

I do a variety of things to keep the stress under control.

3 Emphasise that this is an important exercise because it shows how distraction in the script might lead students to choose the wrong answer. Set this exercise as pair work and then check answers as a whole class.

Answers

E Not true. She mentions doing a bit of sport but does not say it is the main way she deals with stress.

F Not true. She doesn't say how she feels about it.

G Not true. She doesn't mention who told her the techniques she uses.

H Not true. She doesn't mention her brother.

● Prepare for First for Schools

Listening part 3

Task description

The focus of this part is on identifying attitude, opinion, gist, purpose, feeling, main points and detail. Students hear five short related monologues. There are five questions which require students to choose the correct option from a list of eight.

Tip

Tell students to listen for key words and synonyms, and try not to be confused by distracters.

→ See Exam Profile 1, Student's Book page 121.

4 ▶1.11 Tell students to look back at the sentences in exercise 1, and to match the sentences to the speaker. If necessary, with weaker students, pause the recording after each speaker and check answers as a class. They will not need all the sentences. Play the recording. Students should listen to the recording a second time to answer any questions they missed on the first listening and/or check their answers.

Audioscript

Narrator: Two

Speaker 2:   I think people underestimate how stressful life can be for teenagers these days. We've always got loads of deadlines – essays, projects, tests, everything. And then there's always the end-of-year exams coming up. I always do the work and I know I work harder than a lot of other students but <u>teachers never stop telling you how important everything is, how much you need to study now to</u>

<u>get a good job or go to university. That's what worries me the most</u>. My brother is helpful whenever things get me down. He's at university already so he's been through it all.

Narrator: Three

Speaker 3:   I used to be much more sensitive about things and get quite worried about friends, schoolwork, all the usual things. I'd have difficulty sleeping and get really overtired. Then we were discussing stress one day in class and <u>our teacher said that some people find writing a diary helps</u>. I must admit, I thought it all sounded like too much hard work at the time. Then by coincidence someone gave me a really nice notebook and I thought I'd have a go. I don't write loads – and I don't even manage it every day, but it really helps.

Narrator: Four

Speaker 4:   Once in a while, at weekends usually, when I've got a lot to do before Monday, I get a bit stressed. I end up watching TV or just wasting time online. I'll basically do anything to avoid doing the things I need to do! By the end of the day, I'm feeling worse than ever and by then, not at my best. <u>I'll probably be in a bad mood. I know I'm being bad-tempered but I can't help it</u>. I know what they say – running might help, for example. But I'm not really into sport. So I've never bothered with that. Maybe I should just go for a walk or something.

Narrator: Five

Speaker 5:   <u>Sure I worry about things from time to time</u>: when I'm late for something, especially school, or when I have to give a presentation in class. <u>But everyone gets that, don't they? I rarely fall out with friends and ninety-five per cent of the time I get on fine with my parents</u>. I'm not the best student in the world but I work hard. I might be a bit tired in the mornings from time to time, and even a bit grumpy occasionally. I'm not half as bad as my brother. He's really rude sometimes.

Answers

Refer also to the underlined parts of the script.

Speaker 2: D – Students need to listen out for references to *the future*.

Speaker 3: G – *Someone's advice* refers to the speaker's teacher and writing a diary is the *technique*.

Speaker 4: F – Students need to identify bad behaviour caused by stress.

Speaker 5: A – The answer is confirmed by a global understanding of the whole text.

You do not need letters B, E and H.

SPEAKING   Offering help

1 ▶1.12 Ask students to look at the photos and be prepared to take notes. Play the recording once for students to answer the question.

Audioscript

Dan: Hi, Sara. Everything OK?

Sara: I can't miss band practice at eight and I have to finish an essay. And I must take some games back to Ahmed's tonight. He was really annoyed that I forgot to bring them in this morning!

Dan:	I'm seeing Ahmed later. Shall I take the games for you?
Sara:	Are you sure? That'd be fantastic, thanks.
Dan:	OK. I'll text you when I leave here, if you like. It'll be about seven thirty.
Sara:	Thanks but there's no need. I'll have left for practice by then. They can give you the games. My parents will be in all evening, though.
Dan:	OK. Good luck with the essay!

Answer
He's going to pick up some of Ahmed's games from her house and give them to Ahmed.

2 ▶1.12 Give students a few minutes to complete the gaps and then play the recording again. Check answers as a whole class.

Answers
1 Shall 2 sure 3 like 4 need

3 ▶1.13 Ask for a show of hands to see if students ever make dinner or do the shopping for their family. Play the recording for students to answer the questions. Check answers as a class and then play the recording again for students to confirm.

Audioscript
Mum:	I don't know how I'm going to manage tonight. Your Dad isn't back until late so I have to pick your sister up from the station. There's the online shopping which has to be done by eight, not to mention dinner. I haven't even thought about that.
Dan:	Would you like me to pick Lara up? I'll have to borrow your car, of course.
Mum:	Um, it's OK, I can do it myself.
Dan:	Let me do the sho…
Mum:	The dinner? It'd be great if you could. Thanks. I think there's stuff in the fridge and you could get some more on the way home from school.
Dan:	Actually, Mum, I was thinking of doing the shopping.
Mum:	The shopping? No, don't worry. I can manage that. Thanks again, Daniel. Back about seven. OK?

Answers
1 Dan offers to help his Mum.
2 He offers to pick his sister up and to do the online shopping.
3 She wants him to make dinner.

4 ▶1.13 Ask students to tick the phrases they remember hearing. Then play the recording again for students to check their answers. Ask for volunteers to give one more example for each function.

Answers
| Dan: | Would you like me to ..., Let me… |
| Mrs Fisher: | It's OK, I can do it myself, It'd be great if you could. No, don't worry. I can manage. |

5 Introduce this activity by saying three things that you must do this week. One or two could be unusual! Give students five minutes to write a list of things they need to do this week. They can invent things if they don't have much to do. You could ask them to imagine they are a celebrity and to imagine what things this person might need to do.

6 Ask for a volunteer to help you model this first. Start by saying one of the activities you mentioned for exercise 5. Put students into pairs and read the example as a class. Monitor and listen to students' conversations as they are role playing. Help with vocabulary and pronunciation as necessary. Encourage them to use the functions in the *Prepare* box. Choose two strong pairs to act out their conversation to the class.

Cooler
1 Explain to students that a 'rider' is a demand made by a famous singer when they are on tour. Ask students which ones of the following they think are real demands and which ones are false:

a the chauffeur's clothes must be 100% cotton
b four cans of coke zero
c a white couch with three animal print pillows

2 Ask students to match the demands to a celebrity:
1 Rihanna (c)
2 Kanye West (a)
3 Lady Gaga (b)

Project
Bring in some suitable advice pages from a website or magazine. Ask students to brainstorm the type of problems and possible advice they might find. Then tell students to write a letter describing a (real or imaginary) problem. Once students have finished, they exchange their letters with a partner and write a response offering suggestions and advice. They can use some of the ideas from Talking points. Tell students to use vocabulary from this unit when describing their problem, and verbs from page 26 when giving advice.

Teacher's resources
Student's Book
Grammar reference and practice page 151
Vocabulary list page 140
Video
Speaking Part 1
Workbook
Unit 4, pages 16–19
Go online for
- Pronunciation
- Progress test
- Achievement test
- Speaking test video worksheets
- Corpus tasks

Biology
The heart

Learning objectives

- The students learn about how the heart functions and how to maintain a healthy heart.
- In the project stage, students write a paragraph about their own lifestyle and its potential impact on their heart.

Warmer

Ask students to work in small groups to make a list of parts of the body, including organs (e.g. *heart*, *brain*, *liver*, *kidneys*). See which group can make the longest list in just one minute. Ask this group to read their list to the class.

1 Draw a basic heart shape on the board. Ask students to tell a partner what they know about how the heart works (e.g. *the heart is found in the centre of your chest, it is about the size of a human fist, it pumps blood around your body*), and get feedback as a whole class. Monitor and offer help where necessary. If students are all struggling, give them one or two of the answers and then ask them to fill in the rest. Then tell students to read the text and label the diagram in pairs. Check answers.

Answers
1 lungs 2 right atrium 3 left atrium 4 right ventricle
5 left ventricle 6 septum 7 vein 8 left artery 9 capillaries

2 Tell students they will need to read the text very thoroughly in order to complete this exercise. Draw their attention to the glossary and go through it together as a class. If necessary, offer help as they work, for example by showing them where in the text to find the next two answers. Once they have ordered the stages, ask them to compare their answers with a partner and then check as a whole class. When giving the answers, ask for volunteers to say where in the text the answers came from.

Mixed ability

Pair weaker students with stronger students to provide more support for weaker students. Encourage stronger students to explain the reasoning behind their answers.

Fast finishers

Ask fast finishers to close their books and to draw the basic circulation pattern in their notebooks. They can compare their diagram with their partner.

Answers
c 2 left atrium a 3 left ventricle g 4 arteries
b 5 capillaries h 6 veins e 7 right atrium
d 8 right ventricle

3 Ask students which questions they can answer from memory. Then give them time to find the answers in the text. Check as a whole class.

Answers
1 the septum 2 right 3 lungs 4 they are so thin 5 veins
6 atrium

4 Elicit ideas from students about how to maintain a healthy heart (e.g. *eat healthily*). They describe to a partner what they can see in the photos. Then ask them to read the texts and to match them to a picture. Do they need to read the whole text to do the matching? If not, what words gave them the clues they needed? Students can check their answers with a partner before whole-class feedback.

Answers
1 d 2 b 4 a 5 c

5 Ask students to raise their hands if they think they have a healthy lifestyle. Then tell them to read the text again and to rate themselves on each sentence. Ask students to discuss the statements in small groups, and to feed back to the class about things people in their group always / sometimes / never do. On the whole, do they think their class is a healthy group of people?

Fast finishers

Ask fast finishers to write one or two sentences making recommendations about how they could improve their lifestyle. Ask one or two students to share their recommendations after checking the answers to the main task.

Extension activity

Ask students to work with a partner to write down five more health tips. Then put pairs together to make groups of four, and ask students to compare their tips. Ask each group to choose the best three tips and think about why these are the best ones. For feedback, ask two or three groups to share their tips and reasons with the rest of the class.

6 ▶ 1.14 Write these headings on the board: *What Karen eats*, *What exercise she does*, *Dietician's advice*. Tell students that they are going to listen to Karen talking to a dietician about her lifestyle. Ask them to take notes under the headings on the board. Play the recording, and allow students to check their answers with a partner before whole-class feedback. Ask for a show of hands if they think their current lifestyles are more healthy than Karen's.

Audioscript

Dietician: So, Karen. Tell me a little bit about your eating habits.

Karen: OK, um. Where should I start? With breakfast?

Dietician: Sure, that's fine. What do you usually have?

Karen: Well, I always drink a glass of orange juice first. And after that, I usually have some toast, maybe with butter or jam, and sometimes a bowl of cereal, if I'm really hungry and I have enough time. That's about it.

Dietician: OK, that's not too bad. The juice counts as a serving of fruit. And you get enough carbohydrates, with the bread and cereal. But you should probably have more protein too. There isn't enough just in the milk you have on your cereal.

Karen: Really? So what should I eat, then?

Dietician: Well, you could have some peanut butter on your toast, or perhaps have an egg. That would give you enough protein.

Karen: OK, that's easy.

Dietician: And do you usually have five servings of fruit and vegetables a day?

Karen: Mmm, I think so. I usually have fruit at lunch, and I always have some salad or vegetables with dinner.

Dietician: That's fine, but you could also have some fruit as a snack in the morning or the afternoon. A banana or an apple, for example.

Karen: OK, I'll try! And what about my weight? Is it OK?

Dietician: I think so. You weigh fifty-five kilos, and you're one metre sixty-five tall. How old are you, Karen?

Karen: I'm sixteen.

Dietician: Yes, then, you're just fine. And does your weight go up and down a lot?

Karen: Not really.

Dietician: That's good too. OK, one more question. What type of physical activity do you do in a typical week?

Karen: Well, I ride my bike to school. It takes me about ten minutes each way. And when the weather's bad I usually walk.

Dietician: OK, that's a start. But you really need at least 30 minutes of exercise a day. Do you play any sports after school?

Karen: Not really. But I have swimming lessons on Saturdays for an hour, and I usually swim for another half hour after that, but just for fun.

Dietician: Well, that helps. But you should probably do more exercise during the week as well. Think about joining a sports team or a club. Or go jogging two or three times a week. You need a bit more activity every day. It's good for your body, and it also helps you to relax and sleep better at night.

Karen: OK, I'll think about it. Is that all?

Dietician: Yes, that's it. Nice to see you, Karen.

Karen: Nice to see you too, and thanks.

Answers

Karen eats: orange juice, toast, cereal, fruit at lunch, salad, vegetables.
Exercise: walks or rides her bike to school, swims.
Advice: eat more protein, eat fruit as a snack, do more exercise.

Extension activity

Ask students to work in pairs. They should imagine that one of them is a dietician and that the other is a patient. Using the questions in the project work they should role play offering and asking for lifestyle advice. Ask one or two pairs to perform their role play to the class.

Cooler

Ask students to discuss these questions with a partner:
1 What do you think is the biggest health concern in your country?
2 What are some simple changes people can make to improve their health?
Elicit responses from one or two pairs.

Project

Give students a few minutes to read the questions and to brainstorm some ideas with a partner. Then set the writing task. Make sure students choose one or two related questions only and not all six, so that they have a focused paragraph. Encourage them to add detail in this paragraph and monitor so you can help if necessary. Students swap their paragraph with a partner, who ideally has answered different questions. You can take this writing in to mark at the end of the lesson.

5 Past times

Unit profile

Vocabulary: History; Expressing frequency
Reading: A text on sleep
Grammar: Present and past habits
Writing: An article (1)

Warmer

1 Tell students to write down three things that have caused them to feel stressed this week. You could start by giving them an example of your own (e.g. too much homework to mark). Ask students what happens when they feel stressed, and elicit *It's difficult to sleep*. You may need to mime this.

2 Ask students to work with a partner and to give each other advice on reducing stress, and making it easier to sleep.

3 Discuss some ideas as a class and write them on the board for later in the lesson.

Your profile

1 Give students a few minutes to think about their answers before discussing the questions with a partner. As a class, discuss the history of your local area – do any of the students know any particularly interesting aspects?

VOCABULARY   History

1 Tell students that they are going to do a history quiz. Ask them to focus firstly on the meaning of the words in blue and not the answers to the questions. Ask students to define the words without using a dictionary, if possible. Remind them to look at the whole sentence and to use context clues to help them. Check the meanings as a class (*ancestor*: relative who lived a long time ago; *tribe*: a group of people who live together, usually in areas far away from cities, and who share the same culture and language and still have a traditional way of life; *myth*: an ancient story about gods and brave people, often one that explains an event in history or the natural world).

Answers

1 ancestors: relatives who lived a long time ago
2 civilisation: the culture and way of life of a society or country at a particular period in time
kingdom: a country ruled by a king or queen
3 tribe: a group of people who live together, usually in areas far away from cities, and who share the same culture and language
myth: an ancient story about gods and brave people, often one that explains an event in history or the natural world

---

4 century: a period of 100 years
5 citizens: people who have a legal right to live in a particular country
6 inhabitants: people that live in a particular place
7 decade: a period of ten years, especially a period such as 1860 to 1869, or 1990 to 1999
8 launched: made available for the first time

2 ▶1.15 Ask students to answer the questions in pairs and then ask for a show of hands for each one. Play the recording for students to check their answers. Play the recording again and ask students to take notes. Pause it after each section to give students time to answer. They can compare their answers with a partner before whole-class feedback.

Audioscript

Narrator: One
Speaker: Well, man's earliest ancestors appeared about 200,000 years ago, in central <u>Africa</u>. Then, about 100,000 years ago, humans started to move out of Africa into the Middle East and then Asia. The first humans arrived in Europe around 40,000 years ago, and in the Americas only 12,000 years ago.
Narrator: Two
Speaker: The Ancient Greek civilisation started in about 750 BCE. That means 750 years before Year One. It ended in 148 BCE. The Roman Empire was later than that, starting in the first century BCE. <u>But the oldest Kingdom of Egypt started almost thirty centuries BCE</u>. That's almost fifty centuries ago! The first of the great pyramids of Egypt were built during this era.
Narrator: Three
Speaker: Well, you can read about the Amazons, Centaurs and Titans in Ancient Greek myths. According to these myths, the Amazons were a tribe of all-female soldiers, Centaurs were half-man, half-horse and the Titans were Greek gods. Of course, <u>the Amazon River in South America was named after the Amazons</u>. The river was given this name by the Spanish in the 1540s, because they were fighting against the local Indians, including many brave women.
Narrator: Four
Speaker: Cars have been around for about 120 years. Lots of inventors were developing cars at the same time, including Gottlieb Daimler in Germany and Henry Ford in the United States. But it was a German inventor called Karl Benz who produced the first car in the 1890s, <u>at the end of the 19th century</u>. The great era of the car was the 20th century, but now lack of oil means transport will have to change.

Narrator: Five

Speaker: Well, all three of these are very big countries, but with very different population sizes. In 1900, Russia had only four million citizens. India was more populated, with 270 million citizens, but China was the most populated country, with 415 million citizens. Today, 1.3 billion people live in China but India is catching up fast, with 1.2 billion citizens. The world's third largest country in terms of population is now the United States with more than 315 million citizens. Russia's population is about 140 million.

Narrator: Six

Speaker: Most of you probably know that Tokyo is the most populated city in the world now. The Tokyo-Yokohama region has more than 35 million inhabitants. By comparison, London's population is just 8 million today and New York's population is about 19 million. However, in 1900, London had the most inhabitants, with a population of six and a half million people. New York had about three and a half million inhabitants at that time, and Tokyo had only one and a half million.

Narrator: Seven

Speaker: It's difficult for us to imagine life without television now, but in fact it has been around for less than 100 years. There was a race amongst inventors in the UK, the US and Germany to produce the first televisions and there is still some argument about who came first. But the first public broadcasts were in the 1930s. The first commercial TVs in the 1930s showed pictures in black and white. Domestic colour TVs weren't available until the 1960s.

Narrator: Eight

Speaker: Experimental versions of the internet were in use in university departments and by the military in the 1970s. Computers in those days were incredibly slow. They had eight megabytes of memory and they could take a few minutes to download a very basic webpage! The internet wasn't launched publicly until 1995. The twentieth anniversary of the internet was in 2015. In just twenty years, the internet has completely altered how we live. Can you imagine living without any internet access at all?

Answers

1 a 2 c 3 a 4 b 5 c 6 b 7 a 8 b

Extension activity

Put students into groups of four and tell them to write questions using four of the words in blue. Students should try to make their questions challenging to answer. Then put two groups together to ask and answer the questions. Finally, ask groups to read any questions the other group could not answer to the rest of the class to see if anyone knows the answer.

Answers

1 Humans arrived in Asia about 100,000 years ago and in the Americas about 12,000 years ago.
2 The Ancient Greek civilisation started in about 750 BCE and The Roman Empire started in the first century BCE.
3 Centaurs were half-man, half-horse and the Titans were Greek gods.
4 The great era of the car was the twentieth century (the eighteenth century isn't mentioned).
5 In 1900, Russia had only four million citizens. India had 270 million citizens.
6 In 1900, New York had about three and a half million inhabitants, and Tokyo had only one and a half million.
7 Domestic colour TVs weren't available until the 1960s.
8 Experimental versions of the internet were in use in university departments and by the military in the 1970s. The twentieth anniversary of the internet was in 2005.

3 For question 1, ask students to write down three key events for each decade or century. For question two, they should think of at least three differences. Set question three as in the book. Encourage them to think about the ancient past as well as the recent past. Once the students have completed their discussion, feed some of the ideas back on the board and open the discussion to define the key events and the most important inventions. Students could vote to decide what they are.

READING

1 Books closed. Write the first question from the reading text on the board (*What happens if you wake up in the middle of the night?*), and elicit responses from volunteer students. Ask students what word they could use instead of *if* here, and remind them that this is an example of the zero conditional.

Answer
when

🔵 Prepare for First for Schools
Reading and Use of English Part 2

Task description
This task mainly tests awareness and control of grammar with some focus on vocabulary. Students complete eight gaps in a text with a suitable word.

Tip
Remind students to identify the type of word that is missing (e.g. noun, verb, adjective), as well as considering the meaning. Doing this will improve their accuracy.

→ See Exam Profile 4, Student's Book page 127.

2 ● Tell students to read the strategies carefully, as they are useful when dealing with exam questions. Ask students to explain how the first strategy can help them (*it may tell them the part of speech they are looking for, e.g. a noun, adjective or verb*). Then ask students to read the first paragraph and complete the gaps individually. Check answers as a whole class. Were there any which had more than one correct answer? (Yes, questions 1, 3 and 7).

Answers
1 who/that   2 to   3 in/into   4 the   5 no   6 too
7 Although/Though   8 without

3 Encourage students to think back to their advice from the Warmer. Then set the questions for small group discussion. Afterwards, ask each group to summarise their answers to one of the questions.

4 Give students a couple of minutes for this task. Check answers as a whole class.

Mixed ability

Ask stronger students to write one or two more questions about the text. Then tell them to give the questions to a mixed-ability pair who should try to answer them.

Answers
1 the two-sleep habit
2 people could stay up later if they wanted
3 very young and older people tend to get up earlier and go to bed earlier than teenagers and young adults
4 a mid-afternoon sleep
5 the body's function of wanting to be awake or asleep at different times of the day

5 Check students know the meaning of the highlighted words by asking for volunteers to paraphrase them and then set the exercise. Ask students to compare their answers with a partner before checking answers together. Model the pronunciation of *psychologically* /ˌsaɪ.kəlˈɒdʒ.ɪ.kəl/ and ask students to repeat after you.

Fast finishers

Ask fast finishers to write their own sentences using the highlighted words. Ask for an example sentence for each word when checking answers to exercise 5.

Extension activity

Ask students to create a questionnaire to find out about people's sleep habits. Give students support to write their questions. Allow them to write any questions they wish. If any students are struggling, you could give them these questions: *How many hours do you sleep per night? Have you ever suffered with sleep problems? Do you ever stay up late at night?* Then give them a few minutes to interview two or three people. Students should then work with a new partner and discuss their findings. Feed back as a class. Who gets the most and least sleep? What is the average number of hours sleep per night?

Answers
1 tend to   2 psychologically   3 turns out   4 constantly
5 stay up

EP Word profile

Ask students to read the sentences and explain the meaning of each phrase to a partner by trying to substitute the phrase in pink with other words. Then set the exercises on page 133. Discuss their responses to exercise 2 as a class.

Answers
1 take the opportunity to   2 take turns   3 taking; for granted
4 take into account   5 take it easy

Talking points

Ask students to discuss these questions in pairs. As an extension to the final question, you could ask students to draw a pie chart showing what they typically do in a 24-hour period. Ask them to compare their pie charts with a partner.

Cooler

Write the word *sleep* in the centre of the board, and ask students to call out words they associate with it, e.g. *sleeping habits, sleep patterns, awake, fall asleep*. Add their suggestions to the board, connected to *sleep* with a line. You could ask students to copy the resulting mind map into their vocabulary notebooks.

GRAMMAR Present and past habits

1 Books closed. Write *would* and *used to* on the board. Ask students what time they go to bed now, and what time they went to bed when they were five, to elicit an example of the present simple and an example of *would/used to*. Read the examples with the students, and complete the first rule with the whole class. Then ask students to complete the exercise individually before comparing answers with a partner. Check answers as a whole class. Ask students if they can remember how to form questions and negatives with *used to* (questions: *Did* + noun/pronoun + *use to* …, e.g. *Did you use to eat lots of chocolate when you were young?*; negative: *did not / didn't use to*, e.g. *We didn't use to take the bus to school*). Point out that *used to* is more common than *would*.

Answers
a present simple   b present continuous
c present continuous   d used to   e would
f past continuous

→ Grammar reference Student's Book page 152

2 Encourage students to read the whole text before attempting this task as this will help them with meaning and therefore making the correct choices. Set this as individual work before checking as a whole class. When checking answers, ask for volunteers to explain why each choice is correct as this will also provide revision of the differences between simple and continuous tenses in the present and past.

Answers
1 eat   2 are constantly changing   3 have   4 used to be
5 are always telling   6 were constantly worrying
7 never used to have   8 used to think   9 used to need
10 are still changing   11 don't feel   12 are missing

3 Before students do this task, ask them which structure they would use for sentences 1 and 2. Elicit a model for each and write it on the board. Then allow students a few minutes to complete the exercise. Elicit an example for each sentence and write them on the board.

Fast finishers

Ask fast finishers to write further example sentences for each situation, and to feed these back while checking answers to exercise 3.

Corpus challenge

Ask students to correct the sentence and to explain the error (we use *would* with frequency adverbs such as *sometimes*).

Answer
Sometimes I would play this game with my friends.

VOCABULARY Expressing frequency

1 Give students a few minutes to complete the exercise with a partner before writing the answers on the board. Ask students if they know any other words or expressions to add to each group. Alternatively, with a strong class, ask students to close their books and write *always*, *often*, *sometimes* and *almost never* on the board. Next to *always* write *all the time*, then ask for one more synonym for each word. Books open. Students check the expressions in the box to see if the ones on the board are there and then complete the exercise individually.

Answers
always – constantly
often – most days/weeks/months / regularly
sometimes – from time to time / (every) once in a while
almost never – rarely / seldom / occasionally

2 Read the rule together then set this as an individual writing task, encouraging students to use the words in the Vocabulary box. Ask students to work with a partner to ask and answer the questions. As an alternative, with stronger classes, you could set this as a speaking task.

3 Model the exercise by saying two sentences about you (one true and one false), e.g. *I rarely used to have a shower when I was a teenager, I still sleep in my old bedroom from time to time*. Ask students which one they think is false. Then set the task in the book, reminding them to use an expression of frequency in each sentence.

WRITING An article (1)

1 If possible, ask students to bring in the articles they have been reading. Their discussion of the questions can then be extended. If not, simply set the questions as a discussion task with students working in pairs or small groups. Feedback interesting ideas to the class.

2 Give students a few minutes to complete the exercise individually before checking answers as a whole class. Ask them where they found the key words which gave them the answers. Ask students to volunteer what their own talents are.

Answers
1 in a student magazine
2 students and teachers, maybe parents
3 your talent (something that you are naturally good at)
4 chatty. It is a personal text that should be interesting and memorable for readers.

3 Tell students to read the *Prepare* box and the article. Once they have chosen the title, ask a student to explain the reasons for their choice (the writer is an experienced cyclist, who describes their hobby. They do not include any tips).

Answer

B A passion for cycling

4 Ask students to find the topic sentence in each paragraph. When checking answers, highlight the fact that, although here it is always the first sentence, it can sometimes be the second sentence.

Answers

the first sentence in each paragraph
d (possible answer) So what's next for me?

5 Remind students that good articles tend to address the reader directly and this is what gives them a lively, chatty style. Give students a few minutes to underline some examples of this, and ask them to compare answers with a partner.

Answers

In paragraph B they ask the reader two questions (*… is there?* / *Can you imagine that feeling?*).
In paragraph D they ask the reader to watch out for them on TV.

● Prepare for First for Schools

Writing Part 2

Task description

In Part 2, students have a choice of task. They may be asked to write an article, an email or letter, a review or a story. They are given a clear context, topic, purpose and target reader. Students should write 140–190 words.

Tip

Tell students to pay attention to the information given in the input text. This will help them structure their writing and to write in an appropriate register.

6 ● If you have students preparing for the First For Schools exam, set a strict time limit of 40 minutes for this to mimic exam conditions. If not, you could allow your students more time or set this as homework. Remind them to think of a topic sentence for each paragraph when they are organising their ideas and to try and include two or three direct questions. Ask students to exchange their article with a partner. Ask them to comment on: the article's organisation – does each paragraph have a clear topic? Does the introduction refer to the question? Does the conclusion leave a question for the reader? Ask them to underline words they think have been used too often and to suggest replacements. Ask them to circle the language of habits – has the student used a range of structures?

Sample answer

A SENSE OF RHYTHM
Did you play with musical instruments as a very young child? That's my story and I was only two years old when my older brother put a pair of drumsticks in my hands! Right from the start I knew I was good at drumming and so did he. I loved beating out rhythms on anything I could get my hands on – a metal table, an old box, even Mum's saucepans.
As I grew older, my parents noticed my special talent and bought me a drum kit. Then they arranged for me to have classes, which I really enjoyed. Two years ago, I formed a band with a great guitarist from my school and we joined up with a singer he knew. Now, we're getting quite well-known on the local music scene.
My absolute dream is to make it big in the music industry, maybe drumming for someone really famous, and getting to play gigs all around the world. But before that can happen, I know I must improve my technique, and experiment with more complex rhythms. Check me out on YouTube!

Cooler

Ask students to think of a talented person they admire and to note down five reasons why they admire them. Then ask them to tell a partner about the person. Ask one or two students to tell the class about who their partner admires and why.

Project

Ask students to research lifestyles during a period of history they are interested in online. Ask them to use the information they find out to write a short article. If you have a school blog, these articles could be posted there.

Teacher's resources

Student's Book
Grammar reference and practice page 152
Vocabulary list page 141
Workbook
Unit 5, pages 20–23
Go online for
• Corpus tasks

6 Strong emotions

Unit profile

Vocabulary: Expressing emotions; Adverbs: type and position

Reading: An article on fear and phobias

Grammar: *be/get used to*

Listening: Five different situations

Speaking: Favourite things

Warmer

Ask students to think about three past habits and the emotions they associate with them. Tell students to write one or two adjectives to describe each past emotion, e.g. *I always used to feel happy when I went to my granny's house* and to discuss their sentences with a partner.

Your profile

Ask students to discuss the last times they felt the emotions listed in the box. Feed back as a class and discuss some common reasons for feeling happy, angry, worried, etc.

VOCABULARY Expressing emotions

1 Ask students to look at the pictures. Go through each one asking what emotion students can see. For picture 4, ask them how this picture makes them feel. Then ask them to work with a partner to match the questions to the pictures.

Answers
1 c 2 d 3 a 4 e 5 b

2 Set this exercise as individual work. Students can check their answers with a partner before whole-class feedback.

Answers
Fear – scared
Anger – furious
Worry – concerned
Happiness – optimistic
Unhappiness – pessimistic

3 Ask students to ask and answer the questions in pairs. Encourage them to give reasons. Monitor as students discuss, and make a note of any language issues to feed back on.

4 ▶1.16 Check students know the meanings of the bold words by asking them to tell you when they last felt each emotion and why. Play the recording for students to circle the emotion. Then play it again for them to focus on the reason, pausing between speakers if necessary to give them time to write. Check answers as a whole class.

Audioscript

Narrator: One
Sara: This is really annoying. It now stays like this for ages and you can't do anything. Even when it does eventually start, it's so slow.
Narrator: Two
Ahmed: Come on! It's already quarter past! We've still got a bit of time before it starts, but I'm worried there won't be much choice of where to sit if we get there too late.
Narrator: Three
Emma: Oh, can I open it now? Great! No, no! I can't believe it! Thanks so much. It's exactly what I wanted.
Narrator: Four
Dan: Sam! Sam! I'm watching something here. Can you turn that down!
Narrator: Five
Emma: I went on the ticket website at exactly nine, but it had already crashed. When I eventually got it to load, they'd sold out. I just want to forget the whole thing. I wasted all morning on it.
Narrator: Six
Sara: It's only a little one. Aw, he's quite sweet, really.
Dan: Just get it away from me! Seriously. Please, Sara!

Answers
1 fed up with her laptop
2 anxious about being late
3 over the moon about her present
4 irritated because Sam is playing loud music
5 down about wasting time
6 petrified of spiders

5 If you have already checked the meaning of the bold words before playing the recording, then this will be a simple transfer task. You could expand on the task by asking students to write their own example sentences and translations of the words.

Answers
Fear – petrified
Anger – bad-tempered, irritated
Worry – anxious
Happiness – over the moon, relieved, content
Unhappiness – fed up, depressed, down

6 Give students five minutes for this discussion activity. Students can work in pairs or small groups. For feedback, ask some pairs or groups to tell you something interesting from their discussion.

Extension activity

To revise the use of modals from Unit 5, ask students to write a letter to a problem page, based on the three feelings from their discussion for *fed up*, *irritated* and *anxious*. Their partner should then write a response using modals for advice. Share some problems and advice as a class.

READING

1 Before setting this task, ask students to tell a partner about their biggest fear, and listen to some of these as a class. Then ask students to read the text to see if any of the fears they discussed are mentioned. Tell them to make a list of the fears mentioned in the text. Ask one or two students to tell you the answers.

Answers
heights, mice, monsters, the dark, murder, war, looking foolish in front of friends

● Prepare for First for Schools
Reading and Use of English Part 1

Task description
Reading and Use of English Part 1 is a multiple-choice cloze. There are eight gaps, each with four multiple-choice options. It tests students' vocabulary awareness, e.g. of idioms, phrasal verbs and fixed phrases, collocations, and their ability to distinguish between words of similar meaning or use in the given context.

Tip
Remind students not only to think about meaning, but also to consider the grammatical form of the words they are choosing from. This will give them useful clues to the right word.

→ See Exam Profile 2, Student's Book page 123.

2 ● Before setting this task, ask students what strategies they could use if they don't know the meaning of a word. A key one is to notice the grammatical form of the word needed for the gap, and knowing common word endings can help here. Check as a whole class and ask for volunteers to explain why each choice is correct. Stronger students could try to complete the gaps without looking at the options first.

Answers
1 A 2 C 3 B 4 C 5 A 6 D 7 B 8 C

3 Ask students to scan Part B and to underline any names. Then ask them to complete the exercise individually. Check answers as a whole class. With weaker students, you could check they have got the answers to the first two questions correct before asking them to look for the rest of the answers.

Answers
1 Claudia 2 Jacob 3 Jacob 4 William 5 William
6 Claudia

4 Set the matching exercise as individual work, and remind students to look back at the article to use the context to help them. Let them check answers with a partner before checking as a whole class.

Fast finishers
Tell fast finishers to choose one person and their phobia. Then ask them to use the adjectives to describe scary situations for that person, or to describe how the person would feel.

Extension activity
Ask students to think of another common phobia and to create a fictional Case Study for that phobia. Students share their ideas in small groups, and choose one Case Study to present to the class.

Answers
1 distracted 2 distressing 3 extreme 4 foolish 5 deadly

Talking points

Ask students to discuss the questions in pairs. As an extension, ask students to discuss which reactions they have experienced in a scary situation. Increased strength and calm, non-emotional reactions are common reactions.

Cooler

1 Write these fears on the board in a random order, and ask students to work in pairs and to rank them from most to least common fear:

1 (most common) public speaking / public situations
2 spiders/snakes
3 heights
4 open spaces
5 small spaces
6 flying
7 blood
8 water
9 storms
10 (least common) crowds

2 Ask a pair to read their list aloud and see if other pairs agree. Students then raise their hands to show which fear they think is most common. Read out the correct order. Are students surprised by the order?

GRAMMAR *be/get used to*

1 Give students a few minutes to read the information in the box before checking their answers. Make sure they understand the difference in meaning by asking *Is Claudia still surprised by her autophobia?* (No). Write *I am getting used to waking up early in the mornings* on the board. Ask *Am I totally familiar with getting up early in the mornings?* (No). Elicit one more example of each structure to write on the board as a model.

Answers
Verbs in the *-ing* form (*sleeping*) or pronouns/nouns (*her autophobia*)

→ Grammar reference Student's Book page 153

2 Give students five minutes to complete this exercise individually before checking answers together. Explain that they need to look for clues in the sentences which tell them whether something is ongoing or not. This will help them decide if *be* or *get* is needed. If necessary, ask for volunteers to explain why each choice is correct.

Answers
1 'm not **2** we're **3** get **4** get **5** been **6** getting

3 Elicit some ideas from the class about what their friends would have to get used to. You could ask the class whether friends from other countries have visited them, and what they found different. Students can work in small groups, before comparing ideas as a class.

Corpus challenge

Ask students to correct the sentence and to explain the error (*used to* is followed by verb + *ing*).

Answer
I am used to eating this kind of food.

4 Do this exercise as a class. Read the sentences aloud and ask students which one describes a past habit or state. Write the sentences on the board and draw attention to the different forms, the time (past or present) that they are referring to and their meanings. Ask *Is the person still terrified of spiders?* (No).

Answers
2 I used to be terrified of spiders.

5 Do the first sentence on the board as an example. Remind students of the word limit, and then give them a few minutes to complete the exercise. Tell them to look carefully at the tense in the first sentence. Students can check their answers with a partner before whole-class feedback.

Mixed ability

Students can work in mixed-ability pairs to complete the exercise. Check answers after each sentence to ensure everyone is on track and understands the task.

Fast finishers

Ask fast finishers to write sentences about themselves using *be/get used to*, and to share these with a partner who should ask more questions about each sentence. Tell students they can write negative as well as positive sentences. Ask one or two students to tell you what they found out about their partner.

Answers
1 used to be **2** 'm used to/'ve got used to
3 is used to sleeping **4** used to be **5** get used to

VOCABULARY   Adverbs: type and position

1 Read sentences 1–6 with the students, focusing their attention on the adverbs. Set this as an individual task. After students have done the exercise, ask them to add at least one more adverb to each group (e.g. a *yesterday*, b *sometimes*, c *maybe*, d *slowly*, e *at home*, f *Nevertheless*). Create a table with these on the board and elicit as many examples from the class as possible.

Answers
1 b **2** e **3** a **4** f **5** d **6** c

2 Ask this question as a whole class and elicit an example sentence for each of the adverbs in exercise 1. Write the sentences on the board.

Answers
Beginning: time adverbs (for emphasis), connecting adverbs
Middle: frequency adverbs, adverbs of certainty, adverbs of manner
End: adverbs of time, adverbs of manner, adverbs of place

3 Set this as individual work, telling students to look at the examples in the book and on the board if necessary. Then ask students to check answers in pairs. Alternatively, read the sentences aloud with the adverb in the wrong place and ask students to correct you.

Possible answers
1 He can sing beautifully.
2 I have never been afraid of insects.
3 I'll probably get used to it.
4 I had an upset stomach. As a result I had difficulty sleeping.
5 I get anxious about homework from time to time. / From time to time, I get anxious about homework.
6 I've been getting bad-tempered lately. / Lately I've been getting bad-tempered.
7 If we leave now, we'll be home in bed by nine.
8 She definitely left home a few minutes ago.
9 We always have lunch at midday.
10 They were laughing loudly.

LISTENING

1 Tell students that they are going to practise a listening strategy. Tell them to read the questions and underline the key words. As an extension to this, you could ask students to think of synonyms for the words they have underlined (as the speakers will not use the same words as the questions and this will help students to focus on the meaning).

Possible answers
2 passwords, phone, bus, losing things, annoyed
3 support, find out, date, test revision
4 optimistic, progress, concerned, finish, in time, difficult, understand
5 feeling now, furious, concerned, relieved

Listening Part 1

Task description

The focus of this part is on genre, identifying speaker feeling, attitude, topic, opinion, purpose, agreement between speakers, gist and detail. Students hear a series of short unrelated extracts from monologues or exchanges between interacting speakers. There is one multiple-choice question per text, each with three options.

Tip

Encourage students to underline key words in the questions and spend a couple of minutes thinking of synonyms that they may hear in the recording.

See Exam Profile 2, Student's Book page 123.

2 ● ▶1.17 Play the recording once for students to circle *A*, *B* or *C.* With weaker students, you may wish to pause the recording after each speaker.

3 ▶1.17 Play the recording for students to check their answers. For any questions your students are finding particularly difficult, read the part of the audioscript which gives distraction and ask them to say why this would not be correct.

Audioscript

Narrator:	One
Speaker:	I've been doing my degree for three months now. I didn't quite expect it to be as tough as this, but I'm really enjoying it. There's a tremendous amount of reading. <u>It's fascinating stuff – all the experiments that psychologists have done</u> – but I've probably spent more on books since I started than in the rest of my life put together! I haven't really thought beyond the next few years yet, but I'm really happy I chose this subject. The main thing for me is that I'm actually into what I'm studying. Other degrees, like Law, may be more practical, but none of my friends doing stuff like that that are enjoying their degrees much.
Narrator:	Two
Speaker 1:	I was on the bus this morning and an inspector got on. I put the phone on the seat while I was looking for my ticket.
Speaker 2:	No! I've warned you about that before!
Speaker 1:	I know. I know. I don't care about the stuff on it. That's all backed up. It's a good thing you told me to put that password on it. No one will be able to actually do anything with it. But my parents will go mad.
Speaker 2:	Have you said anything?
Speaker 1:	Not yet. <u>The thing is they're always telling me not to put stuff down – they know I forget things easily.</u>
Narrator:	Three
Speaker:	Hi Alex. Where are you? I'm starting to get a bit stressed about tomorrow's History test. I know it isn't a big deal, but I want to do well in it. There's just so much to remember – I'm not used to learning all these dates. Isn't it more important

to understand the events rather than exactly when they happened? Anyway, I've learned most of them now, but it'd be good to talk through our notes and make sure one of us hasn't missed anything important. What do you think? Sorry to go on and on about me when you might be in the same situation. <u>Call me please.</u>

Narrator:	Four
Speaker 1:	How's the project going?
Speaker 2:	Um, OK.
Speaker 1:	Tom! You're just playing with your phone!
Speaker 2:	I was just checking something. <u>I've actually been working on it all morning.</u> I just felt like a break. <u>Mr Murphy took a look earlier and seemed impressed.</u> There's quite a bit more to do of course, but I've got until Friday. By the way, have you done this stuff in Maths, yet? I don't get it at all. And I've really tried.
Speaker 1:	Let's have a look. Oh, these ones take ages. What you have to do is …
Narrator:	Five
Libby:	Hi, Dad. It's me. This is Kay's phone.
Dad:	<u>Libby! You had us worried there.</u>
Libby:	Sorry! My battery died.
Dad:	Well, you could have let us know. Your phone was going straight to voicemail and <u>both your mum and I were getting quite anxious.</u> There wasn't a single thing we could do to check you were all right. And we don't know Kay's number, or her parents' for that matter. We really should get those from you. It's Libby. She's fine.
Libby:	Yeah, sure. Sorry, Dad. I'll let you know next time. Promise.

Answers

Refer also to the underlined parts of the script above.

1 B – Although the speaker says she is enjoying the course, she says she didn't expect it to be as tough, which rules out A as an answer, and C is not true as she doesn't have any career ambitions yet.

2 C – A is not possible as the speaker only refers to one password and there is no indication that he missed the bus, so B is also ruled out.

3 A – The girl doesn't talk about the date of the test, although she does check the time it starts in the message, so B is not true. She doesn't ask about her friend's revision either, which rules out C.

4 A – The boy is confident that he has enough time to complete his project, which rules out B, and C is not true, as there is no indication that he finds the subject difficult – it is maths that he has problems with.

5 C – Although A and B are plausible reactions to the situation, the father says nothing to indicate that he is furious with his daughter, and he is no longer concerned as she has made contact on her friend's phone.

EP Word profile

Books closed. Elicit two or three phrases using the word *thing* and write them on the board (e.g. *For one thing*, *First thing*). Books open. Ask students to compare their phrases with those in the book and discuss the possible meanings of *thing* with the class. Then set the exercise on page 134. Encourage students to record these and collect other phrases with *thing* to add to their list.

Answers

1 a 2 b 3 b 4 a 5 b 6 b 7 b

SPEAKING   Favourite things

1 ▶1.18 Ask students which days of the week they like and dislike and why. Play the recording and ask them to decide which person is most like them. Afterwards, you could ask students to write a similar short text about themselves and discuss their ideas with a partner.

Audioscript

Ahmed: My best day is Saturday. <u>What normally happens</u> is I wake up about ten. The first thing I do is check my phone for messages – someone might have come up with a good plan for the day. <u>Nine times out of ten</u> my parents have already gone out, so I go into the kitchen, put on some loud music and make myself some breakfast. It's my favourite start to a day.

Sara: <u>Virtually every Monday</u> we have tests at school. So my worst day is often Sunday. I spend most of it revising and end up going to bed too late and feeling a bit tense. <u>As a rule, I</u> don't have difficulty in sleeping, <u>with the exception of</u> Sunday nights. Sometimes I lie awake for hours.

2 ▶1.18 Ask students to write S or A depending on who said the phrase as far as they can remember. Then play the recording and check. Ask students what they think the function of each phrase is (1–4 generalise, 5 points out an exception) and which words tell them (e.g. *normally*).

Answers

1 A 2 S 3 S 4 A 5 S

3 ▶1.19 Tell students that they are going to listen to two more people talking about days they like. Give students a few minutes to read the sentences and then play the recording for students to complete them. Play the recording again if necessary. Check answers.

Answers

1 Science, ICT   2 players on her football team
3 Sunday nights   4 public speaking

Audioscript

Emma: <u>Generally speaking</u> my best days are Wednesdays. It's a good day in terms of lessons – lots of <u>Science</u>, um, no Music! And over an hour of <u>ICT</u>. I get really into that. Then after school, I have <u>football</u> practice. <u>Ninety per cent of the time</u>, we all go for a snack or something afterwards. <u>There's a great bond between the players on my team</u>.

Dan: No one likes <u>Sunday nights</u>, of course, especially if you haven't done your homework, but <u>I make every effort to get it done on Friday or Saturday</u>. <u>For the most part</u> I don't have bad days – although <u>one exception is</u> possibly Tuesdays. We do <u>public speaking</u> at school then, and from time to time I have to give a speech in front of the whole school. <u>I'm always really nervous</u> – though <u>on the whole</u> I'm actually quite good at it and it turns out fine.

4 ▶1.19 Set this as individual work. Students can to write down who says what from memory. Check answers by playing the audio again.

Answers

Emma: Generally speaking, Ninety per cent of the time
Dan: For the most part, one exception is, on the whole

5 Give students time to read the questions and think about their answers before setting this as a pair work discussion. Monitor and give help with vocabulary and pronunciation where necessary. Ask pairs to feed any interesting answers back to the class.

Extension activity

Ask students to write up a short summary of their partner's responses, but to not include the person's name. Take the summaries in and redistribute them randomly around the class. Ask students to read the summaries and to guess who wrote them.

Cooler

Monday is often considered the worst day of the week. Put these reasons on the board and ask students to change them so that they reflect a teenager's feelings rather than an adult's.

1 You dread working 9 to 5 every day.
2 You had a particularly busy weekend looking after the children and visiting your parents.
3 You always have a mountain of emails to catch up on.
4 You spent much of the weekend driving your family around.

Project

Ask students to interview a member of their family using the questions from exercise 5 and the information from the Cooler. In the following class, students should report back on their findings to the class. Were there any interesting or surprising findings? Did adults and children differ in their favourite days of the week / times of the year?

Teacher's resources

Student's Book
Grammar reference and practice page 153
Vocabulary list page 141
Video
Speaking Part 2
Workbook
Unit 6, pages 24–27
Go online for
- Pronunciation
- Progress test
- Speaking test video worksheets
- Corpus tasks

Culture
Colours around the world

Learning objectives

- The students learn about the significance of different colours around the world.
- In the project stage, students write advice for tourists visiting their country about the meaning of different colours.

Warmer

1 Hold up different coloured paper or card and ask students to write down the first thing that comes into their mind when they see that colour.

2 Ask students to compare their ideas with a partner. Encourage them to ask each other questions to find out more about their responses.

3 Tell pairs to raise their hands if they had similar ideas to their partner. If so, ask them to explain why they think their answers are similar.

1 Explain to students that they are going to do a quiz on colours. Ask them to work with a partner to answer the questions. Once they have answered them, ask for a show of hands to find out the most popular answer for each one.

Fast finishers

Ask fast finishers to write a similar question about colours in their own country or language. When discussing the answers to the quiz, ask the fast finishers to read out their question to the class.

2 Ask students to read the text to check their answers to the quiz. Find out which pair guessed the most answers correctly.

Answers

1 b 2 a 3 c 4 a 5 c 6 a 7 c 8 b

3 Give students time to read the text individually, before discussing each situation with a partner. In feedback, encourage them to explain why they have chosen the colours.

Extension activity

Ask students to make a list of the countries in the reading text and to make a note of what the colour mentioned means in that country. Then ask students to discuss with a partner whether they think the meaning is similar or different in their own country.

Possible answers

1 green
2 black
3 red and orange
4 purple

4 ▶1.20 Tell students they are going to listen to four people talking about colour. Play the recording and ask students to listen and complete the chart. Check answers. Ask students if any of the colours mentioned have a significance in their country.

Mixed ability

Ask weaker students in the class to work in pairs. Student A should note down the country and the colour, student B should note down its significance and/ or use. Stronger students can complete the exercise individually.

Audioscript

Presenter: Hi there, everyone. For today's programme about colours and culture, our reporter, Sandra Connelly, went to Heathrow International Airport, here in London, to ask people about special colour meanings in their native countries. Here's what some of them had to say:

Sandra: Excuse me, Miss. Can I ask you some questions about colours?

Speaker: Sure, what do you want to know?

Sandra: Well, first of all, I should ask you where you're from.

Speaker: I'm from China. I'm here studying English here at university.

Sandra: Oh, perfect! And is there a special, lucky colour in China?

Speaker: Yes, there is. It's <u>red</u>.

Sandra: Really! And why is red special?

Speaker: Well, it symbolises <u>fire, life, and good fortune</u>.

Sandra: And do people use the colour red for special occasions?

Speaker: Yes, they do. It's a colour for many happy <u>festivals</u> in China.

Sandra: For example?

Speaker: For example, during <u>the New Year festival</u>. People put up red decorations, and they also give each other presents or money, in red packages.

Sandra: How interesting! Thank you for answering.

Speaker: No problem at all.

Sandra: Excuse me, Sir. Can I ask you some questions about colours?

Speaker: Yes, why not?

Sandra: Thank you! My first question is where are you from?

Speaker: I'm from Brussels, in <u>Belgium</u>.

Sandra: Oh! So colours probably mean the same things there as they do in the UK, right?

Speaker:	Yes, I think so. Except for <u>pink and blue</u>, of course.
Sandra:	Really? Why is that?
Speaker:	Well, here in the UK, people dress baby girls in pink, but we don't do that in Belgium.
Sandra:	Oh! And <u>what colours do you use for baby girls</u>?
Speaker:	<u>Blue</u>. Well, light blue, actually. And <u>we dress baby boys in pink</u> – the opposite of what you do here in the UK.
Sandra:	I've never heard that! And do you know why?
Speaker:	I have no idea! But that's the way we do it in Belgium.
Sandra:	That's interesting. Thanks very much!
Speaker:	You're welcome.
Sandra:	Hello, Ma'am. Do you mind answering some questions about colours?
Speaker:	Of course. I have an hour before my plane leaves!
Sandra:	Oh, good! So first of all, where are you from?
Speaker:	Me? I'm from São Paulo, in <u>Brazil</u>.
Sandra:	Brazil! What a beautiful country. And compared to the UK, are there any colours that mean something different in Brazil?
Speaker:	Hmm … something different? Oh, yes. <u>Purple</u>.
Sandra:	Purple! And what does it mean there?
Speaker:	Well, it doesn't mean royalty, like it does here in the UK. For Brazilians, purple is a colour for <u>sad</u> occasions, <u>like when someone dies</u>, and people are in <u>mourning</u>.
Sandra:	Oh, well that is very different. Here in the UK, we wear black when someone dies.
Speaker:	Oh, we do that in Brazil, too. But you also see purple.
Sandra:	OK, well thanks for answering my questions. Have a nice flight!
Speaker:	Thank you!
Sandra:	Excuse me. Can I ask you some questions about colours, sir?
Speaker:	About colours? Yes, I suppose so.
Sandra:	Thanks! But first of all, where are you from?
Speaker:	Well, I live in London now, but I'm originally from Bangkok, in <u>Thailand</u>.
Sandra:	Oh! I love Thailand! People often wear <u>yellow</u> there, don't they?
Speaker:	Yes, they do. It's a very popular colour.
Sandra:	And why is that?
Speaker:	Well, Thailand is a Buddhist country, and <u>yellow is a special colour for Buddhists</u>. <u>It symbolises the Earth</u>. It's also our <u>King's royal colour</u>. <u>He was born on a Monday</u>, you know.
Sandra:	On a Monday?
Speaker:	Yes, and for Buddhists, <u>yellow is the special colour for Monday</u>. Many people wear yellow clothes on Mondays.
Sandra:	How interesting! And does every day have a colour?
Speaker:	Yes. Every day is different.
Sandra:	How nice! Well, thanks very much for stopping!
Speaker:	You're very welcome. Bye, bye.

Answers

1 China; red; fire, life and good fortune, used in festivals, e.g. New Year
2 Belgium; pink and blue; boys wear pink and girls wear blue
3 Brazil; purple; sad, death, mourning
4 Thailand; yellow; Buddhism, the Earth, the King, Mondays

5 Ask students to discuss the questions with a partner. Elicit ideas for different colours from different pairs.

6 Ask students to read the sentences and to choose what they think the underlined expression means. Tell students to guess if they don't know the meaning. Check answers as a whole class.

Answers

1 angry   2 ecological   3 What's wrong?   4 couldn't
5 surprised

7 Ask students to do this exercise with a partner. When they have completed the list and explanations, encourage them to find out whether there is a direct translation equivalent or a different way of saying the same thing in English.

Cooler

Ask students to work with a partner and to think of colours that would seem strange in certain situations. For example, white at a funeral in the UK would be quite unusual. Then ask them to explain to another pair what colours they have chosen and why they think they would be strange. Elicit responses from one or two pairs, and discuss as a class.

Project

Ask students to discuss points 1–4 in small groups, and to write a short text giving advice. They can make this into a poster to present in the next lesson, using colourful photos and relevant advice. Ask each group to talk about their poster. Do the other groups agree or disagree with their advice?

7 Telling stories

Unit profile

Vocabulary: Verbs of movement; sounds; Time phrases
Reading: An extract from a novel
Grammar: Narrative tenses
Writing: A story

Warmer

1 Tell students to imagine moving to a new country or city. Ask them to write down all the things they think they would have to get used to. They can focus on a country they know well, either from visiting it, or from TV and film. Alternatively you could give students a factsheet with information about the lifestyle in a given country.

2 Tell students to imagine they have been living there for six months and are visiting their home city or country. They should tell their partner about the last six months. Tell them to focus on things they are now used to and things that they are still getting used to. Ask one or two pairs to feed back to the class.

Your profile

Give students a few minutes to discuss these questions in small groups. Ask students to raise their hands to find out the most popular genre in the class and then ask why it is so popular. You could also ask students to discuss these questions: *Who is your favourite author? What was the last book you read? What was it about?* Monitor and give positive feedback for interesting ideas. Ask for a couple of volunteers to share their ideas with the class.

VOCABULARY   Verbs of movement; sounds

1 Before students do this exercise, ask individuals to explain what they can see in each picture and to suggest what the difference is in each pair of pictures (the first is a gentle action, the second a stronger action). Then ask students to match the sentences to the pictures and check answers as a class. Ask students to write the infinitive of the words in bold, and to check their answers with a partner before whole-class feedback.

Mixed ability

To support weaker students, revise the spelling rules for the past simple verbs in exercise 1. Do this together on the board as a whole class, encouraging stronger students to volunteer the rules. For example, silent -e (*close* = *closed*), vowel + w (*show* = *showed*), consonant + y (*marry* = *married*), consonants after a stressed vowel (*stop* = *stopped*), and in British English the doubling of a final *l* (*travel* = *travelled*). You could also revise the pronunciation patterns of -ed endings (*-t*, *-id*, *-d*) and focus on any your students struggle with.

Answers

1 lean, tap **2** burst, bounce **3** rush, shake **4** kneel, slap
5 charge **6** swing, wander

2 ▶1.21 Play the first sound (*whisper*) as an example. Then ask students to demonstrate the other sounds to a partner before playing the rest of the audio. Check answers as a whole class. Point out that the difference between *mutter* and *mumble* is quite subtle (*mutter*: to speak quietly and in a low voice that is not easy to hear, often when you are worried or complaining about something; *mumble*: to speak quietly and in a way that is not clear so that words are difficult to understand).

Audioscript

Narrator: One
So, don't tell anyone, but I think the best thing to do would be to …
Narrator: Two
Someone whistling
Narrator: Three
Hey! What are you doing there?
Narrator: Four
He's always taking my stuff without asking, and he never gives it back …
Narrator: Five
Someone sighing
Narrator: Six
Good afternoon, my name … and I'm here to talk to you about …

Answers

1 whisper **2** whistle **3** yell **4** mutter **5** sigh **6** mumble

3 Ask students to do the matching exercise individually. In pairs, they could choose three of the beginnings and invent their own endings to these sentences. Then ask them to practise the pronunciation of the past simple verbs in pairs. You could also drill this as a whole-class exercise. Students may have particular difficulty with *mumbled* /ˈmʌm.bld/.

READING

1 Set a short time limit (e.g. 30 seconds) for students to tell you their answer. Ask them what *clues* in the pictures or text helped them decide. For weaker groups, you could give options for students to decide between, e.g. *murder mystery, horror, romance*. Check the answer. Ask students if they have heard of Sir Arthur Conan Doyle and Sherlock Holmes and find out any details they know from the TV programmes, movies or books. Read out the information in the Cultural background, if necessary.

Cultural background
Sir Arthur Conan Doyle was a Scottish doctor, famous for writing the crime stories about the detective Sherlock Holmes. The four Sherlock Holmes novels and 56 short stories were published between 1887 and 1901. Holmes solves cases, such as *The Hound of the Baskervilles*, through his logical reasoning and use of forensic science.

Answer
murder mystery

● Prepare for First for Schools
Reading and Use of English Part 5

Task description
Reading and Use of English Part 5 is a multiple choice task. It consists of a text followed by six questions, each with four multiple-choice options. Part 5 tests students' understanding of gist, specific detail, attitude, opinion, implication and meaning from context.

Tip
Pronoun referents are a common question type in this part. Often the pronoun will refer back to one of the previous nouns in the sentence immediately before. Tell students to check this as a first option before considering other possibilities.

→ See Exam Profile 2, Student's Book page 122.

2 ● Draw students' attention to the tips in the boxes and encourage them to use each strategy to answer the questions. They could try and answer each question for themselves, before looking at the options. When they think they have the answer, they should choose the option which matched it most closely. Ask them to individually choose the best answer and then compare with a partner. In whole-class feedback, ask students how they decided on the answers. Find out which tip students found most useful, which tips are new, and which tips they have already used.

Fast finishers
Ask fast finishers to write down any other tips they can think of for reading and answering exam questions. Ask these students to share their tips with the class. The rest of the class votes on the most useful tips. Ask for a volunteer to write these tips on the board.

Extension activity
Ask students to work in small groups and to think of a scene in a murder mystery story. It can be from their own imagination or a scene from something they have read or watched. Ask them to plan what happens. Do not ask them to write the whole story; just an outline of ideas. Share some ideas as a class.

Answers
1 D – The final part of the paragraph describes Holmes's inability to sit still: *He wandered restlessly around our sitting-room; he bit his nails; he tapped the furniture nervously; and he complained about the inactivity.* A is not true as it is Watson who is reading the newspaper; B is ruled out because Holmes was only working on the music project for the first three days, Monday to Wednesday; and C is not possible as Holmes is clearly frustrated with their 'dull existence'.

2 B – This question tests vocabulary above B2 level, where the meaning can be worked out from context (here, with the reference to a *tiger in the jungle*, before making a move).

3 C – Holmes says *My abilities demand something far more worthy than that* when referring to the recent thefts. A and B are not suggested in the text and although Watson talks of *a large number of small thefts*, there is nothing to indicate that the weather has caused an increase.

4 A – This question tests backwards reference and Holmes has been talking about an imagined murder.

5 B – Holmes describes Mycroft's behaviour in terms of a train that stays on its rails, which suggests a fixed routine. A is not possible because Mycroft lives in London and works nearby; C is ruled out as Mycroft spends his time in indoor places – his home, his club, his office; and D is not possible as he rarely visits his brother and no other family is mentioned.

EP Word profile
Books closed. Write *patiently* on the board and tell students to write an example sentence using it. Books open. Ask students to compare their sentence with the one in the book. Read the other example, then set the exercise on page 134. Ask students to write two more sentences using each form of the word.

Answers
1 patience 2 patiently 3 impatient 4 patience
5 impatience

Set this as a small group task. For the first question, ask students to list the three key ingredients for a good story. Then as a whole class, see if you can agree on the three most important ingredients. You could extend the second question by asking students what people might miss or lose from only watching the film. Encourage students to think about the pros and cons of each (e.g. there is more time and space in a book for extra detail, and more is left to the reader's imagination; with films you can share the experience with your friends or the rest of the audience).

Cooler

Invite a volunteer to the front of the class and whisper a word from exercise 1 and 2 to them. They mime the word for other students to guess. Then ask them to choose the next student to come up. Repeat until students have mimed and guessed *lean*, *tap*, *bounce*, *rush*, *shake*, *slap*, *wander*, *whisper* and *sigh*.

GRAMMAR Narrative tenses

1 Ask students which tenses they can remember seeing in the story. Then ask them to look back at page 43 and identify the tenses. Check answers as a whole class.

Answers
had settled; had ... been: past perfect
wandered; bit; tapped: past simple
was asking: past continuous

2 Books closed. Write *past continuous*, *past perfect* and *past simple* on the board. Elicit an example sentence for each (e.g. *She was sitting in a chair by the window*; *He'd moved in the week before*; *She mumbled something to the person next to her*) and the form of the past continuous and the past perfect (was/were + ing; had + past participle). Then ask students to explain any uses of these tenses they know (past continuous: to say that something was in progress around a particular past time; past perfect: to talk about something that had already happened at the time we are talking about). Books open. Give students a few minutes to read and complete the rules.

Answers
1 past simple   2 past continuous   3 past perfect

→ Grammar reference Student's Book page 154

3 Set this as individual work and then ask students to compare their answers in pairs. Check answers in whole-class feedback and encourage students to explain why each answer is correct.

Answers
1 was travelling   2 sat   3 were all sitting
4 had just reached   5 rushed   6 had left

4 Look at this sentence together as a whole class. Ask students whether Inspector Lestrade spoke first or listened first (Answer: spoke first). Ask which action took longer – speaking or listening (Answer: listening). Then ask students to find another example of the past perfect continuous in the story on page 43 (*Holmes has been patiently studying ...*). Ask students to complete the rule and check answers.

Extension activity

Ask students to look back at their story outlines from the previous Extension activity and to think about how they could use these three narrative tenses to write their story. Ask students to write one or two sentences for each of the main points of their story. They should include at least one example of each of the three narrative tenses. Ask one or two students to explain their story briefly and which tenses they might use in each part.

Answer
had, been

5 Ask a volunteer to briefly explain the difference between the past perfect and the past perfect continuous before setting this as an individual task. Remind students to look back at the rules in exercises 2 and 4. Monitor and give help if necessary. With a weaker class, you may want to do this in mixed ability pairs. Check answers as a whole class.

Answers
1 had been calling   2 had been playing   3 had been crying
4 had been rushing   5 had called   6 had left

Corpus challenge

Ask students to correct the sentence and to explain the error (the past perfect is not needed as the sentence starts in the present simple).

Answer
It is amazing to think all this happened less than 30 years ago.

VOCABULARY   Time phrases

1 Do the first sentence as an example on the board and then set the rest of the exercise for individual work. Ask pairs to compare answers before checking as a whole class. Ask students if they can think of any other time phrases using these prepositions and write them on the board. Encourage students to make a note of any new ones in their vocabulary notebooks.

Answers
1 in   2 for   3 before   4 for   5 before   6 on

2 Ask students to complete the sentences individually. Monitor and give help where necessary for weaker students. Students then discuss them with a partner. Give positive feedback for interesting ideas. Elicit an example for each sentence from students. If there are any incorrect ones, ask a volunteer to correct them, ensuring students remain polite to one another!

Extension activity

Tell students to ask at least one follow up question about each sentence their partner has written in exercise 2. Ask one or two students to tell you what else they found out about their partner.

WRITING   A story

1 Ask students if they have ever looked after someone else's pet or children and whether this was a positive or negative experience. Students then look at the picture and explain what they can see. Then ask the class to read the task. Ask them to work with a partner to describe what they think will happen in the story. Ask one or two pairs to tell you their ideas, and ask the rest of the class whether they have a very similar or different story.

2 Ask the students to read the story and to compare it to their own version. Of the one or two stories your class heard, which was the most similar to the story on page 43?

Answer
Yes

3 Books closed. Ask students what they think a good story should include and write ideas on the board. Take a class vote to decide on the most important order. Books open. Give students a few minutes to read the *Prepare* box. Ask whether they think the story in exercise 2 includes all of these features or not. Then ask them to match paragraphs a to d to the functions in the box. Check answers as a whole class.

Answers
a background information   b opening events
c developing story   d ending

4 Give students a few minutes to complete the gaps and then check answers.

Answers
1 Just then   2 Before long   3 After   4 Later

5 Students discuss this in pairs for a few minutes. Ask three different volunteers to each explain the reason for the use of the three verb forms to the whole class.

Answers
- *had been raining* – it started raining before Oliver sighed and it was raining continuously until that point (past perfect continuous)
- *had disappeared* – the action of the dog running out of the door started and finished before the action of Oliver moving (past perfect)
- *were shaking* – the action of shaking was happening continuously when the boys got on the bus (past continuous)

6 Tell students that in creative writing, it is good to use a wide range of vocabulary. Encourage them not to use the same word too often. Ask students to replace the highlighted words in pairs. They should check they have chosen the correct replacement by re-reading the whole sentence with the replacement in place.

Answers
ran – rushed
shouted – yelled
disappeared – vanished
looked – glanced
see – make out
happily – cheerfully

7 Give students a couple of minutes to read the task. Then ask them to discuss what they think might happen with a partner. Give them five to ten minutes to organise their ideas and to plan their story further. They could then compare these plans with a different partner.

⬤ Prepare for First for Schools
Writing Part 2

Task description
In Part 2, students have a choice of task. They may be asked to write an article, an email or letter, a review or a story. They are given a clear context, topic, purpose and target reader. Students should write 140–190 words.

Tip
Tell students to make sure that their story has a clear story line, with coherent linkers and good use of narrative tenses.

8 ⬤ If you have students preparing for the exam, then set a strict time limit of 40 minutes for this to mimic exam conditions. If not, you can be more flexible with time, or even set it as a homework task. Encourage them to use a variety of narrative tenses in their answer. Afterwards, ask students to exchange their story with a partner. Their partner should look at the essay and check that the student has paid attention to each point in the *Prepare* box. Using their partner's story, they should underline the different verbs used. How many different tenses has their partner used? Have they used them accurately?

Teacher's resources

Student's Book
Grammar reference and practice page 154
Vocabulary list page 141
Video
Stories
Workbook
Unit 7, pages 28–31
Go online for
- Video extra worksheet
- Corpus tasks

Sample answer

Hannah rushed over to Dan's house as soon as she heard the news. Her friend had sent her a text to say that Dan had just got back from the hospital. Two days before, he had broken his arm and injured his right leg playing football, so he really needed her help, especially as his parents were away on holiday and his older sister would be out at work all day.

But when she got to his house, Hannah saw that there were three cars parked outside. She wondered whether she should leave immediately – it looked as though Dan already had a lot of visitors, and she'd hoped to be on her own with him. Just then, the front door opened and she recognised the football coach, who came out to get something from his car. He waved at Hannah and said, 'Have you come to see Dan? The whole team's inside and we're cooking him spaghetti. Why not come and join us?'

Hannah went red and said she couldn't stay for lunch. She asked the coach to tell Dan she had called round. Then she headed home, wondering whether she would ever be able to see Dan on his own.

Cooler

Ask students to work in groups of four and imagine they are the judges of a short story competition. They should read three other student's stories and award each one gold, silver or bronze. Then ask each group who won the gold award and why.

Project

Ask students to find a graded reader. If possible, you could bring of a selection from your school's library. Once they have read the story, they should write a review, including a brief summary of the main plot. The reviews could be displayed on the classroom wall or posted on the class blog for students to read. They can then decide which one to read next.

8 A great place to live

Unit profile

Vocabulary: Community; *as if / as though*
Reading: Five texts about different cities
Grammar: Future (1): Review
Listening: A new skate park
Speaking: Comparing photographs

Warmer

Ask students to make notes to plan a story about something real or imaginary that has happened recently in their home town. After five minutes planning time, ask students to tell their story to a partner. Monitor as students do this and help with narrative forms. Ask one or two students to tell their story to the class.

Your profile

In pairs, students discuss these questions. Ask them to look at the picture and say whether they would like to live in a place like this and why / why not. If your students have lived in other places, extend the task by asking them to compare the different places. Elicit answers from some students. You could also ask students about other places they would like to live and why.

VOCABULARY   Community

1 Check students understand the meaning of the words in blue by asking questions such as *Which word is the opposite of urban? Which word is the opposite of similar? Which word is a synonym of friendly?* Then ask students to match the two halves of the sentences and decide whether the adjectives are used for people, places or both. Ask students to check their answers with a partner before whole-class feedback.

Answers
1 c, relaxed – both
2 e, urban – places
3 a, remote, rural – places
4 b, welcoming – both
5 g, close – places (collocates with *community*)
6 d, industrial – places; inner – places (collocates with *city*)
7 f, diverse – places

2 Ask students to read the sentences in exercise 1 and to rank them from 1–7 in the order of most to least appealing place to live. Tell students to do this individually. Then ask them to discuss their ranking and reasons with a partner.

3 ▶1.22 Ask students to read the questions. Play the recording twice for students to take notes. Allow students to check their answers with a partner before whole-class feedback. Ask students where John could study in their country.

Audioscript
I've just started my degree, I'm doing Architecture at Bristol University. As part of my degree, <u>I'm going to study at a university abroad in my second year</u>. I have a massive long list of universities. It's so long I don't know where to start and I need a bit of help. I come from a small town in Devon, half an hour from the nearest city. My parents' place is in a quiet, residential neighbourhood and it's quite a <u>close community</u>, so everyone seems to know everyone else's business. On the one hand it's nice, but it's also very <u>rural</u> and a bit <u>remote</u> and I find it a bit dull. Bristol's much better. There are a lot of <u>industrial</u> estates in the suburbs but the student areas have a really <u>relaxed</u> atmosphere and a lively social life. So in terms of what I want from my year abroad, I'm looking for somewhere <u>urban</u>, that's interesting and <u>culturally diverse</u>, where the people are very <u>welcoming</u> – somewhere that's good for young people, basically. If you have any suggestions, please post them on my blog. It'd be great to hear from you.

Answers
1 He is going to study abroad.
2 remote, rural, close community
3 industrial, relaxed
4 urban, culturally diverse, welcoming

READING

1 Write *Istanbul, Milan, Barcelona, Sydney* and *Mexico City* on the board and ask students what they know about each place. Can they identify the places shown in the photos? Give them a few minutes to read the texts quickly.

Answer
The pictures show Barcelona (top) and Mexico City (bottom).

2 Explain that using key words from the questions can help students locate information. Go through the steps as a class, and then give students one minute to find the answer.

Answer
A Doruk (line four of text A) says *It would make a big difference if you learnt some Turkish before coming*.

Prepare for First for Schools
Reading and Use of English Part 7

Task description

Reading and Use of English Part 7 requires students to match ten options to different parts of a text. The text can be one long text or, as in this example, a number of short texts. This part tests students' understanding of opinion, detail, implication and specific information.

Tip

When there are several short texts, encourage students to write a brief summary (just one or two words) of the main idea of each one. For example, text C on page 47 could be summarised as 'rural location'. This will help them to find the correct text for each question.

3 Before students do the exercise, ask them to underline the key words in each question. Give students five to ten minutes to find the answers. Ask them to compare with a partner before whole-class feedback. With weaker students, you could monitor and provide assistance for the first two or three questions. Remind students that the people can be chosen more than once.

Fast finishers

Ask fast finishers to think about where they would choose to study and why. Ask them to share their ideas with the class.

Answers

1 E Cristina (*you should definitely make use of the ski slopes ...*)
2 C Simon (*my bus leaves once an hour, so if I miss it I'm in trouble!*)
3 A Doruk (*It has a reputation for excellent teaching*)
4 D Marco (*we visit relatives there every New Year*)
5 B Natalia (*incredible contemporary buildings*)
6 E Cristina (*There are restaurants from every continent*)
7 D Marco (*opera and pop concerts*)
8 E Cristina (*the Aztec pyramids in the ancient city*)
9 A Doruk (*the campus seemed quite a close community*)
10 C Simon (*The campus is in the suburbs, surrounded by parkland*)

4 Encourage students to write down any answers they can remember without having to look back at the text. Do the first item together as an example and then ask students to work individually. Check answers. Then ask students to find other new words in the texts that they think would be useful for describing places and activities, and to make a note of them in their vocabulary notebooks.

Extension activity

Ask students to read the texts again and to underline any place words (e.g. *city centre*, *woods*) and to circle any activity words (e.g. *walking*, *performance*). Then ask them to use these words to write a paragraph about a place they know well. You can display these around the classroom for other students to read.

Answers

1 campus 2 overseas 3 suburbs 4 location 5 lifestyle
6 scale

EP Word profile

Look at the examples. Then set the exercise on page 134. Ask students to write three sentences using three of the phrases in pairs. Ask different pairs to share a sentence with the whole class, who decide whether or not they have written it correctly. They should not repeat a phrase that another pair has already used.

Answers

1 make sense 2 make the most of 3 make your way
4 made a; difference 5 Make the most of
6 makes no sense

Talking points

Ask students to work with a partner to come up with four points for each one, and to rank them in order of importance. They should then compare their ideas and ranking with another pair. Elicit some ideas from a couple of groups.

Cooler

Write these words on the board: *urban*, *dull*, *industrial*, *inner-city*, *welcoming*, *diverse*. Ask students to work in pairs and to note down the opposites of these words (*rural*, *interesting*, *residential*, *remote*, *unfriendly*, *similar*). In feedback, add the opposites to the board. Then erase the original words, and see if students can remember them from the opposites remaining.

GRAMMAR   Future (1): review

1 Books closed. Write on the board *I'm about to start at Koc[cidilla] University.* Ask: *Have I already started at the university?* (No), *Am I going to start there soon?* (Yes). Books open. Ask students to find the corresponding rule in the box (g). Read sentence 2 and find the corresponding rule as a class. Students work individually to identify which future form is being used in each sentence. Then tell students to complete the rules. Check answers together as a whole class and elicit a further example for each one.

→ **Grammar reference Student's Book page 155**

2 Set this task as individual work. When students have finished, ask them to discuss whether they use the same forms in their language with a partner.

3 Students should read the texts all the way through first before making their decisions so they get a feel for the overall meaning and timeframe. Then ask them to work in pairs to choose the correct form. Remind them to look at the rules in exercise 1 to help them and if necessary, give them an overview of the general present situation. Check answers.

Fast finishers

Ask fast finishers to write true sentences about themselves using the future forms in the box in exercise 1. They can share some examples after checking answers to exercise 3.

---

4 Ask students to complete the sentences, and then to discuss them with a partner. Monitor and give help where necessary. Remind them that we usually use *be going to* (rather than the present continuous) for intentions or plans that have not yet been arranged (e.g. 'One day I'm going to learn to sail'). Tell them to ask their partner at least one question about each sentence.

Corpus challenge

Ask students to correct the sentence and to explain the error (we use the present simple (*go*) after time conjunctions, such as *before*).

Answer
Before I go home, I'll go shopping.

VOCABULARY   *as if / as though*

1 Explain that in this exercise *as if* and *as though* are synonyms (not words they have to choose between). Read the sentences 1–4 aloud and ask for a show of hands for the two options each time. If there is disagreement, ask one person who voted for *a* and one who voted for *b* to explain their choice.

2 Choose one of the people in the picture and model an example sentence on the board (e.g. 'Her umbrella looks as though it's going to fly away'). Then ask students to write sentences for the other people. Ask different students to read out a sentence for each one, and see if others in the class agree.

LISTENING

1 Ask students if any of them go skate-boarding and if so, what they think of their local skate park. Tell them that predicting information is a useful listening strategy, especially for an exam. Ask students to guess what the missing words are, and to compare their predictions with a partner. Elicit some ideas from students. Can they agree on what 'type' of word is missing, even if not the 'actual' word?

Prepare for First for Schools

Listening Part 2

Task description
Listening Part 2 requires students to complete ten sentences while listening to a monologue. The focus is on listening for detail and identifying specific information and opinion.

Tip
Tell students to read the sentences with the missing words carefully before listening, and think about the type of information that might be needed to complete each one.

See Exam Profile 4, Student's Book page 127.

---

2 ◉ ▶1.23 Play the recording for students to complete the gaps. Make sure they realise they will not hear the exact same sentences as those written on the page but that the words they write down *must* be the same as those they hear on the recording. Ask students to compare their answers with a partner but do not confirm answers at this stage.

Audioscript

Andy: I just love skateboarding, but I live in a small town where until recently there were no facilities for this activity. But, three years ago, my friends and I decided to convince our local community of the need for a proper skate park. Most people were really supportive of our ideas and we soon formed an action group consisting of teenagers and adults – teachers, parents and others – all led by local restaurant owner Martin Ashton. He was brilliant, as he had good contacts with companies in the area, who began to offer financial help. Martin also knew how to apply for a government grant to develop the park, and he got involved in making that happen straightaway.

The next thing the action group had to do was to start raising serious money. We persuaded our school to organise a concert and all the ticket money went towards the skate park fund. Apart from this, my friends and I did everything we could think of to raise money – I washed cars and others organised sales of second-hand books and DVDs and stuff like that. Of course, we didn't get a huge amount in this way, but local businesses contributed money too, and at the end of six months, there were funds of £185,000 available, slightly short of our target of £200,000, but more than enough to allow the building work to get started. In fact, within a year, we managed to raise nearly £300,000, which meant we were also able to afford lighting within the budget.

In the meantime, local resident John Richardson was helping out with the planning stage of the project. He works as an architect in London and has got close links with colleagues in the United States. Through them, he found a specialist business in California called Xcite, who have won awards for their skate park design. We all found their website very impressive, especially the video clips of similar parks they'd done. There was some interesting feedback posted on the website and it seemed that they'd satisfied quite a lot of clients over there.

We knew that these guys – Ricky and Bob – were perfect for us! So the action group held a community meeting and we held a vote on the matter. Almost ninety eight per cent said yes to using Xcite. Things moved pretty quickly after that. John asked three of us to join him in a few transatlantic discussions on Skype™, where we explained what we wanted to achieve, not only for skateboarders like us, but for the BMX riders too. For example, they requested a great feature called a whale tail, which is basically made of steel, with thin strips of wood on top. Xcite came up with some very imaginative ideas for this, and did some rough designs for other features, which they emailed to us.

Then, Ricky flew over for three weeks to show us his drawings and to get to know the town. He stayed at my house, actually, and he was really cool. Although he was a bit older, he didn't mind hanging out with us skateboarders, and we often chatted late into the night, which helped him to improve his work. We also walked around the place where the skate park was going to be constructed. It was an empty piece of land that used to belong to a factory and had been bought by the town council. Luckily for us …

Once Ricky was back in the States, it didn't take him long to produce the final plans and paperwork, and after getting official approval this end, everything went ahead. And now, we have this fantastic new skate park, which keeps us extremely happy, morning, noon and night.

3 ▶**1.23** Play the recording again for students to check/complete their answers. Confirm answers as a whole class. If necessary, explain why distraction in the script was not the correct answer.

Answers
1 restaurant owner   2 government grant   3 washed cars
4 £185,000   5 planning   6 video clips   7 vote   8 steel
9 drawings   10 a factory

SPEAKING   Comparing photographs

1 Ask students to look at the photographs and say where in the world they may have been taken. Explain that this type of task will require comparative language, and if necessary, review simple comparative adjective structures (*-er than, more/fewer/less than, not as … as*). Then ask students to think about the questions and compare their ideas with a partner. Monitor and help with ideas if necessary.

2 ▶**1.24** Play the recording once and ask students to answer the three questions. For question three, you might need to play the recording again.

Audioscript

Examiner: In this part of the test, I'm going to give each of you two photographs. I'd like you to talk about your photographs on your own for about a minute, and also to answer a short question about your partner's photographs. Ana, it's your turn first. Here are your photographs. They show two villages. I'd like you to compare the photographs, and suggest some advantages and disadvantages of living in each village. All right?

Ana: Yes, thank you. Both of these places are small, rural villages. Neither place looks as though it's busy or industrial. Both seem quiet and peaceful but as they're in the middle of nowhere, there probably aren't many facilities like shops or youth clubs. And they probably aren't very culturally diverse, like a city is. In the top photograph there's some mountain scenery. It looks cool and damp, whereas the other village is in a hotter country. The hills are brown, dry and dusty, so it obviously doesn't rain that much. I think that the villages may have very different standards of living. While the village in the top photograph has quite large cottages, the village in the second photograph has much smaller, simpler houses. I reckon that the people in the top photograph are probably quite wealthy, the people in the bottom photograph probably have less money.

Answers

1 five (similarities: small and peaceful, not many facilities, not culturally diverse; differences: weather, standards of living)
2 four (size, facilities, crime, weather and lifestyle)
3 Students' own answer.

3 ▶ 1.25 Set this as a pair work task and then play the recording. After completing this exercise, you could ask students if they know any other expressions for making comparisons, e.g. *at the same time*, *however*, etc.

Audioscript and answers

Ivan: The main difference is the size.
Ana: Both of these places are small, rural villages.
Ana: Neither place looks as though it's busy or industrial.
Ana: It looks cool and damp, whereas the other village is in a hotter country.
Ana: While the village in the top photograph has quite large cottages, the village in the second photograph has much smaller, simpler houses.
Ivan: On the other hand, I assume that the villages would have less crime.

4 ● Use this as a practice task before setting a time limit on the task in exercise 5. Ask one or two pairs to model their dialogues and then ask the other students to comment on the strengths and weaknesses of what they hear. Encourage them to be as positive as possible in their feedback.

● Prepare for First for Schools

Speaking Part 2

Task description
This involves an individual 1-minute 'long turn' for each student with a brief 30-second response from the second student. In turn, students are given two photographs to talk about.

Tip
It can feel quite unnatural to speak about a picture for one minute as it's not something most people do in normal life. Give students a range of pictures just to practise speaking about to make the task seem more natural.

→ See Exam Profile 5, Student's Book page 129.

5 Give a similar limit to the exam for this task (one minute for the first speaker, with a 30-second response from the second speaker). If students can record on their phones, encourage them to record themselves so that they can listen back later and assess their own strengths and weaknesses. Ask them to tick the phrases in the *Prepare* box that they used.

Mixed ability

You could brainstorm some ideas here as a whole class, if students are struggling with ideas. Or you could write some advantages and disadvantages onto cards or the board for students to categorise in mixed-ability pairs.

Cooler

Ask students to write a short paragraph about their ideal place to live. Tell them they should not name the place, but that it should be somewhere real. Afterwards, they should give their description to a partner who should try to guess the place. Ask two volunteers to read their texts to the class to see if other students can guess the place.

Project

Ask students to bring in photos of very different places. These could be pictures from the internet or photos of places they have visited. Collect the photos in and redistribute them so that each pair has two photos. Set a task similar to the speaking exam practice in exercise 5. Ask one or two pairs to perform their conversation to the class.

Teacher's resources
Student's Book
Grammar reference and practice page 155
Vocabulary list page 142
Video
Where we live
Speaking Part 3
Workbook
Unit 8, pages 31–35
Go online for
• Pronunciation
• Progress test
• Achievement test
• Video extra worksheet
• Speaking test video worksheets
• Corpus tasks

Literature
Poetry

Learning objectives

- The students read and react to a range of different poems displayed on the New York underground.
- In the project stage, students research a poem that they like and write a brief description of the poem.

Warmer

1 Write these types of reading material on the board: *newspapers, magazines, short stories, novels, poetry, blogs.* Tell students to rank them in order from their least favourite to their most favourite. Ask students to work with a partner to explain their order.

2 For feedback, find out which type is the most popular in your class. Ask students if they had to give up reading two of the types for a year, which two they would choose.

1 Tell students to read the poems and to choose their favourite. Point out there is a glossary to help them at the bottom of the page. If they don't like any of them, ask them to explain why. For each poem, ask for a show of hands from the students that chose it. Then ask for a volunteer for each one to read the poem out loud.

Cultural background

Grand Central is a train station in New York City. It is a popular visitor attraction and the largest station in the world by number of platforms.

Billy Collins is an American poet and professor, based in New York. He is regarded as America's most popular poet.

Robert Frost was one of America's most popular poets of the 20th Century. His poems look at social and philosophical themes.

Bronislaw Maj is a Polish poet, renowned as one of the finest of his generation.

Alicia Partnoy is an Argentinean poet and human rights activist, based in the US.

2 ▶1.26 Ask students if any of them know what 'Grand Central' is and where it is. Tell them that they are going to listen to a student talking about *Grand Central* and give them a few minutes to read the rest of the questions. Play the recording (you may need to play it twice). Alternatively, you could play the recording once without the students having to answer the questions; just simply ask them to summarise what they heard.

Audioscript

Teacher: OK, class. Today Janet here is going to give us a short presentation about the poem *Grand Central*. I hope everyone read it for homework! Right then. You can start when you're ready, Janet.

Janet: OK, I'm going to talk about the poem *Grand Central* by Billy Collins. First, I'll read the poem aloud. '*Grand Central* by Billy Collins. The city orbits around eight million centers of the universe and turns around the golden clock at the still point of this place. Lift up your eyes from the moving hive and you will see time circling under a vault of stars and know just when and where you are.'

Teacher: Very nicely done, Janet. Now tell us about the poem.

Janet: OK, so everyone knows what Grand Central is, right? It's a big train station in New York City. I saw Grand Central last year when I visited New York with my family. It's the biggest train station in the world, with forty-four different platforms. I mean, it's huge! I think it was built like a hundred years ago, or something like that.

Teacher: That's interesting, Janet. But what about the poem? What do you think it means?

Janet: Oh, well, in the first line of the poem, the author says 'the city orbits around eight million centers of the universe'. And New York City has a population of about eight million people, so I think he means that each person in New York is the center of the universe, or their own little universe, maybe. I like that idea! Anyway, after that, Collins talks about 'the golden clock at the still point of this place'. Well, in the middle of Grand Central, there's a really big golden clock that people look at to check the time. Everyone walks around it, but the clock doesn't move, so it's the still place.
That's what Collins means when he says 'lift up your eyes from the moving hive, and you will see time circling'. A hive is a place where bees live, and bees are always busy and moving around, just like the people in the station. And when the people look up, they see 'time circling' because the hands of the clock are moving in circles.
Then in the next line, it says, 'under a vault of stars', which sounds strange, inside a building. But when you're in Grand Central, and you look up, you can see lots of stars painted on the big, round ceiling over your head. And the word 'vault' can mean 'ceiling'. So, you look up and you see time circling on the clock, under a ceiling with stars.
Finally, the poem ends with the line, about 'you'll know just when and where you are'. So that means, when you see all those things, like the busy hive of people, and the stars on the ceiling, you'll know exactly where you are: at Grand Central. And you'll know 'when' you are, because you'll see the time on the golden clock. OK! That's all!

Teacher: That was very good, Janet. Thank you for that. You can sit down now. OK, now does anyone have any questions about …

Answers
1 A train station in New York City 2 the people in New York
3 In the middle of the station 4 how busy the station is
5 the ceiling 6 that you'll know exactly where you are

3 Ask students to choose one of the other poems on page 50. Group students with other students who have chosen the same poem, and ask them to discuss the relevant questions. Monitor and help with ideas if necessary. If you have time, you could discuss more than one poem together. Ask groups for a summary of their discussion. Try to cover each poem.

Possible answers
A leaf
1 'parts', 'spinning', 'falls', 'stops', 'fades': the verbs are important because they track the short journey of the leaf.
2 By repeating it three times, the writer emphasises the loneliness of the place.
3 The last three lines look lonely on their own and this emphasises the isolation of the writer.
Fireflies in the garden
4 Fireflies shine like stars at night time.
5 They are not as big ('they never equal stars in size') and they do not live as long ('they can't sustain the part').
6 'At heart' means 'in reality'.
Communication
7 It is about a conversation and Partnoy speaks with the reader directly ('you').
8 Partnoy may be hungry for conversation (or possibly hungry for food).
9 The short lines are like a quick conversation.

Fast finishers

Ask stronger students to discuss more than one poem, and to share their ideas with the class.

Extension activity

Find one person who likes each of the poems in the book and ask them to read the poem to the class. Before students read, point out features that might affect how they read it, e.g. the use of commas and full stops for pausing. Alternatively, you could do this activity in small groups with students taking turns to read a poem.

4 Give students a few minutes to read the text, and elicit their ideas about what *shards* are. Extend the task and check comprehension further by asking students the following questions: *What does the word barefoot refer to? How long are haiku? Where are they from? Which line contains the most syllables? What do traditional haiku refer to?*

Answer
pieces of someone's broken heart

5 Ask students to write their own haiku. Provide support as necessary. You could brainstorm some ideas as a class. Ask them what season they can see (*winter*), and what references to the natural world they can see (*the sky, snow, trees,* etc.). Check that students understand *syllables* by tapping each one as you read the example poem in the text. Ask students what the photo makes them feel, e.g. *cold, lonely*. You could bring in a selection of haiku to show students (search online for examples).

6 Students should share their poems either with the whole class or in small groups. Hold a vote for the most beautiful, funny and unusual poem, and display the haiku around the classroom for other students to read.

Cooler

Ask students to discuss these questions in pairs.
1 Is poetry popular in your country? Why / why not?
2 What things are displayed on the underground or buses in your town? Do you think poetry would be popular?
Elicit responses from one or two pairs.

Project

This project can be done in a class with computer access or set as homework. Once students have completed the project, display it around the classroom. Give students a few minutes to move around the classroom and read the different poems. Then ask students to choose their favourite. You could follow this up by asking students to find another poem by the writer of the one they chose.

Unit profile

Vocabulary: Collocations; Adjective and noun suffixes
Reading: An online competition
Grammar: Future (2): Continuous and perfect
Writing: An essay (2)

Warmer

1 Ask students to write six sentences about their future. Tell them that they should use a variety of different future forms, (i.e. *will*, *be going to*, present continuous, present simple, present perfect, future continuous, future perfect) and to include topics such as work, travel and families.

2 Put students into pairs. They should read their sentences and ask each other questions to find out more.

3 Ask two or three students to tell the class about their partner.

Your profile

In pairs, students discuss the questions. Ask one or two students to feed back on their discussion. Take a class vote to find out if most students in the class are optimistic or pessimistic?

VOCABULARY Collocations

1 Ask students to look at the middle arrow and say what they think *realism* means (behaviour in which you deal with the true fact of a situation and do not hope for things that will not happen). Set the exercise for students to complete individually. Tell students not to do the quiz yet, but just to complete the sentences. Check answers as a whole class.

Answers
1 making **2** looks, put **3** have, take, make **4** go **5** have
6 make **7** achieve **8** see

2 Ask students whether they already know the meaning of any of the bold words, but don't ask for the answers yet. They should do the matching exercise individually and then compare answers with a partner. Check answers. Ask students to identify antonyms and synonyms (e.g. strengths/weaknesses, the best of / the most of).

Answers
b have a go **c** make the best of **d** make a difference
e see the best/worst **f** look bright **g** achieve your goals
h take every opportunity **i** have strengths/weaknesses
j go wrong **k** make the most of

3 ▶ 2.02 Draw students' attention to the scoring system at the top of the quiz. Explain that they will hear two people doing the quiz and that they need to write down Dan's scores for each question. Ask students what kind of information they are listening for, and elicit *numbers*. Play the recording and then check answers as a whole class.

Audioscript

Dan: Hi, Sara. What have you got there?
Sara: It's a quiz about how optimistic you are. Apparently, I'm very optimistic!
Dan: Oh, yeah. Let's have a go.
Sara: OK. So for each of these statements, you have to give yourself a score from one to five. One means you strongly disagree. Five means you strongly agree.
Dan: OK. There aren't loads of questions, are there?
Sara: No, just eight. Here's the first. 'I'm good at making the best of a bad situation.'
Dan: Hmm, <u>two</u>? I get in a bit of panic when things go wrong.
Sara: OK. 'I think the future of mankind looks bright. For instance, one day, science will put an end to major diseases.'
Dan: Well, yes, one day that might happen. But not for a long time, I reckon. And between now and then we'll have loads of problems to deal with. Some things though, especially technology, are going to be really cool soon. And not just stuff like smartphones and tablets. Important things. Things that might make a difference to the world.
Sara: So …?
Dan: Four. No, <u>three</u>.
Sara: OK. Question three. 'I'm always willing to have a go at something new. I always take opportunities that come my way, and I make the most of them.'
Dan: You know the answer to that one! I'm pretty lazy and I don't always take opportunities that come my way.
Sara: One or two then?
Dan: <u>Two would be too generous</u> I think …
Sara: OK. Number four, 'I rarely consider myself to be at fault when things go wrong'. Actually, you're the least likely person to blame someone else, aren't you?
Dan: Well, …
Sara: You're always apologising, even when it's definitely not you. <u>One</u>?
Dan: <u>Yes</u>, sure. What's five?
Sara: 'I have more strengths than weaknesses.'
Dan: That's pretty hard to answer. I guess I do. I mean, I don't spend a lot of time worrying about things I'm not very good at.
Sara: Or your hairstyle, or the clothes you wear …
Dan: Ha ha. Overall, I'm happy with myself – I'd give that one a <u>four</u>.
Sara: That's almost a 'strongly agree'! Number six. 'I'd really like to make a difference to the world and I believe that I can achieve this.'
Dan: Well, I might have some strengths, but I'm not Einstein or anything. But yes, I'd say another <u>four</u>. I won't be saving whales, but I'm definitely going to try to do a job that's useful to the world.
Sara: Like what?

Dan:	I don't know. Maybe I'll teach!
Sara:	Really? What would you teach?
Dan:	I don't know. I haven't thought about it that much. What are the last two?
Sara:	Seven. 'I expect I will achieve all my goals in life.'
Dan:	Hmm. I don't think I have any goals in life.
Sara:	Hold on! That's not true. You just told me one of them. You want to be a teacher, don't you?
Dan:	I only said 'maybe I'll teach'. I guess I do have some goals though – or at least ideas about what I want. But will I actually achieve them? I don't know. I'm not completely confident. <u>Three</u> I guess.
Sara:	Last one. 'I often see the best in people, rather than the worst.' This is definitely you. I've never heard you say anything bad about anyone … Strongly agree. <u>Five</u>. Your only one. OK. So here's your result. You got a total of …

Answers
1 2   2 3   3 1   4 1   5 4   6 4   7 3   8 5

4 Tell students to do the questionnaire themselves. Remind them to score 1 if they strongly disagree with the statement, and 5 if they strongly agree. Students should then work in pairs and discuss their answers. Encourage them to give an example for each point.

5 Ask students to add up their scores and to read about themselves and Dan on page 130. Ask students whether they agree with the interpretation or not.

Extension activity
Give students these quotations on optimism and pessimism. Ask them to work in groups and discuss what they mean, which ones they relate to and why.
Don't cry because it's over, smile because it happened. Dr. Seuss
We are all in the gutter, but some of us are looking at the stars. Oscar Wilde
The man who is a pessimist before 48 knows too much; if he is an optimist after it he knows too little. Mark Twain
Discuss some ideas as a class.

Answer
Dan scores 23 and is described as Realistic.

READING

1 Set a short time limit of two minutes for students to answer these questions. Students should then compare their answers with a partner before whole-class feedback.

Answers
1 people's feelings about the future
2 Ruby and Hannah are optimistic. Glen is pessimistic.
3 Adam

2 Remind students that underlining key words in the question can be a helpful strategy. You could also ask students to underline the parts of the text that helped them decide on the answer. Monitor and help weaker students by confirming the first one or two questions with them before they move on to the next. Check answers as a whole class.

Answers
1 Glen   **2** Adam   **3** Ruby   **4** Hannah

3 Give students a few minutes to answer these questions quickly, and check answers. If they already have a good grasp of the text, you could go through these orally as a whole class.

Fast finishers
Ask fast finishers to find words in the text that mean (answers in brackets):
1 end something unpleasant (*get rid of*)
2 develop an opinion based on things you notice (*get the impression*)
3 not make any progress (*never get anywhere*)
4 have the opportunity to do something (*get to do*)
5 obtain something, usually after some difficulty (*get hold of*)
6 annoy someone, especially by doing something again and again (*get on somebody's nerves*)
Ask fast finishers to feed back after checking answers to exercise 3.

Answers
1 She spoke to teachers and friends about her problem and read a book. She also developed new interests, including playing the guitar and learning Spanish.
2 He thinks university will be harder than school. He knows he'll need to borrow a lot of money, and eventually find a job.
3 She looks forward to the things she enjoys doing, like surfing, or she listens to music or watches comedy shows.
4 He avoids negative things and people.

4 Draw their attention to the opening paragraph as students may have overlooked this up until now. In pairs, students should discuss who should win and why. Then hold a class vote with a show of hands. Ask them what they think the prize is, directing them to the end of the first paragraph. Explain that it is a pair of sunglasses, and comes from *The future's so bright, I gotta wear shades* (*shades*: sunglasses).

Extension activity
Ask students to read the introductory paragraph of the text on page 55 again and to write their own post. Then put them into small groups. Ask them to read their posts and decide who the winner is in their group. In whole-class feedback, ask one or two groups to explain who the winner was and why.

EP Word profile

Books closed. Elicit three sentences from the class using the word *hold*. Books open. Ask students to read the sentences and say if any of the meanings are the same as on the board. They should explain the meaning of *hold* in each one to a partner. Then set the exercise on page 135.

Answers

1 Hold on   **2** holding my breath   **3** get hold of   **4** holding on
5 get hold of   **6** holds the record

Talking points

In pairs, students discuss the question. Monitor and help with ideas if necessary. For example, being too pessimistic might stop you doing things you might enjoy, while being too optimistic might lead to disappointment if things don't turn out well later. Ask the class to vote on the first question by raising their hands. Elicit some reasons why the class feel this way.

Cooler

Ask students to work in groups of four to six with other students they know quite well. Each person should take a piece of paper and write their name at the top. They should then pass this to their left and the next person should write a sentence about something this person will have done or will be doing in the future (e.g. 'Max will have moved to Paris', 'Anna will be studying architecture'). Students then fold the piece of paper so that only the name can be seen and not the prediction. They then pass this on to their left again and repeat until the piece of paper gets back to the named person. Students then open their paper and see if they agree with their friends' predictions. Share some funny or interesting predictions as a class.

GRAMMAR   Future (2): Continuous and perfect

1 Ask students to look carefully at each example and elicit the structure for how each one is formed (future continuous: *will / won't* + *be* + verb + *-ing*; future perfect: *will / won't* + *have* + past participle; future perfect continuous: *will / won't have been* + verb + *-ing*).

Mixed ability

If some students are struggling, write the gapped structures on the board and encourage stronger students to complete them. For example:
Future continuous
will + ... + ...
Future perfect
.... + *have* + ...
Future perfect continuous
will + ... + *been* + ...

Answers

Future continuous: *will* + *be* + *-ing*
Future perfect: *will* + *have* + past participle
Future perfect continuous: *will* + *have been* + *-ing*

2 Tell students to read the examples in exercise 1 and to complete the rules individually. Ask them to give you one more example sentence for each structure and write it on the board. Remind them that we don't use the future perfect for states; we use *will* instead. For example, 'You'll be very hungry by dinner time if you don't eat breakfast' (not 'will have been very hungry').

Answers

1 continuous   **2** perfect   **3** perfect continuous

→ **Grammar reference Student's Book page 156**

3 Ask students if they think life will be better or worse in 50 years. Then ask them to complete the predictions individually before comparing answers with a partner. Monitor and give extra help if necessary, explaining which predictions refer to the actual moment in the future and which refer to what has happened between now and that point in the future. Check answers. Which predictions do students agree/disagree with?

Answers

1 will have put; will be generating
2 won't have found; will be living
3 won't be working; will have earned
4 will, be living; will have discovered

4 Ask students to write their sentences individually. Then tell them to work with a partner and to ask questions to find out more information about each statement. Once students have finished, ask two or three students to tell the class about their partner.

Extension activity

Ask students to imagine themselves at the age of 40. Tell them to write a paragraph about things they think they will be doing and things they will have done in their life. Then ask students to exchange their paragraph with a partner who should check their use of future forms. Tell students to put their hand up if they think their partner is a pessimist. If anyone raises their hand, ask them to explain why, but encouraging the conversation to remain light-hearted. Repeat the same for optimists.

Answers

1 I will/won't be studying at university.
2 I will/won't have travelled abroad without my parents.
3 I'll have been learning English for … years.
4 I will/won't be living with my parents.
5 I will/won't have learned how to drive.
6 I will/won't be doing an interesting job.

Ask students to correct the sentence and to explain the error (we use the future continuous to talk about an action that will be happening at a point in the future).

Answer
I would like to go on holiday in July because I don't know if I will be working or not in September.

VOCABULARY   Adjectives and noun suffixes

1 Write an example word with each suffix (word ending) on the board (for example: *sociable*, *collective*, *magical*, *attraction*, *enjoyment*, *infinity*, *ownership*). Underline the suffix, and ask students whether the word is an adjective or a noun. Then set the exercise as individual work. Check answers.

Answers
1 valuable   2 effective   3 practical   4 competition
5 encouragement   6 responsibility   7 friendship

2 Look at the example together and discuss what clues tell us that the missing word needs to be an adjective (after verb, before noun). Then ask students to complete the exercise in pairs. Check answers.

Answers
1 adjective (comes after *can be*)
2 noun (comes after adjective)
3 noun (*a lack of* + noun is a fixed expression)
4 noun (comes after adjective)
5 noun (adjective not possible)
6 noun (adjective not possible)
7 adjective (comes after *the least*)
8 adjective (comes before *95%*)

● **Prepare for First for Schools**
Reading and Use of English Part 3

Task description
The focus of this task is on word formation, in particular the use of affixation, internal changes and compounding. Students are given a text with eight gaps. Each gap corresponds to a word. The stem of the missing word is given beside the text and must be changed to form the missing word.

Tip
Encourage students to look around the gap to identify the other words. This will give them a clue to the type of word they need. Often they will need to read further away from the gap to identify whether a negative prefix is needed or not.

→ See Exam Profile 3, Student's Book page 124.

3 ● Set a strict time limit of ten minutes here to mimic exam conditions. Allow students to check their answers with a partner before whole-class feedback.

Extension activity
Ask students to use the words from this section to write three or four questions on health and happiness. Then they should ask ask and answer their questions in pairs. Ask one or two pairs to perform their conversations to the class.

Answers
1 beneficial   2 relationship   3 enjoyment   4 personality
5 satisfaction   6 majority   7 active   8 remarkable

WRITING   An essay (2)

1 Ask students to look at the photos and say what is happening in each. In pairs, students discuss the questions. Ask them to describe some of the differences between their childhood and their grandparents' childhood.

2 In pairs, students brainstorm extra ideas for the essay. Elicit some ideas from different pairs and write them on the board.

3 Tell students to read the example essay and answer the questions. They should ignore the highlighting for now. Check answers together and then ask students whether they agree with the opinions in the essay.

Answers
1 Students' own answers.
2 technology and safety

4 Set this as an individual task. Check answers, and then ask students to work with a partner to add one or two more phrases to each category. Stronger students could give synonyms for the highlighted words before looking at the functions in exercise 4.

Answers
1 Furthermore, Moreover   2 In my view   3 As a result
4 On balance

5 Give students time to read the *Prepare* box and make sure the meanings are clear. Then ask them to complete this task individually.

Answers
1 Unlike   2 In comparison with   3 whereas   4 Compared to
5 on the other hand

6 Work through *home life* as an example on the board, eliciting ideas from students. Then ask students to work with a partner to add more ideas to the other points. Elicit some ideas from the class and add them to the board. Remind students of the tenses they will need to make predictions about the future.

Fast finishers

Ask fast finishers to use their notes to write sentences using the expressions to compare and contrast ideas. Elicit an example of each expression after checking answers to exercise 5.

Prepare for First for Schools
Writing Part 1

Task description
This part is a compulsory task. Students are required to write an essay giving their opinion on the essay title using the ideas given and providing an idea of their own. Students should write 140–190 words.

Tip
A very simple paragraph structure you can teach students to remember for the essay is: topic sentence containing the main opinion, an example, an explanation or reason, a concluding sentence. Keeping this simple structure in mind can help students communicate their ideas clearly.

7 Give students a time limit of 40 minutes to write their essay. Remind them to use the bulleted checklist as they write their answers. Collect in the essays and provide feedback on the items listed in the bullet points. Once you have given the work back, ask students to redraft the essay and improve it.

Sample answer
Although there is no way of predicting the future with any accuracy, the idea that life for young people will be harder in 25 years' time seems unlikely. With all the technological aids that are already available and the many new ones that are sure to be invented between now and then, things can only improve. This is certainly true of home life, where labour-saving devices and smart technology will make our existence trouble-free, unless we run out of electricity, or suffer a major war.

As far as education is concerned, better use of the internet should make learning far more accessible than it is today, and there could even be brain implants to assist us in our studies. Research is already happening in this area, so this may well be the case.

In my view, climate change is the only factor that might make life harder in the future. If we fail to protect the environment over the next few years, there will be negative results for us humans, and life could become a real struggle.

On balance, however, I believe that the next generation will have an easier life than ours.

Cooler

Write three topics on the board, for example, *space*, *energy* and *computing*. Ask students to write sentences comparing fifty years ago to today in each area. Then tell them to write sentences about each one using the future forms from this unit. Ask students to compare ideas with a partner, and discuss some as a class.

Project

Tell students to choose a topic from the Cooler and to research predictions in this area online. In the next class, ask them to work in small groups and share their research. Ask students to write a short text on the similarities and differences in their predictions.

Teacher's resources

Student's Book
Grammar reference and practice page 156
Vocabulary list page 142
Workbook
Unit 9, pages 36–39
Go online for
* Pronunciation
* Corpus tasks

10 Surprise!

Warmer

Write the following on the board:
In twenty years' time you will:
be married and have had three children
have gone to university and be living in another country
Ask students to discuss which one of these events they would find most surprising about their own life, and to change them to make them more realistic for themselves. Ask students to discuss their ideas with a partner, and then ask for volunteers to tell the class about their partner.

Your profile

In pairs, students discuss the questions. Ask them to feed back on any interesting surprises their partner has had.

VOCABULARY Phrases with *in, out of, at, by*

1 Tell students they are going to hear five people talking about unexpected or surprising things that happened. Ask them to read through the list of options and then play the recording.

Audioscript

Narrator: One
Speaker: I couldn't believe it. There were only a few hundred people left at the venue. Most people had left, but it had taken us ages to get our coats. It was only by chance that I glanced through the door and noticed him coming back onto the stage. He played for another hour, so the whole concert lasted for three hours in all. It was really special.

Narrator: Two
Speaker: Unfortunately he found out about it in advance. I'd left an email open by accident, and he saw it when he borrowed my tablet to watch some video. After that there was no point in trying to keep it secret. I don't think it mattered, though. I think he enjoyed himself on the night. Almost everyone we'd invited made it.

Narrator: Three
Speaker: He scared the life out of me, bursting into my room out of nowhere. I was on the phone to Rob and I nearly dropped my brand-new phone! Actually it's not exactly out of character for my brother to turn up like that, especially on my birthday, but I was impressed that he'd made the effort to come home from university just for the evening.

Narrator: Four
Speaker: United are now at risk of finishing the season without any trophies. They were expected to beat City easily, but instead the game ended two-two due to a last minute effort from City's new eighteen-year-old Brazilian player. The goalkeeper was partly at fault for the goal when he …

Narrator: Five
Speaker: … still talking about this week's surprise news from the singer Melissa Zane. She refused to speak in detail about the ceremony, but said that it had taken place in secret a few months ago. The singer's agent is expected to make a longer statement this evening. The announcement was particularly surprising after the very public break-up the couple went through a year ago.

Answers
1 d a surprise party   **2** c an unexpected visit
3 f a shock result   **4** a an unexpected extra
5 e a surprise wedding
Extra topic: b a surprise win

2 **▶2.03** Tell students to complete the phrases and then to compare their answers with a partner. Play the recording for students to check their answers, pausing after each one if necessary.

Answers
1 in all   **2** in advance   **3** by accident   **4** out of nowhere
5 out of character   **6** at risk   **7** at fault   **8** in detail; in secret

3 Ask students to work in pairs and to match the phrases to the definitions. Then tell them to think of more phrases which use these prepositions. Check answers. Elicit some of the other phrases from students and write them on the board. Ask students to explain their phrases and to give you an example sentence for each one.

Answers
1 c **2** a **3** g **4** f **5** e **6** j **7** i **8** b; d

4 Ask students to discuss the meaning of the phrases in bold with a partner. After a few minutes check the meaning of the phrases as a whole class. Then set the questions for pair work discussion. Elicit one or two answers for each question from different students.

Answers
1 as active or as intelligent as you can be
2 learn something so you can say it from memory
3 communicate with someone
4 no longer popular or seen as stylish
5 share interests or experiences with someone
6 in a place where people can see you

READING

1 Ask students if they have ever heard of a flash mob, and ask a volunteer to explain what it is. If possible, find a video clip of one and show it to the class. If students haven't heard of a flash mob, tell them to read the article quickly to find out what they are. Then ask students to read the article quickly and choose the best title.

Answer
c

2 Books closed. If you have time before class, type the sentences without the underlining and project them onto a screen. Ask students to make a note of any words or phrases that they think will help them fit these sentences into a text. Books open. Ask students to compare their words to the underlined ones in the book. If you do not have time to do this, focus students' attention on the underlined words, and remind them that it is a good strategy to focus on key words before deciding which sentence fits where.

Mixed ability
Give weaker students one or two of the sentences. Stronger students can work through the exercise in the book.

● Prepare for First for Schools
Reading and Use of English Part 6

Task description
Reading and Use of English Part 6 tests students' awareness of cohesion, coherence, and text structure. It consists of a text from which six sentences have been removed and placed below the text in jumbled order. Students must put the sentences in the correct place.

Tip
Tell students to skim read the text first to get the general sense, before reading the sentences immediately before and after each gap. This will help them to identify the correct place for each missing sentence.

3 ● Remind students that the underlined words will be related to ideas in the sentences before and after each gap. Give students time to complete the gaps and compare answers with a partner before checking as a whole class.

Fast finishers
Ask fast finishers to write two or three sentences expressing their reactions to the text, and to share these with the class after checking answers to exercise 3.

Answers
1 G – *he* refers back to Bill Wasik, and his *60 friends* are referred to in the sentence after the gap as They.
2 D – the missing sentence mentions seven more events and these are referred to in the phrase *Each time* immediately after the gap.
3 B – the underlined phrases in sentence B are matched in the text by *everywhere* before the gap and *modern urban culture* afterwards.
4 F – the paragraph is describing the annual *international* pillow fight and the missing sentence talks about this event occurring in *25 cities around the world*.
5 A – the missing sentence refers to *incidents* caused by flash mobs, and immediately before the gap, one such incident is described, where thousands of rail passengers were seriously inconvenienced.
6 E – the missing sentence talks about product promotion, which is matched in the text by *commercial opportunities*.
Extra sentence: C

4 Do the first sentence on the board as an example to highlight that the form of the phrasal verb changes. Then ask students to complete the exercise individually before checking answers as a class.

Extension activity
Ask students to write questions using the phrasal verbs. Monitor and check while they are writing these to help with any vocabulary. Then tell them to ask and answer their questions in pairs.

Answers
1 turning up   2 carrying out   3 's come up with
4 had already cleared up   5 put you off

Talking points
In pairs, students discuss these questions. Elicit any reasons about the serious purpose flash mobs might have (e.g. to raise awareness of a charity or social issue).

Cooler
Ask students to work in small groups to plan a flash mob. Where and when will it be? What will participants do? How will they advertise it? Will it be for fun or will it have a serious purpose? Ask one or two groups to report back to the class.

GRAMMAR   Modals (2): Modals in the past

1 Ask one student to read the first four sentences aloud. Then ask the class what the form of the word is that follows each modal.

Answer
a past participle

2 Ask students to complete the rules and to compare their answers with a partner. Check answers as a whole class and elicit an example sentence using each structure.

Answers

b shouldn't **c** needn't have **d** didn't need to

→ **Grammar reference Student's Book page 157**

3 Ask students to complete the exercise individually. When checking answers, ask students to give you a reason for their choice.

Answers

1 shouldn't 2 needn't 3 didn't need to be 4 would
5 shouldn't 6 should

Prepare for First for Schools

Reading and Use of English Part 4

Task description

Reading and Use of English Part 4 is a key word transformation task that tests grammar, vocabulary and collocation. It consists of six questions, each with a lead-in sentence and a gapped sentence. Students must complete the gapped sentence in two to five words, including the given 'key' word.

Tip

Make sure students understand the importance of sticking to the word limit given in the rubric.

4 Do the first sentence together as an example and then ask students to complete the exercise in pairs. Check answers as a whole class.

Answers

1 should have asked (me) / should have asked my permission
2 needn't have got
3 he should have checked
4 should have kept my mouth
5 should have let

Corpus challenge

Ask students to correct the sentence and to explain the error (we use *would have* + past participle to imagine something in the past that didn't happen).

Answer

I don't know what I'd have done without your help because I didn't know where to go.

5 Tell students to complete the sentences with information about themselves. In pairs, students should ask questions to find out more information. Elicit an example for each sentence from the class.

VOCABULARY Extended meanings of words

1 Ask a student to read both sentences aloud and discuss the questions as a whole class. If possible, think of an example verb in the students' own language which has both a literal and figurative meaning to help them see the difference.

Answers

frozen – not moving; turned into ice
flooded – quickly entered; covered in water

2 Ask students to complete the exercise individually and to compare their answers in pairs. Check answers as a whole class, and ask students if they can define each word's literal meaning.

Answers

1 bright 2 hit 3 boiling 4 weighed 5 froze 6 flooded

3 Ask students to work in pairs to explain the meaning of each word. Afterwards, elicit definitions for the words from the class.

Answers

1 very good and kind
2 unclear
3 asked a lot of questions for a long time
4 improved
5 easily passed
6 involving a lot of arguments and shouting

LISTENING

1 ▶ 2.04 Ask students if they have had any surprises this week. Tell them they are going to listen to an extract from a radio interview about a surprising event. Ask the class to make a prediction about what happened to Rachel.

Audioscript

Presenter: Hi, Rachel. Now we understand you've just had a rather special and surprising weekend. Tell us all about it.

Rachel: Thanks. Yes, yes, I did. I, er …

Presenter: Did you know something special was going to happen?

Rachel: Absolutely not. <u>I had no idea anything was happening, especially as it isn't even my birthday until tomorrow.</u> On Saturday, my best friend, Lucy, suggested seeing a film in the evening. We met at the cinema, but were a bit early. Lucy suggested some new café she'd heard of. To get a coffee.

Presenter: Suspicious …

Rachel: Yes, well, I remember being a bit confused. We usually just got something at the cinema. Anyway, she insisted on it …

Answer

She had a birthday surprise.

2 Ask students to read the question and to discuss with a partner what they might need to listen for, to be able to answer this question, e.g. what Rachel thought they were doing.

3 ▶2.04 Ask students to compare their ideas from exercise 2 with the questions in exercise 3. Did they have the same or different ideas? Play the recording and ask students to answer the question.

Answer
C. Saturday wasn't actually her birthday.

● Prepare for First for Schools

Listening Part 4

Task description
The focus of this multiple-choice task is on identifying opinion, attitude, detail, gist, main idea and specific information. Students hear an interview or exchange between two speakers, and answer seven three-option multiple-choice questions.

Tip
Encourage students to look at each question and identify whether they need to listen for an opinion, the speaker's attitude, a main idea or specific information.

→ See Exam Profile 5, Student's Book page 128.

---

4 ● ▶2.05 Give students a few minutes to read through the questions and to think about what they need to listen for.

Audioscript

Presenter: Hi, Rachel. Now we understand you've just had a rather special and surprising weekend. Tell us all about it.

Rachel: Thanks. Yes, yes, I did. I, er …

Presenter: Did you know something special was going to happen?

Rachel: Absolutely not. I had no idea anything was happening, especially as it isn't even my birthday until tomorrow. On Saturday, my best friend, Lucy, suggested seeing a film in the evening. We met at the cinema, but were a bit early. Lucy suggested some new café she'd heard of. To get a coffee.

Presenter: Suspicious …

Rachel: Yes, well, I remember being a bit confused. We usually just got something at the cinema. Anyway, she insisted on it …

Presenter: And all your relatives and friends were waiting there.

Rachel: Well, yes, but a few things happened before that. The café turned out to be a restaurant. But they seemed happy for us to just have a drink. Then something really strange happened. My uncle turned up! When he saw me, he looked as though he was going to pass out! He mumbled something about meeting a friend and being late. Obviously his friend wasn't there. I didn't know what to say. He just looked really embarrassed, but sat down with us.

Presenter: He could have ruined everything! Presumably he genuinely was late …

Rachel: I expect so!

Presenter: But once he'd seen you …

Rachel: Exactly! Anyway, then Lucy got a text message. She suddenly stood up and said 'Let's go and sit downstairs.' I remember thinking 'The film will be starting soon. Is there any point?' But at the same time it was getting busy and they probably needed the tables for people ordering food. So we started going down – I was first. At the bottom, there was a door. I pushed it open, but it was dark inside. I was about to turn round when the lights went on and I heard a huge 'Surprise!'

Presenter: What did you do? I would have fainted!

Rachel: I almost did. My sister, typically, got the exact moment on film. My mouth falls open! I look like a fish! I immediately saw my favourite cousin. I haven't seen him for months and he's at uni in Scotland. So I definitely wasn't expecting to see him! He'd come home especially! Then everyone starting singing *Happy Birthday*. I was almost in tears.

Presenter: I bet you were! So what happened then? Did you make a speech or anything like that?

Rachel: No, I didn't. I hope no-one expected me to. My mum did, though. She didn't say much about me, fortunately. I would have been really embarrassed. My dad and his friends played some music – he sings in a band. He'd even rewritten the lyrics to some Beatles song so that it was about me. It was really funny. After about an hour, my parents said that the adults were leaving. I pretended I was a bit disappointed, but I don't think they believed me!

Presenter: So then the real party started …

Rachel: Yeah, it went on until about midnight and then some parents started arriving to pick my friends up.

Presenter: Whose idea was it? Your parents' again?

Rachel: My sister's. At first my parents weren't really sure about it. They were OK about having a party, and they knew I'd love it but they were worried a surprise party would involve a lot of organisation for them. So my sister promised to find a venue and sort out the invitations. My parents just had to, er, pay for it.

Answers
Refer also to the underlined parts of the script above.

2 A – B is not correct because the uncle only invented the story about the friend to prevent Rachel from finding out about the surprise; C isn't true because he did sit with them.

3 B – A is incorrect because the restaurant had an eating area upstairs; C is not supported by what Rachel says, but is plausible as the upstairs area was getting busy.

4 A – B is suggested by the fact that the sister was filming the event but there is no suggestion that Rachel was uncomfortable with this; C is incorrect as Rachel says she was *almost in tears*.

5 B – A is ruled out because the adults, including her parents, only stayed for an hour; C is wrong as Rachel said that her mum didn't say much about her and that she *would have been really embarrassed* if her mother had done so.

6 C – A is not correct because even if the parents paid for the event, there is no suggestion that they were concerned about its cost; B is ruled out because Rachel says that her parents *knew I'd love it*.

 **Word profile**

Ask students to define the meaning of *expect* in each sentence in the book. Then set the exercises on page 135. Discuss their responses to exercise 2 as a class.

Answers

1 expectations 2 expected 3 be expecting 4 I expect
5 unexpectedly 6 expected

SPEAKING Surprising news

1 ▶2.06 Explain that students will hear Emma and Ahmed talking about a competition she entered. Play the recording and check the answer together.

Audioscript

Emma: Do you remember that short story competition I entered?
Ahmed: Of course. It was ages ago, wasn't it? Don't tell me …
Emma: No, not me! But Sally Frost did. She won!
Ahmed: Did she? That's amazing! What was the prize again?
Emma: The school gets some money and her story will be published online. The head came into our English lesson to tell us. He was really pleased.
Ahmed: I bet he was. Wow! I'd never have guessed Sally was a good writer.
Emma: We sit next to each other in English once in a while. She's quiet but really creative. By the way, have you heard about Dan's bike?
Ahmed: No, what happened?

Answer

He's surprised that Sally Frost won.

2 ▶2.06 Play the recording again for students to complete the gaps. Check answers and ask the students how the phrases were used (*to express surprise*).

Answers

1 amazing 2 guessed

3 ▶2.07 Explain that students will hear another conversation about a surprise. Play the recording for students to answer the question. Check the answer as a class. Play the recording again if not all students were able to answer the question.

Audioscript

Ahmed: Hi, Dan. Emma told me what happened to your bike at the weekend. But, no lock! I mean, seriously.
Dan: I know, I know. I should have locked it. That's what my dad said. He was absolutely furious with me.
Ahmed: Was he? I'm not surprised to be honest. Did you report it?
Dan: Yes, and the police said there was no chance of getting it back. But get this! I got a call from them this morning. They found my bike.
Ahmed: Really?
Dan: Yeah. Someone, they didn't know who, took the bike back to the shop where I lost it.
Ahmed: You're kidding!

Dan: It was the last thing I expected too. I'm going there after school to pick it up.
Ahmed: No way! That's so lucky! I wonder what happened. Do you think someone felt …

Answer

They were surprised that someone took the bike back to the shop.

4 ▶2.07 Play the recording and ask students to write the expressions they hear.

Answers

Ahmed: Was he?, Really?, You're kidding!, No way!
Dan: It was the last thing I expected

5 Ask students to make notes on three of the ideas in the box, or other ideas they can think of. Monitor and help students with ideas and vocabulary.

6 Tell students to work in groups and to discuss their ideas from exercise 5. Remind them to use the *Prepare* box language to react. Ask one or two pairs to act out their dialogues to the class.

Cooler

Ask students to write down something that would surprise them onto a piece of paper. In small groups, each student should mime their surprise and the rest of the group should guess what the surprise is.

Project

Tell students to research another internet craze (*craze: something that is very popular for a short time*). They should prepare a short presentation to explain the craze to the class, including information about what the craze is, where it started and how popular it is. If possible, their presentation could include screenshots or videos.

Teacher's resources

Student's Book
Grammar reference and practice page 157
Vocabulary list page 143
Video
Surprises!
Speaking Part 4
Workbook
Unit 10, pages 40–43
Go online for
• Pronunciation
• Progress test
• Video extra worksheet
• Speaking test video worksheets
• Corpus tasks

Culture
World music

Learning objectives

- The students learn about the invention of world music and the WOMAD festival.
- In the project stage, students produce a fact file about a singer who has been influenced by a range of music around the world.

Warmer

1 Find six images of some of the most popular musicians in your country and the world. Ask students to name each of the musicians.

2 Put students into groups of four and tell them to create a quiz about the musicians. They should write one question for each musician.

3 Put two groups together and ask each group to take turns reading out their questions to the other group. Each correct answer gets a point.

4 Find out which team did the worst. Ask for their questions to be read out to the whole class to see if the class can do better together.

1 ▶ **2.08** Tell students to look at the flags, and ask if they know anything about music from these countries. Explain that students are going to hear music from each country. Tell them to guess which country the music is from. Play the recording, and check answers.

Audioscript
Extracts of music from eight countries.

Answers
1 India   2 Ireland   3 Morocco   4 China   5 Brazil
6 The USA   7 Russia   8 Australia

2 ▶ **2.08** Ask students to look at the adjectives in the box. Check that they know the meaning of the words. Play the recording again and ask students to choose adjectives to describe each piece of music. Students check in pairs before feedback.

Extension activity

Ask students to discuss their favourite music and whether they listen to world music or not. You could do this in small groups, or students could create a questionnaire to find out the most popular style of music, the most popular country's music, etc.

3 Ask students to read the text quickly and to raise their hand when they have found the answer. When half the class have their hands raised, elicit the answer.

Answer
Robert E Brown, a music professor from New York (see *Early Years* panel)

4 Ask students to read the text again and find the answers to the questions. Check answers as a whole class.

Answers
a flamenco   b David Guetta   c WOMAD
d Youssou N'Dour   e Graceland

5 Ask students to discuss these questions with a partner. Elicit ideas for each sentence in a whole-class discussion.

6 ▶ **2.09** Ask students to share anything they already know about WOMAD. Tell them that they are going to listen to a discussion about the festivals. Play the recording. Allow students to compare answers with a partner before whole-class feedback.

Audioscript
James: Hello, everyone. In today's podcast, we'll be hearing from Angela, who volunteers for the WOMAD organisation, here in the UK. Good afternoon, Angela! It's nice of you to be here.

Angela: Good afternoon, James. It's my pleasure!

James: Well, Angela, for those listeners who are wondering, what exactly is WOMAD?

Angela: Good question! Well, WOMAD is an international organisation that promotes inclusive, multi-cultural values, such as peace, human rights, international cooperation, and environmental protection. And it also organises music festivals, of course!

James: Yes, that's probably what most people think of when they hear the name WOMAD. And how long has it existed?

Angela: Since 1980, really. But the first WOMAD festival wasn't held until two years after that. It took place in Shepton Mallet, a town in south-west England. That particular event was one of the world's first truly international music festivals, and it attracted about fifteen thousand spectators.

James: That wasn't too bad for the first year, was it?

Angela: No, it was quite good, although the first festival wasn't really a commercial success, since it didn't make a profit. It just cost too much to organise everything.

James: And is the festival still held in Shepton Mallet now?

Angela: No, it isn't. Now the UK festival takes place in Charlton Park, in Wiltshire. And there are lots of WOMAD events in more than twenty-five different countries around the world.

James: I read somewhere that there have been about one hundred and fifty WOMAD festivals since it was established. Is that true?

Angela: More than a hundred and sixty, really. And there are more every year. Some of them are small, one-day events, but most are week-long celebrations.

James: Wow, and all of those events are organised by WOMAD in the UK?

Angela: Oh, no. There are also national WOMAD organisations in other countries, like New Zealand, Australia, Spain and Russia. And there's also an organisation in the United Arab Emirates, which organises a WOMAD festival in Abu Dhabi. It attracts about a hundred thousand people!

James: Impressive! And the festivals, do they just offer concerts, or is there more to them?

Angela: Well, the concerts are the main attraction, of course, but there are always other activities as well, like musical workshops, street theatre, or markets with food and art from around the world. There's always something for everyone!

James: Well, that sounds great, Angela. We have to take a break there, but thank you for coming in today. It's been a pleasure.

Angela: No problem, and thanks James.

Answers

1 15,000
2 It didn't make a profit.
3 one day to one week
4 New Zealand, Australia, Spain, Russia, United Arab Emirates
5 musical workshops, street theatre, food markets and art from around the world

7 ▶ **2.10** Tell students that they are going to hear a presentation about the singer, Shakira. Ask students what they know about her. Give students time to read the text and try to predict the words from the box for each gap. Play the recording for students to check their guesses and fill any incomplete gaps. Check answers as a whole class.

Audioscript

Teacher: OK, everyone. Today we're going to hear the first presentations of the world music projects that you've been working on. And the first people to present will be Alicia and Janice. You two can start whenever you're ready.

Alicia: OK. Well, our presentation is about the singer Shakira, whose full name is Shakira Isabel Mebarak Ripoll. She was born in the city of Barranquilla, in 1977. Now you go.

Janice: Er, Shakira is Colombian, but she also has ethnic roots in other countries. Her mother's family is Spanish and Italian, and her father is Lebanese, although he was born in the USA. I think this international background has always influenced Shakira's musical taste and style.

Alicia: Me too! But when Shakira first started her music career, she mostly sang Latin pop and rock. Her first two albums weren't very successful, but in 1996 she recorded the pop album *Pies Descalzos*. That means 'bare feet' in English. And that's when her musical career really took off.

Janice: That's right. And since then, she's made six other successful albums, including *Laundry Service* in 2001, and *She Wolf* in 2010. She's also performed songs with famous American pop singers, like *Beautiful Liar*, which she sang with Beyoncé, in 2007.

Alicia: Shakira has had lots of hits, like *Whenever, Wherever* in 2001, *Hips Don't Lie* in 2006, and *Can't Remember To Forget You* with Rihanna in 2014. But one of her most famous songs is probably *Waka Waka*, or *This Time for Africa*, which she sang for the FIFA World Cup in South Africa. It features traditional African rhythms and musical instruments, which makes it a good example of modern world music.

Janice: Shakira's music always has always had an international feel, with sounds from Andean folk music, Middle-Eastern music, and Indian music. You can also notice sounds from Spanish Flamenco music and Brazilian Bossa Nova. There's a bit of everything in there! I think that's why her music is so popular. It has a little something for everyone – it appeals to people of different ages, young and old, in many different countries and cultures. OK, that's all! Thanks!

Alicia: Thanks! Phew!

Answers

1 Colombia 2 Italian 3 Lebanese 4 Latin 5 1996
6 Beyoncé 7 Middle-Eastern 8 Brazilian

Cooler

Ask students to work in pairs and to think about festivals in their own country or around the world. Ask them to make brief notes about the festival, including when and where it happens, the type of music played, how popular it is, etc. Elicit ideas from one or two pairs.

Project

Ask students to do their research online and produce a blog post about the singer. In the following class, they can present this in small groups. Ask each group to choose one presentation to share with the whole class.

Unit profile

Vocabulary: Phrasal verbs: relationships; Compound adjectives

Reading: Three family history texts

Grammar: Relative clauses

Writing: An article (2)

Warmer

1 Tell students to write five sentences with *would have … but / shouldn't have / didn't need to / needn't have / should have* about members of their family. Three of the sentences should be true and two should be false.

2 Students read their sentences aloud to a partner who should guess which ones are true.

3 Tell pairs to ask each other a question about the two true sentences. Ask two or three pairs to report back to the class.

Your profile

In pairs, students describe what they can see in the photos and say whether they have seen photos like these of their own family. Then they discuss the first question. For the second question, ask students to come up with at least three differences. After the discussion, encourage students to write full sentences about these differences to revise comparative structures.

VOCABULARY Phrasal verbs: relationships

1 Ask students to match the sentence halves individually. Monitor and give clues where necessary. Check answers as a whole class, and ask students to explain the meaning of each phrasal verb.

Answers

1 h 2 b 3 a 4 e 5 f 6 d 7 i 8 c 9 g 10 j

2 ▶ 2.11 Tell students that they are going to listen to six conversations about relationships, and that they should answer the questions they hear on the recording. Tell them there is one question for each conversation. Play the recording. Check answers by asking one of the questions at a time and eliciting the answers from the class.

Audioscript

Narrator:	One. Who can count on their father?
Emma:	Hi, Ahmed. Who are you waiting for?
Ahmed:	My dad. He's always late though.
Emma:	Oh. My dad's really reliable. He said he'd be here at six o'clock, and …
Dad:	Hi, Emma. Jump in!
Emma:	Do you want a lift?
Ahmed:	No, I'd better wait, thanks.
Narrator:	Two. Who does Sara take after?
Sara:	My mum found all these old black and white photos in a box the other day. Look at this – it's of my mum when she was about twenty!
Dan:	Wow. You don't look at all like her.
Sara:	I know, but look at my grandma, here, when she was my age.
Dan:	She looks just like you!
Sara:	I know. It's amazing, isn't it?
Narrator:	Three. Did Emma hit it off with Sara's cousin?
Dan:	Hi, Emma. How was the evening at Sara's?
Emma:	It was OK, but it was a bit embarrassing at first. I got there early and Sara's cousin was there.
Dan:	I've never met her, I don't think.
Emma:	I'd never met her either. I didn't have anything to say to her and there were lots of awkward silences. We just didn't have anything in common. I was glad when everyone else turned up.
Narrator:	Four. Who does Dan feel he has let down?
Emma:	How were your maths results?
Dan:	Hmm, lower than last time. The maths teacher said he thinks I understand the material and he's sure I'll do better next time, but I know my parents will be really disappointed. I promised them I'd get a higher grade in this test.
Narrator:	Five. Does Ahmed's brother look down on him or look up to him?
Emma:	What's up with your brother? He used to be so friendly.
Ahmed:	I know. It's since he's been at university. I think he thinks he's better than me.
Emma:	Than 'us' you mean. He obviously can't be bothered to spend time with any of us.
Narrator:	Six. Has Dan finished with or fallen out with his cousin?
Sara:	Why does Dan always avoid his cousin? It's ridiculous. They've been friends since they were little.
Emma:	I know. It's a pity. I heard they had a big argument.

Answers

1 Emma

2 her grandma

3 No. They didn't have anything in common.

4 his parents

5 Ahmed's brother looks down on him.

6 Dan has fallen out with his cousin.

3 Books closed. Say *Have you ever let anyone down?* and ask for a volunteer to reply with a full sentence. Then ask *How did you let them down?* Books open. In pairs, students ask and answer the questions. Tell students to ask at least one follow-up question each time. Monitor and give positive feedback for accurate responses and questions. Elicit some responses from different pairs.

READING

1 Ask students if their families have always lived in the same area, and tell them that they are going to read three interesting family stories from around the world. Write a verb (*have*), conjunction (*however*), adverb (*as*), determiner (*another*), preposition (*of*) and article (*the*) on the board and ask students to identify the parts of speech. Then tell students to look at the example gap and elicit what type of word is missing.

Answer
verb

2 Ask students to work with a partner and to discuss what they think the missing word could be.

Answer
being

● Prepare for First for Schools

Reading and Use of English Part 2

Task description
The main focus of this task is on awareness and control of grammar with some focus on vocabulary. Students complete the eight gaps in the text with a suitable word.

Tip
In this part, the students are not given options to choose from, so it is important that they use their language knowledge to predict the type of word needed and to also think about issues such as collocation.

3 ● If you have students preparing for the First For Schools exam, set a time limit of ten minutes for this task. Tell students to complete the gaps, and remind them to think about what type of word is missing. After students have completed this individually, ask them to compare their answers with a partner, reminding them that sometimes more than one answer is possible. Check answers as a whole class.

Answers
1 another   2 Although / Though / While / Whilst   3 the   4 as
5 their   6 of   7 whether / if   8 in

4 Give students a two-minute time limit to encourage them to skim read the text. Check answers as a whole class, and then ask students to underline the part(s) of the text that helped them to find the answer. As an alternative, with stronger students, you could ask them simply to skim the text and then come up with headings of their own for sections A–C. They then compare their suggestions with options 1–5 in the book and choose the nearest.

Answers
1 C
2 B
3 not needed
4 A
5 not needed

5 Ask students to read the texts individually and answer the questions. Monitor and provide assistance where necessary. Tell them to compare their answers with a partner before whole-class feedback.

Fast finishers

Ask fast finishers to think about which of the three texts they found most interesting and why. After checking the answers to exercise 5, ask one or two of the fast finishers to tell the class their reasons.

Extension activity

Ask students to think about their own family. Do they have any interesting family history stories? Give students a few minutes to make notes on their story. Students should then tell a partner their story. Ask one or two students to tell the class their partner's story. If they cannot think of an interesting story, tell students to invent one, using the texts for inspiration.

Answers
1 He dialled the wrong number.
2 Because he was on his own.
3 Because she and her parents have lived in lots of different places and they are probably going to move again.
4 Greece, Belgium, Japan, Chile, Morocco, British, Indian, the UK, India, Afghan, Scottish, American, Thailand

EP Word profile

Ask students to write a follow up sentence to each phrase to help explain the meaning. For example, *He decided to start all over again. There were just too many mistakes in his first one.* Then set the exercise on page 135.

Talking points

In pairs, students discuss these questions together. Ask students to think about how far back they can name people in their family. For the second question, students should think of at least three things that make a family happy. Elicit ideas from the class.

Cooler

Ask students to draw their own family tree. Then ask them to describe their family to a partner. They should ask about each other's family to try to find out any interesting stories or facts. Ask one or two students to feed back to the class.

GRAMMAR   Relative clauses

1 Go through the first two sentences on the board as an example. Explain the difference between the two types of relative clauses (see the information in the rules box in exercise 2). With stronger students you could ask for volunteers to come up with the differences and write these on the board. Then ask students to complete the exercise. Do not check the answers together yet, as students will do this in exercise 2.

2 Ask students to read the rules to check their own answers. Tell students to compare their answers in pairs. If they have different answers, they should use the rules to discuss and agree on which one is correct. Ask if all students are in agreement and clear any disagreements up by checking answers as a whole class. If you feel that students need more support, elicit one or two more examples of defining and non-defining clauses.

Mixed ability

Pair stronger and weaker students together. This challenges stronger students to explain the rules and gives weaker students more support.

Answers

1 Marie Wouters, who had just moved to Greece, answered the phone. Non-defining.
2 Attis couldn't stop thinking about the woman he had spoken to. Defining.
3 Attis re-dialled the number that he had called by accident. Defining.
4 There was something in her voice which had really appealed to him. Defining.
5 Lucinda's father, whose work is mainly in the UK, was born in India. Non-defining.
6 Nobu travelled to Santiago, where Huachipato was going to play against Palestino. Non-defining.

→ **Grammar reference Student's Book page 158**

3 Ask students to analyse the sentence with their partner. Remind students that we use certain prepositions with particular verbs (e.g. *speak to*). Tell them that when we use these combinations in relative clauses, the preposition usually comes at the end of the clause. Ask if they can think of another example of this (e.g. *I need to give you information (which) you don't know about*).

Answer

at the end of the relative clause

4 Look at the example together. Then ask students to complete the task individually. When checking answers, ask students to explain why they have/haven't put the pronoun or adverb in brackets (*it can be left out if it is the object of the clause*). Monitor and provide support for weaker students.

Answers

I'll never forget the time (**when**) we had a family holiday in Greece. We went to the island of Rhodes, **where** my ancestors used to live. It's an area **that/which** has a fascinating history, and my parents wanted to find the village **where** they used to live. We couldn't find any records **that/which** could help us, but eventually we found a village just like the one in the old photos (**that/which**) we had been given. We asked in a café and we were introduced to an old man **whose** great-grandparents had lived next to our old family home. The house had been knocked down, but it was nice to make a connection with someone **who** knew a bit about our family history.

5 Tell students that when completing written tasks, relative clauses will make their work more sophisticated than if they use several short sentences. Do the first sentence as an example on the board and then ask students to complete the task individually. Check answers.

Extension activity

Ask students to complete these relative clauses with their own ideas.
1   Studying is something …
2   I tend to like people …
3   I'll never forget the moment …
4   My family, …
Then tell students to work in groups of four or five. They should share their sentences together. Ask them to choose the sentence they think is most interesting for each one. For feedback, get each group to tell you the most interesting sentences and explain why they chose them.

Answers

1 This is our family home, where four generations have grown up.
2 Our apartment, which was built five years ago, has views across the whole city.
3 My uncle, who always played with us as children, is now a teacher at our school.
4 Last year we visited Poland, where my grandparents came from.
5 This is a photo of my grandparents, who got married in 1967.

VOCABULARY   Compound adjectives

1 Books closed. Write *old-aged*, *balanced* and *behaved* on the board. Ask students if they know any adjectives which can go before *balanced* and *behaved*. Books open. Look at the example together, and ask a student to explain the meaning of *well-built*. Then ask students to complete the exercise individually. Check answers and ask students to explain the meaning of the words. Can they think of the opposites of any of them (e.g. *badly-organised*)?

Answers

1 organised   2 aged   3 balanced   4 paid   5 behaved

2 Ask students to first put the words in combinations without looking at the sentences, and to compare their combinations with a partner. Check the combinations and then tell students to complete the sentences. Check answers.

Fast finishers

Ask fast finishers to write three questions using the vocabulary from the exercise, e.g. *At what age do you think a person is a grown-up? Why?* Students should then ask a partner their questions. Elicit some example questions and answers, and discuss any interesting questions as a class.

Answers

1 self-confident   2 short-term   3 grown-up   4 high-tech
5 last-minute

WRITING   An article (2)

1 Tell students they are going to read an article called *Someone I admire*. Ask them to write down the name of someone they admire and to then tell their partner why they admire this person. Ask students to read the text and answer the question. Check the answer with the whole class.

Answer

1 His brother taught him to be more thoughtful.

2 Draw students' attention to the notice and tell them to read it quickly. Then ask students to read Dan's article again and answer the questions with a partner. Elicit ideas from one or two pairs.

Answers

1 Students' own answers (e.g. My brilliant brother!)
2 and 3 Yes. 'Which family member or friend do you most admire?' is answered in paragraph 1.
'Why?' is explained in paragraph 2.
'How has this person influenced you?' is the subject of paragraph 3.
4 He asks the reader questions (e.g. *Can you think of someone who you really look up to?*), which encourage them to compare Dan's experiences with their own.

3 Give students a few minutes to do the matching exercise. Check answers as a whole class.

Answers

questions – *Can you think of someone who you really look up to? Who has been a big influence in your life?*
-*ing* forms a subjects – *Talking to my parents didn't help.*
structures which add emphasis – *The thing I admired most about him was … , What I've learned more than anything is …*

4 Tell students to use the sentences from the article as a model for these sentences. You may choose to go through the first question as an example. Give students a few minutes to complete the rest and to compare them with a partner. Check answers as a whole class.

Extension activity

Give students the following stems for further practice of these structures:
1   The thing I enjoyed the most about my primary school was …
2   What I like more than anything about this school is …
3   The thing I admire the most about my (grand)father/(grand)mother is …
4   What I hope to achieve more than anything is …
Ask students to choose one of the sentences to expand into a paragraph. Tell them to write a paragraph and then give it to their partner. After reading their partner's paragraph, ask them to write three follow-up questions. Tell students to use their partner's questions to write a further short paragraph on the topic.

Answers

1 Meeting   2 admire most   3 I love most   4 Spending time
5 I find really   6 I really like is

5 Ask students to work through each step. Monitor and help with ideas and language. Then ask students to work with a partner to provide some feedback or additional ideas to help with their plan. Remind students that they should give opinions and comments to engage the reader.

Prepare for First for Schools

Writing Part 2

Task description

In Part 2, students have a choice of task. They may be asked to write an article, an email or letter, a review, an essay or a story. They are given the context, topic, purpose and target reader. Students should write 140–190 words.

Tip

Ask students to think about the target audience before they start writing, and to consider the types of things that would interest their reader. This will help them to write in a suitable style and register.

6 If you have students preparing for the First For Schools exam, remind them that writing an article is one of the Writing Part 2 tasks, and set a strict time limit of 40 minutes. Once students have finished, ask them to swap articles with a partner and to highlight examples of the target structures their partner has used. Ask them to underline any opinions and comments they think are interesting, and discuss one or two examples as a class.

Sample answer

MY EXCEPTIONAL GRANDMOTHER

How could a poor girl born on a small farm in the middle of nowhere grow up to be such an important person? My grandmother was the youngest of seven children and they had a tough life, even going short of food sometimes, but she has succeeded in life. Working hard from an early age, she now runs a major company in our city and has brought up three children of her own.

Although she never went to university, she made sure that her own children had that opportunity. She has always been both determined and optimistic, and has encouraged me to behave in a similar way. I think her sense of humour is the quality I most admire in her because in the most difficult moments, she manages to put a smile on people's faces and makes everyone feel at ease.

She is always ready to listen when I have a problem and gives me very good advice. She has influenced my life in many different ways, from the novels I enjoy reading to the clothes I wear. My grandmother truly is 'one in a million'.

Cooler

Ask students to write three sentences with non-defining relative clauses. Tell them to read their sentences aloud to a partner without mentioning the thing that they are defining. Their partner should try to guess what is being defined. Share any fun or challenging ones as a class.

Project

Tell students to interview someone in their family about their family history, and to bring in some photos to show who some of the people in the family are. In a future class, students can work in small groups to show the photos to each other and talk about some of the things they discovered.

Teacher's resources

Student's Book
Grammar reference and practice page 158
Vocabulary list page 143
Video
Families
Workbook
Unit 11, pages 44–47
Go online for
- Pronunciation
- Video extra worksheet
- Corpus tasks

12 Making a difference

Unit profile

Vocabulary: Communication and effect; *both, either, neither*
Reading: A text about acts of kindness
Grammar: The passive (1): Review; Causative
Listening: A surprising experience
Speaking: Discussing options

Warmer

1 Ask students to think about people, events, dates and places that have been important in their life. Tell them to write down a sentence for each one using a relative clause, e.g. *I really liked my first primary school teacher who taught me to read.*

2 Tell students to discuss their sentences with a partner who should ask more questions about each one. Ask one or two pairs to feed back on their discussion.

Your profile

Tell students which photo you like best and why. Then ask pairs to discuss the questions together. Elicit from pairs how these things can make a difference to people. Have any of the students ever seen something similar? If so, what was it and where did they see it?

VOCABULARY Communication and effect

1 Ask students to work in pairs to match the sentences and photos. Tell them that there is not a definite right or wrong answer, but that they will need to justify their choice. After a few minutes, go through each sentence, asking different pairs to explain their choices.

Possible answers
1 a   2 a, b, d   3 d   4 b   5 c, e   6 c, e   7 a   8 d

2 ▶2.12 Ask different students to read out each sentence from exercise 1 and check pronunciation of the verbs in pink. Then play the recording for them to match two verbs to each photo. Check answers.

Audioscript

Narrator: A
Sara: I love things like this. You see more and more of them these days. They're just supposed to amuse you, aren't they? I mean, they're not more serious than that?
Dan: I guess so. You could call it 'art'. There's no real message though: just 'love'.
Sara: I do actually think that little things like this can improve your day, you know, I think they can actually inspire you to feel more hopeful.

Dan: Cheerful, too. Yes, they do make a difference to your day.
Narrator: B
Dan: You see these messages by the side of the road all the time. They're often there to congratulate people on their birthday or to wish them a happy anniversary.
Sara: Or to apologise for things!
Dan: I guess they're there to cheer people up, really, just to help them to have a nice day.
Sara: To be honest, I think they're a bit annoying and messy. Imagine if everyone's birthday was celebrated with these signs!
Narrator: C
Sara: I really like this sort of street art. It looks like graffiti but it's actually much more thoughtful than that.
Dan: Well, it makes a point, doesn't it? You know, about huge businesses taking over our lives, that sort of thing. The artist is obviously trying to express some kind of philosophy. Especially by painting the trolley there. It's right in the street, not in a gallery.
Sara: It's interesting, and it certainly stimulates you to think about things.
Narrator: D
Dan: This last one's obviously there to promote a business.
Sara: Maybe a second-hand clothes shop or an independent shop of some sort. I don't think a high street chain would advertise like this, it's too homemade.
Dan: True. It's humorous. I mean, it is quite funny! But it's also trying to persuade you to go along to the shop and take a look.
Sara: Yes, at least it's funny. They've made an effort to get people to laugh.

Answers
a amuse, inspire   **b** congratulate, cheer up
c express, stimulate   **d** promote, persuade

3 ▶2.12 Ask students to read through the sentences before playing the recording again. Check answers as a whole class.

Answers
1 S   2 S   3 D   4 S

4 Ask students to discuss these topics in small groups. As a whole class, find out if there are any particularly common things for each category.

Fast finishers

Ask fast finishers to think of one more thing that cheers them up, inspires them, and that they'd like to express their opinion about. Ask students to share these ideas during feedback to exercise 4.

READING

1 Elicit ideas on what *random acts of kindness* may mean. Then ask students to read through the text quickly to answer the questions. Ask one student to define *random acts of kindness* and another student to give you two examples from the text.

Answers
Doing a favour to someone you have never met before, and for no special reason, e.g. picking up litter from someone's garden, swapping places with the person behind you in a queue

2 Ask students to read the text individually, before comparing their answers in pairs and checking as a whole class. Ask students to correct the false sentences.

Answers
1 False. He was a bit suspicious. 2 True
3 False. This hug started her interest in random acts of kindness.
4 True 5 False. He could hardly believe what heard. 6 True

3 Tell students to complete the exercise individually. When checking answers, ask students to define the words.

Fast finishers
Ask fast finishers to write definitions and example sentences for the highlighted words, and to share these during feedback to exercise 3.

Answers
1 barista 2 philosophy 3 random 4 suspicious 5 viral
6 generosity

4 Ask students to discuss the questions in pairs. Ask them to also think about how different random acts of kindness might make them react differently. Briefly discuss students' responses as a whole class.

Extension activity
Tell students that a beggar finds an engagement ring in his cap. Ask them to work in pairs and discuss what he should do with it. Share some ideas as a class. Then tell students this true story: a woman accidentally dropped her engagement ring into Billy Ray Harris' (a homeless beggar in the USA) cup. He gave the ring back to her. The woman and her fiancé started a website to raise money for Billy Ray Harris in thanks for his act of kindness. By the end of the collection, people from all around the world had donated just under 200,000 dollars. Billy Ray Harris bought a house and a car, and found a job.

EP Word profile
Ask students to explain the meaning of each phrase using *as*. Then set the exercise on page 136.

Answers
1 As far as I'm concerned   2 As far as I know
3 as a result of   4 As a matter of fact

Cooler
Ask students to discuss with a partner which act of kindness from the text sounds like the best one: *free hugs, free coffee, other random acts of kindness*. Which one would they prefer to receive? Which ones would they be happy to do? What other ideas for random acts of kindness can they think of?

GRAMMAR   The passive (1): Review

1 Remind students of the form of the passive on the board (a form of *be* + past participle) and add one or two sentences as examples. Ask students to read the examples on page 70 and identify the tenses used.

Answers
1 past simple   2 present perfect   3 past continuous

2 Ask students to read the rules and to explain to a partner why the passive is used in each. Check answers as a whole class.

Mixed ability
While students are completing exercise 2, write two possible verb forms of the words needed to complete the gaps in exercise 3 on the board – the right one and a distractor in each case. Then if students get stuck with the exercise, they can refer to the board for choices.

Answers
1 a. The hugger is unknown but it seems important to add 'by a stranger' because it is an unexpected situation.
2 c. By starting the sentence with the number of people, we are emphasising the number.
3 b. The speaker is obviously being served by a waiter.

→ Grammar reference Student's Book **page 159**

3 Elicit the different forms of the passive that are used in the text (*present simple, present continuous, present perfect* and *past perfect*) and write an example of each form on the board. When checking answers, ask students to explain their choice.

Answers
1 had been invited   2 were blocked   3 are being advised
4 might be affected   5 have been impressed
6 have never been hugged

⊙ Corpus challenge
Ask students to correct the sentence and to explain the error (you need an auxiliary verb, e.g. *is*, before the past participle).

Answer
Each cycle route is shown in a different colour.

Causative

4 Ask students to read the example sentences and discuss the questions with a partner. Elicit an explanation for each one.

> **Answers**
> 1 himself   2 someone else
> 3 someone else; No, the customer didn't pay.

5 Work through the example together on the board. Ask students to complete the exercise individually before students compare answers together. Check answers.

> **Extension activity**
> Ask students to write three or four sentences like those in exercise 5. They should then give these to a partner who should write causative sentences to explain what they could have done. Monitor and help whilst students do this. Put any incorrect sentences on the board for the class to correct.

> **Answers**
> 1 She could have/get it cut.
> 2 She could have/get it washed.
> 3 I could have/get it repaired.
> 4 I could have/get it redelivered.

VOCABULARY   *both, either, neither*

1 Give students a few minutes to read the examples and then complete the matching exercise with a partner.

> **Answers**
> 1 b 2 a 3 c

2 Read these sentences aloud and ask students for a show of hands for each option.

> **Answers**
> 1 are 2 is 3 were

3 Ask students to complete this exercise individually before whole-class feedback.

> **Answers**
> 1 either; both   2 neither of   3 both of

LISTENING

1 ▶2.13 Tell students that they are going to hear someone talking about a surprising experience on the way to work. Elicit some ideas from the class about what this may be. Check students understand *the underground* (a railway system in which electric trains travel along passages below ground, e.g. the London Underground) and then play the recording for them to check their answers.

Audioscript

Hi, my name's Amy Linton and I want to tell you about something which happened to me one day on my way to work in London. It was a cold winter's morning and I was walking towards my local station on the underground railway. It was a journey I'd made thousands of times because <u>I'm a journalist</u> employed by a newspaper and I go into the office most days. It was about half-past eight and I was surrounded by other people dashing to work: shop assistants, waiters, all the people who keep the busy city working.

Arriving at the station, I ran down the steps and into the warm air of the <u>ticket office</u>. That's when I realised I could hear beautiful violin music and I wondered where it was coming from. I made my way through the automatic ticket barriers and took the escalators down to the trains. That's when I spotted a female violinist sitting beside the entrance to my platform.

Her playing was quite <u>exceptional</u>; fast, accurate – and yet delicate – that's what made me stop and listen. Her eyes were closed and every time she drew the bow across the strings, she moved her head as well. Her whole body seemed to be filled with this wonderful music. She was wearing the kind of clothes you might wear at home or for popping out to the shops – a pair of jeans, a thick sweater and <u>a pair of trainers. I had to smile at that – how much more sensible in this weather than the high heels I was wearing</u> for work.

I stood absolutely still and listened to her. By her feet was a <u>violin case</u> with an old teddy-bear sitting in it, and a cap with a few coins shining in the bottom. Every now and again, passers-by would throw a coin, but nobody else stopped to listen. Then a man with a little girl came past, holding hands. He was obviously her father. He kept on walking, but she stopped and turned to look, so he had to stop too. The violinist seemed to sense that she was there, because she <u>opened her eyes</u> for a few seconds. I thought she might've smiled or given some sort of greeting, but she was soon immersed in her playing again.

It was a very moving piece that I recognised from somewhere. I tried to think where. Was it the theme from a TV series perhaps, or used in a well-known advert? Then it came to me: I'd listened to it recently on <u>a radio programme</u>. It was lovely. Busy commuters rushed past but nobody else stopped to listen. After about ten minutes, the man persuaded his little daughter to move on as well.

The music ended and I clapped, impressed with the performance, but <u>embarrassed</u> at the small pile of coins the violinist was putting into her pocket. 'That was fantastic. You were amazing!' I said. Thanking me, she put her violin back into its case and we started to chat.

Then I realised who she was. I'd seen her playing at a concert in London three months earlier. The show had been a sell-out and my ticket had cost <u>£85</u>, but some people said they'd paid £150 on the internet for the best seats. I couldn't believe it. What was she doing here, playing for just a few coins in the underground? She explained that she had to practise somewhere and that she enjoyed playing in public places, because each location produced a slightly different <u>sound quality</u> and that interested her. With that, off she went – one of the country's best violinists had just performed for half-an-hour, and nobody apart from me and a little girl had even cared.

Answer

The violinist was a professional musician playing for pleasure.

Task description

Students are required to complete ten sentences with information they hear in a 3–4 minute monologue. This part focuses on detail, identifying specific information and stated opinion.

Tip

Tell students to look at the gap and to link it to a question word such as *who*, *where*, *when* etc. This can help to identify the type of missing information.

2 ● ▶ **2.13** Ask students to think about the type of word needed for each gap. Do the first one as an example, e.g. *It's a company or organisation*. You could ask students to fill in the gaps with guesses or from memory before they listen again. Play the recording. Allow students to compare their answers with a partner before whole-class feedback.

Answers

1 journalist **2** ticket office **3** exceptional **4** a pair of trainers
5 violin case **6** opened her eyes **7** radio programme
8 embarrassed **9** £85 **10** sound quality

SPEAKING Discussing options

1 ▶ **2.14** Ask students to look at the photo and describe what they can see. Give help with vocabulary if necessary (e.g. *wheelchair*). Tell them to read the questions and words in the box and then play the recording. Check answers.

Audioscript

Examiner:	I'd like you to imagine that your school is starting a system to help disabled children in the local community. Talk to each other about how each of these ideas could help disabled children in the local community.
Hans:	Where shall we start?
Elena:	Let's start with access to school. We could collect people on our way to the bus stop and help with getting on and off transport, and getting into school.
Hans:	Yes, I agree.
Elena:	How about computer gaming?
Hans:	Again, depending on the disability, people might need help with actually playing games.
Elena:	What exactly do you mean?
Hans:	Well, pressing buttons and things like that.
Elena:	I'm not so sure that would help. Computer games are all about our own reactions, so I think it would be frustrating to be helped with that sort of thing.
Hans:	Maybe you're right. How about going shopping?
Elena:	Well, I think this is an obvious area where we could help quite a lot. Lots of shops have steps or are difficult to access, especially if you're in a wheelchair. I think we could definitely help.

Hans:	I'd add that it should be boys helping boys and girls helping girls with the shopping though.
Elena:	Agreed! What about going out at the weekend, you know, to the cinema and things like that?
Hans:	Again, as with shopping, we could easily help with this sort of thing. We could organise lifts for people and help them in and out of places. Anything else?
Elena:	I was just going to say that we may be able to take them to places they or we don't normally get to.
Hans:	True. Do you want to add anything?
Elena:	I guess we'd have to match up people with similar interests.
Hans:	Good point. Last of all, what about tidying up? Is that something we could help with?
Elena:	It's really hard keeping places tidy, even if you do tidy every day, so this is definitely an area people would appreciate help with.
Hans:	Of course. And it would be easy to set up a timetable for something that is very regular.
Elena:	Good point.
Examiner:	Thank you. Now you have a minute to decide one area you would both like to help with.
Hans:	Right, well I can tell you what I wouldn't want to do: tidying up would be my least favourite.
Elena:	Mine too. I'd also rule out computer gaming. I think we agreed that would be too complicated.
Hans:	Yes, and more to the point, it's probably not that helpful anyway.
Elena:	I think access to school would be hard, too. I find it impossible to get up and out of the house in the mornings, and I think it would be really stressful if I had lots of things to do in the morning before school.
Hans:	I agree about not doing access to school. That leaves going out at the weekend and going shopping. Do you have a preference with either of these?
Elena:	I think I'd go for the shopping.
Hans:	Hmm. I'm not a great fan of shopping to be honest. But you could argue that going out at the weekend includes shopping.
Elena:	That's a very good point.
Hans:	Shall we agree that going out at the weekend is the area we'd both be happy to help with?
Elena:	Absolutely.
Examiner:	Thank you.

Answers

1 access to school, computer gaming, going shopping, going out at the weekend, tidying up
2 going out at the weekend

2 ▶ **2.15** Tell students they will hear all of the expressions apart from one. Play the recording for them to identify which one and elicit the answer from a volunteer.

Audioscript

Hans:	Where shall we start?
Elena:	Let's start with access to school. We could collect people on our way to the bus stop and help with getting on and off transport, and getting into school.

Hans:	Yes, I agree.
Elena:	How about computer gaming?
Hans:	Again, depending on the disability, people might need help with actually playing games.
Elena:	<u>What exactly do you mean?</u>
Hans:	Well, pressing buttons and things like that.
Elena:	I'm not so sure that would help. Computer games are all about our own reactions, so I think it would be frustrating to be helped with that sort of thing.
Hans:	Maybe you're right. How about going shopping?
Elena:	Well, I think this is an obvious area where we could help quite a lot. Lots of shops have steps or are difficult to access, especially if you're in a wheelchair. I think we could definitely help.
Hans:	I'd add that it should be boys helping boys and girls helping girls with the shopping though.
Elena:	Agreed! What about going out at the weekend, you know, to the cinema and things like that?
Hans:	<u>Again, as with</u> shopping, <u>we could</u> easily help with this sort of thing. We could organise lifts for people and help them in and out of places. <u>Anything else?</u>
Elena:	<u>I was just going to say that</u> we may be able to take them to places they or we don't normally get to.
Hans:	True. <u>Do you want to add anything?</u>

Answer

Hans and Elena use all the expressions except *Are you referring to … ?*

Prepare for First for Schools

Speaking Part 3

Task description

This part is a two-way conversation between the students. They are given spoken instructions with written stimuli. The focus is on sustaining interaction, exchanging ideas, expressing and justifying opinions, agreeing/disagreeing, suggesting, speculating, evaluating and reaching a decision through negotiation.

Tip

Highlight to students the importance of the concept of interaction. Students should actively listen to and respond to their partner and not just simply think of, and state, their own opinion.

See Exam Profile 5, Student's Book page 129.

3 ● ▶ 2.16 Tell students to work with a partner. Play the recording and then give students two minutes to prepare. Students should then speak to their partner. If possible they should record each other and provide feedback.

Audioscript

Examiner: I'd like you to talk about something together for about two minutes. I'd like you to imagine that your school is starting a system to help elderly people in the local community. Talk to each other about what services students could offer to help elderly people in the local community.

Extension activity

Before class, record a weak response to the task. Ask students to listen and to tell you what they think is wrong with the answer. This will depend on what you choose to focus on, but it could include things such as going off topic or spending too much time on one point.

Cooler

Write this saying on the board and ask students what they think it means:

'*There is no such thing as a selfless good deed.*'

Ask students to discuss whether they agree with it or not, and why. Discuss some ideas as a class.

Project

Ask students to research community projects in their area. They should find out what the organisations do and how people can get involved. Ask them to report back in the next class, and say which one they would prefer to help and why.

Teacher's resources

Student's Book
Grammar reference and practice page 159
Vocabulary list page 144
Workbook
Unit 12, pages 48–51
Go online for
• Pronunciation
• Progress test
• Achievement test
• Corpus tasks

ICT
Crowdsourcing

Learning objectives

- The students learn about the concept of crowdsourcing to produce something collaboratively.
- In the project stage, students design their own crowdsourcing project.

Warmer

1 Write *computer technology* on the board and ask students to brainstorm as many things as possible that use computer technology in our daily lives.

2 Ask students to discuss the things on their lists and to decide which two would be easiest to give up and which two would be hardest.

3 Read the following out loud (not the years) and ask students to write them down:

Twitter™ (2006), YouTube™ (2005), Facebook™ (2004), Wikipedia™ (2001), Google™ (1998)

Ask students to put them into order from oldest to newest company. You could add any other similar companies, too. Check answers and ask students if they are surprised by the order.

4 Ask students whether they have heard of crowdsourcing. If so, which of the companies above is an example of crowdsourcing? (*Wikipedia*). Ask students if they use Wikipedia, how often and for what reasons?

1 Ask students to read the text and find out what the different companies and organisations are. If your students are expected to use academic sources in their own schoolwork, you could ask them to discuss what the strengths and weaknesses of Wikipedia are. (Example strengths: anyone can contribute, it gets corrected all the time, convenient, free; example weaknesses: anyone can contribute, can contain factual errors, nothing is complete or finished.)

Answer

Wikipedia is an online encyclopedia created and managed by volunteers. Memrise is a community learning website that offers free courses. Goldcorp is a mining company that offered a prize for the best list of locations for finding gold.

2 Ask students to choose the best definition and then check the answer as a class.

Mixed ability

Ask stronger students to write their own definition of crowdsourcing before comparing their answer with the information in the text.

Answer
2

3 Ask students to read the questions and the text again. Encourage them to identify the key words in the questions to guide their reading. Tell them to compare answers with a partner before whole-class feedback.

Extension activity

Ask students to work in pairs and to discuss:
1 Which of the crowdsourcing activities sounds the most fun. Which is the most worthwhile?
2 What volunteering activities they have done? Why did they do them and what did they like / not like about them?
Discuss some ideas as a class.

Answers

1 All the articles are written by volunteers.
2 They include games and quizzes.
3 They learnt how animated films are made.
4 Because they wanted to find gold and make a lot of money.

4 Ask students to discuss the questions in small groups. Monitor and give positive feedback for interesting ideas. Then elicit ideas and responses from different groups. Have any students been involved in crowdsourcing projects?

Extension activity

Ask students to discuss these questions in groups:
How could crowdsourcing help
    during a natural disaster?
    to catch a criminal?
    someone find members of their family they are not in touch with?
Discuss some ideas as a class. You could get students to research one of the topics and to present it in the following class. Ask them to include real-life examples.

5 Set a short time limit (e.g. 20 seconds) for students to scan the text and find the information.

Answer
information about after-school clubs

6 ▶ 2.17 Tell students that they are going to listen to a meeting related to the web post in exercise 5. Explain that students will hear the recording twice. Ask them to read the tasks, and then play the recording for them to put the tasks into the correct order. Allow students to compare answers with a partner before checking as a class.

Audioscript

Mr Prentice: Good afternoon, Tina and John. Are you ready to start the meeting?

Tina: Yes, Mr Prentice.

Mr Prentice: Excellent. Let's get started then. Have you thought of any ideas to start the project?

Tina: Yes, we have. First of all, we've written a short web post with three survey questions. We're going to post it on social media websites, like Facebook and Twitter. Then students everywhere can send in their answers to our questions.

Mr Prentice: Well, that sounds like a good strategy. And where did you get that idea?

John: We were looking at a crowdsourcing website, and that's one of the suggestions it gave for projects.

Mr Prentice: Fine, and what will you do with the answers that people send you?

Tina: Well, we thought one person should be in charge of reading the messages and keeping track of the different answers. That will be me! I'll check the email once a week and add new ideas to our list. And I'll make notes about how many people suggest the same idea. For example, if lots of people suggest an arts and crafts club, or a photography club.

John: Exactly. And then Tina will give the information to me, so I can create a shortlist for a vote at our school. I think we should make a list of the twenty most popular suggestions.

Tina: Then I can post those twenty ideas on the website, and everyone here at our school can vote for the three clubs they like best. I'll be in charge of counting the votes afterwards.

Mr Prentice: Well, that sounds like a good idea. But how will students vote? Will they do it in class? Or will they have to vote online?

Tina: Well, some students wanted people to vote online, but I think they should vote in class, because some people might not have internet at home. But then we'll need a leader in each class to hand out the votes and then collect them afterwards. John says he can ask for volunteer leaders in each classroom to do that.

Mr Prentice: OK, I think that's probably best. But what day would the vote take place? You'll need to wait for answers to the online survey, first.

John: Well, I think we should wait a month for answers to the survey, and then vote here at school about two weeks after that.

Mr Prentice: Well, that makes sense. And what will happen after you count up the votes? Will you choose the three most popular clubs? Or the top five? Tina?

Tina: Umm, well, I think we should choose the top ten really. And then we'll both meet to discuss it with you, because some clubs might be more expensive, or they might need equipment, like a sports club, for example.

John: If that happens, then we might need to raise money for some clubs … but then we can start another crowdsourcing project for that!

Mr Prentice: Well, that's true, but let's do one thing at a time, shall we? Send me a copy of your webpost and survey questions, and then we can get started. OK? Let's meet again in a week, and see how things are going.

Answers
c, f, d, b, e, a

Cooler
Ask students to work in groups to discuss the questions in the webpost in exercise 5. Elicit responses from one or two groups.

Project
This project can either be done in class with internet access or set as homework. If they are stuck for ideas, encourage them to think about the 'type' of project that appeals to them – e.g. asking people to observe something (e.g. wildlife in their garden), getting people to write reviews on a topic, social change, journalism, etc. Once students have designed their project, ask them to give a short presentation. The class can then vote on the best suggestion. Depending on time and resources, you could encourage the students to carry out the project and discuss its progress in future lessons.

13 Leading the way

Unit profile

Vocabulary: Leadership and achievement; Phrasal verbs with *up*

Reading: The Three Dot Dash challenge

Grammar: The passive (2): Other structures

Writing: A review (1)

Warmer

1 Ask students to think about a person who is a good leader and why. The person can lead anything, e.g. a sports team, a business, a political party.

2 Students should then work in groups of four and tell each other who their person is and the reason for their choice.

3 Ask students to come up with three sentences using *both, neither…nor and either…or* to talk about the similarities and differences between their leaders (e.g. 'they both inspire optimism', 'neither x nor x gives up easily when they face difficulties'). Ask one or two groups to feed back to the class.

Your profile

Ask students to discuss the questions in groups. Write *A good leader …* on the board and ask students to complete the sentence. Ask two or three groups to read out their sentences to the class.

VOCABULARY Leadership and achievement

1 Students read the sentences in pairs and check with each other that they can define the words. Tell students they can use a dictionary if necessary. Elicit the meaning of each word from the students.

Answers

1 doubt: feel uncertain; motivated: enthusiastic
2 fairly: equally
3 adventurous: happy to try new or challenging things; cautious: avoids risk
4 my own company: alone
5 sympathetic: understanding and caring
6 appreciation: gratitude
7 criticism: negative comments
8 influence: power
9 targets: things to achieve; strict: firm
10 stand out: be very noticeable

2 Ask students to do the quiz on their own and then to compare their answers with a partner. Encourage students to explain the reason for their score.

3 Tell students to add up their scores and read the information on page 131. In pairs, students should discuss their opinion of the results. Ask for a show of hands to find out who agrees and who disagrees with the quiz.

4 ▶2.18 Give students a few minutes to complete the table and then play the recording for them to check their answers. Go over any words you think your students will have difficulty pronouncing (e.g. 'appreciative' /əˈpriː.ʃə.tɪv/, 'doubt' /daʊt/).

Audioscript

Speaker 1: sympathy, sympathetic, sympathise
Speaker 2: appreciation, appreciative, appreciate
Speaker 1: criticism, critical, criticise
Speaker 2: motivation, motivated or motivating, motivate
Speaker 1: doubt, doubtful, doubt

Answers

1 sympathy 2 sympathetic 3 appreciation 4 appreciate
5 criticism 6 critical 7 motivation 8 motivated/motivating
9 doubtful 10 doubt

5 ▶2.19 Tell students that they are going to listen to four people talking about leadership. Play the recording and ask students to discuss who would make a good leader with a partner. Ask two pairs to explain their choices to the class. Do any of the speakers remind students of themselves?

Audioscript

Narrator: Phoebe
Phoebe: I think I lead more than I follow when I'm in a team situation, but actually I don't always work well as part of a team. My problem is that I can't stand people who make excuses. 'I couldn't do it because I didn't have enough time.' 'I wasn't well.' 'I had too many other things to do.' Whatever. If you want to do something, and if you want to do it well, you will do it. But these people – they don't want to do anything and I haven't got time for them.

Narrator: Mo
Mo: I just want to be one of the crowd. I hate standing out and I think I'll always be this way. I'm generally happy to fit in with others' plans. It's no big deal. What I enjoy most is just spending time with my friends.

Narrator: Nathan
Nathan: I used to be a much more cautious person. I didn't want to look different. I just wanted to be the same as everyone else. But in the last year, I've changed a bit. One of our teachers has been really helpful. I'm not the best on the soccer team, but he made me captain a year ago. I'm so grateful he did that. I've really enjoyed the experience.

Narrator: Ruby

Ruby: <u>I'm often the one in charge of things</u>. I guess I like it that way. And <u>ninety-nine per cent of the time I don't have a problem with that. I don't think my friends do either</u>. My parents say I'm always telling them what a bad idea everything is. How someone should have done something, how I would have done it. I should try and stop that. It's just that I often say what I'm thinking a bit too quickly.

Possible answer

Nathan and Ruby would make the best leaders. Mo just wants to be one of the crowd, and Phoebe doesn't work well as part of a team. Nathan has leadership experience (soccer team captain) and Ruby enjoys being in charge.

6 ▶2.19 Students read the sentences and try and complete them from memory. Then play the recording again for students to complete the rest of the sentences. Check answers as a class.

Extension activity

Ask students to extend their *A good leader…* sentence from Your profile into a full paragraph using at least five of the words from exercise 4.

Answers
1 Mo **2** Nathan **3** Phoebe **4** Ruby

READING

1 ▶2.20 Ask students if any of them lead a local club or organisation. Tell them that they are going to listen to someone talking about a challenge set for teenagers by a charitable organisation. Check they understand the meaning of *in common* (in the same way as someone else). Play the recording for students to answer the question. Check answers as a whole class.

Audioscript

Speaker: Have you ever had an idea that might possibly change the world? Could you lead a team of people so that idea became a reality? This is the challenge that Three Dot Dash sets for thirty teenagers every year. <u>This charitable organisation</u>, founded by the musician Nile Rodgers, <u>supports teenagers who have had ideas about how to solve problems related to basic human needs</u> – things such as food, health, shelter and education. The challenge starts with a conference in New York, where teenagers work with leading experts in relevant areas to develop their ideas. They then have one year to lead their project to success. In its short life, Three Dot Dash and the projects it has sponsored have already influenced the lives of millions of people all over the world.

Answer
They all want to solve problems related to human needs.

2 Check meaning of *addressing* (dealing with a problem). Ask students to scan the texts to find what need each teenager is addressing. Give them a time limit of two or three minutes to do this. Tell them to compare their ideas with a partner before checking answers as a whole class.

Mixed ability

Write these answers on the board in a jumbled order, and ask weaker students to match the need to the text. Tell stronger students to complete the exercise without looking at the board.

Answer
A environmental education
B health
C food
D family and friends

⬤ Prepare for First for Schools
Reading and Use of English Part 7

Task description
Reading and Use of English Part 7 requires students to match ten multiple options to different parts of a text. The text can be one long text or, as in this example, a number of short texts. This part tests students' understanding of detail, opinion, specific information and implication.

Tip
Highlight that this task can be one long text instead of four short texts. When dealing with longer texts, encourage students to make brief notes next to each paragraph to indicate the main idea. This will help them to identify the answers to the questions.

3 ⬤ Tell students to read the questions before reading the text again and remind them to underline key words in each sentence to provide focus for their reading. Give students a time limit of ten minutes to match each question to a person. Monitor and provide help where needed. With weaker students, you could go through two or three of the questions with them, demonstrating your strategies for this type of task. Check answers as a whole class.

Fast finishers

Ask fast finishers to summarise the main aim of each person in one sentence only. After checking the answers to exercise 3, elicit a summary for each one from different fast finishers.

Extension activity

Tell students to work in groups of four. They should imagine that they are judging an Inspirational Young People competition. Together they should decide which person on page 77 should receive the award. Take a class vote to decide on the winner.

Answers

1 D. *Anoop was recently included in the '20 under 20' list, which celebrates Canada's future leaders.*
2 B. *[Yash's project has] given thousands of young children the glasses they need.*
3 C. *Natasha set up FoodSync in New York but really wants her project to be adopted all over the country.*
4 D. *Anoop … started volunteering at homeless shelters at a young age.*
5 C. *With the help of friends and family, Natasha began collecting food from two local bakeries and delivering it to homeless shelters and retirement homes.*
6 B. *Yash Gupta's project was inspired by breaking his glasses … While he was waiting for a new pair, Yash had to go to school for a week without them. Unable to see clearly, Yash soon found keeping up in class difficult.*
7 A. *The initial target of the project is 7–11 year olds …*
8 B. *Yash went online to find out more about poor sight and discovered that around 130 million people worldwide depend on their glasses every day. Furthermore, he learned that an astonishing 300 million need glasses but can't afford them.*
9 D. *[Project HELLO] aims to put homeless residents in Vancouver, Canada, in touch with lost family and friends.*

EP Word profile

Ask students to look at the uses of the word *lead* in the box. Put them into pairs to take turns saying a sentence with *lead* and then identifying its use. Then set the exercise on page 136.

Answers

1 leader   2 led to   3 lead   4 lead   5 leading   6 led
7 leads to   8 lead

Talking points

In pairs, students discuss the two questions. For the second question, ask students to list at least five qualities. Elicit the qualities needed from the class and write them on the board. Then ask each pair to choose just three qualities and to rank them in order of importance. Ask two or three pairs to tell the class their order and explain their reasons.

Cooler

Ask students to discuss these questions in groups: *Do all teams or groups need a leader? Why? What qualities would you dislike in a leader? Would you rather be a leader or a follower? Why?* Share some ideas as a class.

GRAMMAR   The passive (2): Other structures

1 Books closed. Say *I want to be given a big present on my birthday* and write this phrase on the board. Elicit that this is the passive voice and explain to students that they are going to look at further examples of the passive. Elicit the forms and uses they saw in Unit 12. Books open. Read the first sentence together and ask them to compare the sentence with the one on the board. Elicit the form used, then ask students to match the use and form with the correct rule (b). Then students read the sentences alone before you check the rules as a class.

Answers

a being   b to be   c being   d to be   e be

→ Grammar reference Student's Book **page 160**

2 Work through the example and sentence 1 on the board. Then ask students to complete the task individually before comparing their answers with a partner. Check answers. For an extra consolidation exercise, ask weaker students to match the sentences in exercise 2 to a rule in exercise 1.

Answers

1 being criticised   2 being blamed all the time
3 be appreciated if you were on time   4 be treated fairly
5 to be made captain of the team soon   6 to be told

3 Complete the first sentence on the board and then set this as individual work. Remind students that every sentence will need some form of the verb *be*. Elicit answers from the class.

Answers

1 Everyone expects to be criticised from time to time.
2 He instead on being put in charge.
3 The first student to be awarded a prize was from my class.
4 You will be given the results of your exam this week.
5 The singer would like to be taken seriously as an actress.

4 Tell students to spend a few minutes completing the sentences before comparing their ideas with a partner. In feedback, ask students to volunteer their answers, and tell the other students to raise their hand if they agree or disagree with them.

Extension activity

Ask students to work in pairs and to add two more example sentences to the stems in exercise 4. Next to each stem they should write a scale of 1–5, where 1 is strongly agree and 5 is strongly disagree. Then students should work in groups of six and complete one another's surveys. Ask each group to report back on one or two interesting things they found out, e.g. *Everyone strongly agreed that they can't stand being …*

Corpus challenge

Ask students to correct the sentence and to explain the error (we use a form of *be* + the past participle in passive structures).

Answer
I am very happy to be asked my opinion about this subject.

VOCABULARY   Phrasal verbs with *up*

1 Set this exercise as individual work and then ask students to compare their answers against the profiles.

Answers
1 turned up   2 set up   3 keeping up

2 Ask students to do the matching exercise in pairs. Then tell them to write an example sentence for each phrasal verb. Ask for an example for each as you check answers.

Answers
1 set up   2 turn up   3 keep up

3 Invite volunteers to suggest definitions for the words in bold but don't correct them at this stage. Write the suggestions on the board. Ask students to work in pairs to do the matching exercise. Check answers as a whole class. Were the definitions on the board correct? If not, correct them together.

Answers
1 c   2 a   3 b   4 d

4 Ask students to discuss the questions in small groups. Monitor and give positive feedback for correct usage and interesting ideas. Then ask each group to report back on which question had the most interesting answer.

WRITING   A review (1)

1 Ask students what their favourite TV show is. Tell them to read the task and to answer the questions. Check answers.

Answers
1 a review about a TV show you like or dislike
2 students, and possibly teachers and parents
3 what the show is about and why you like or dislike it

2 Following the discussion, ask students to feed back to the class. Find out if there are some commonly loved and disliked shows and for what reason. Ask students to use their discussion to write a brief plan for a review based on one of the shows they discussed. They can work in pairs to help one another with their plans.

3 Do this exercise as a whole class and explain any of the vocabulary students find challenging (e.g. *fire*: remove from a job).

Extension activity

Ask students to use three of the phrases to write sentences about a TV programme they like. Elicit some ideas and write any good examples on the board.

Answers
1 Yes
2 massive fan, absolute favourite, brilliantly entertaining, totally addicted, a fantastic show, thoroughly recommend it
Students' own answers.

4 Give students time to read the *Prepare* box. Concept check some of the ideas by asking students what they would expect to see in a well-organised review (*title and paragraphs*), what language is used to make recommendations (*descriptive vocabulary*) and how a writer can express their views (e.g. *by making recommendations*). Ask students to do the matching exercise and check answers.

Answers
a – introduction   b – description of show
c – strengths/weaknesses   d – recommendation

5 Start by doing the task as a whole class. You can highlight the first examples for questions 1 and 2 (i.e. *reality TV shows* and *surprisingly challenging*). Then ask students to work individually. Check answers as a whole class.

Fast finishers

If you have a show similar to *The Teenage Boss* in your country, ask fast finishers to think about their opinion of it. If not, ask them to think about whether they would want to watch it or not. Elicit ideas during feedback to exercise 5.

Answers
1 reality TV shows, episode, celebrity, contestants, series, show
2 surprisingly challenging, cool experience, extremely critical, difficult and even arrogant personalities, brilliantly entertaining, totally addicted, fantastic
3 I thoroughly recommend it to anyone of my age.

6 Tell students to classify the expressions and decide whether the first word(s) in each expression mean a lot (*brilliantly, extremely, absolutely*) or a little (*rather, not very*). Then ask students to work with a partner to add more examples to the table. Add a fun, competitive element by giving them just one minute to write as many as possible. After one minute, ask which pair has five or more examples, then six or more, etc. until you find the pair with the most examples. Get this pair to come and write their examples on the board.

⬤ Prepare for First for Schools

Writing Part 2

Task description

In Part 2, students have a choice of task. They may be asked to write an article, an email or letter, a review or a story. They are given a clear context, topic, purpose and target reader. Students should write 140–190 words.

Tip

Description and explanation are key to this task. Encourage students to think of interesting ways to describe what has happened. For example, instead of 'the contestants argued', students could write 'the contestants argued fiercely'.

7 ⬤ Tell students to write their review individually. Then ask them to swap reviews with a partner, and to use the features from the *Prepare* box to check each other's work. They should give positive suggestions for how their partner's writing could be improved, but encourage students to be tactful with their advice. They swap back and edit their own work to improve it.

Sample answer

BAD EDUCATION

My favourite show on TV at the moment is the comedy series Bad Education, starring popular comedian Jack Whitehall, who is also the writer of the show. Jack plays a fairly useless history teacher called Alfie Wickers, who works at the fictional Abbey Grove secondary school. Alfie is desperate to be liked by his class and does all kinds of weird things to impress them! He's really funny and wears the strangest clothes.

Some of the other characters in the series are a bit predictable – the weird headteacher, his very ambitious deputy, the class bully, and a very hard-working Chinese student – but I think the aim of the programme is partly to make fun of previous shows set in schools, so it needn't be taken too seriously.

I'd thoroughly recommend the programme, especially the second series, where the plot gets really strange and extremely odd things happen! It attracts huge audiences, so why not see for yourself? I'm sure you won't regret it!

Cooler

In groups, students swap reviews until they find one reviewing a show they haven't watched. After reading the review, they should decide whether they want to watch the show or not. Ask two students who are going to watch a new show to explain the show and why they want to watch it. Then ask two students who don't want to watch the show they read about to explain why.

Project

Ask students to research other young people who have helped good causes or the basic needs of others, either in their town, their country or abroad. Ask students to write a short text or blog post giving information about the project, what it has done and what it aims to achieve. In the following class, ask students to work in pairs or small groups and to tell each other about the person they researched.

Teacher's resources

Student's Book

Grammar reference and practice page 160

Vocabulary list page 144

Workbook

Unit 13, pages 52–55

Go online for

- Pronunciation
- Corpus tasks

14 Getting there

Unit profile

Vocabulary: Phrasal verbs; Reporting verbs
Reading: A holiday guide
Grammar: Reported speech
Listening: Travel problems
Speaking: Making decisions

Warmer

1 Tell students to imagine they get lost in one of these situations: trekking in the jungle / climbing up a mountain / driving in the desert / walking around a city for the first time. They should imagine they are with three of their friends or family. Tell them to write down the characteristics of their friends/family that would help them in this situation.

2 Ask students to work in pairs. Tell them to describe their team and how they would help each other get out of the situation. Ask one or two pairs to share their ideas with the class.

Your profile

Ask students to work with a partner and to take it in turns to describe each journey. Monitor and help with ideas if necessary. In feedback, ask students who heard an interesting story to tell it to the class.

VOCABULARY   Phrasal verbs

1 Before students do this exercise, ask them to describe to a partner what they can see in each picture. Allow them just a few minutes to do this. Then ask students to work individually to match each picture to a sentence. As an alternative, put students into small groups. See which group can complete the exercise correctly and most quickly. Check answers. Check they have correctly understood the meaning by inviting two or three students to offer definitions of the words in bold, in particular *be held up* (something slows you down or makes you late), *pull over* (if a vehicle pulls over, it moves to the side of the road and stops), *make out* (just see).

Answers

1 a **2** g **3** l **4** h **5** c **6** b **7** j **8** d **9** k
10 f **11** e **12** i

Fast finishers

Ask fast finishers to use some of the phrasal verbs from exercise 1 to write a brief description of one of the journeys they described in Your profile. Ask one or two of the students to tell their stories to the class.

2 ▶ 2.21 Play the recording and ask students to decide what is happening. Go through the first one as an example. In pairs, students should describe what they heard using the phrasal verbs from exercise 1. If necessary, pause after each situation to allow students time to think. Check answers as a whole class.

Audioscript

Narrator:	One
Dad:	Sophie. I have to go. I'll be late!
Sophie:	Just five minutes, Dad.
Dad:	Sorry, Sophie. You've still got time to walk. I'm leaving now.
Narrator:	Two
Speaker:	Oh, no! Not more traffic jams! Look at this. Something must have happened.
Narrator:	Three
Speaker:	Oh, no! I thought the garage had fixed the problem! We'd better put the warning lights on.
Narrator:	Four
Speaker 1:	Want me to wait?
Speaker 2:	No, go ahead. I just need a minute.
Narrator:	Five
Speaker 1:	I think I'm lost. Oh, there's someone. Excuse me are you local?
Speaker 2:	Yes, how can I help?
Speaker 1:	I'm looking for …
Narrator:	Six
Speaker 1:	Watch out for that box in the middle of the road.
Speaker 2:	Where? Oh, I didn't see. Oh dear! I guess we'd better stop and pick it up.
Narrator:	Seven
Speaker:	The next station is Liverpool Lime Street. This train terminates here. Please make sure you have all your belongings and luggage with you.
Narrator:	Eight
Speaker 1:	So, what's wrong with the car this time?
Speaker 2:	It needs water. Look, that red light's come on. But the engine's too hot to put it in at the moment. We'll have to wait a few minutes.

Answers

1 It sounds like Sophie's dad has driven off without her.
2 It sounds like they're slowing down.
3 It sounds like they've broken down.
4 It sounds like he's having trouble keeping up with his friend.
5 It sounds like she's pulling over to the side of the road.
6 It sounds like they almost ran over a box.
7 It sounds like they're about to pull into the station.
8 It sounds like their car needs to cool down.

READING

1 Ask students if anyone went on holiday last year, and if so what type of holiday it was. Check students understand the differences between each type of holiday (A to E) by asking them to explain what typically happens on each one. Ask students to discuss the questions with a partner, and to report back on any particularly interesting holidays.

2 Give students just one or two minutes to complete the exercise. If students struggle, remind them that they can often do this type of task by just reading the first one or two lines of each paragraph. This is a useful exam skill to practise. When checking answers, ask students to identify the key words or phrases that helped them make their choice.

Answers
1 B   2 A   3 E   4 D   5 C

3 Give students more time to do this exercise, and monitor and help as necessary, whilst encouraging them to guess the meaning of any new vocabulary. Allow students to compare answers with a partner before checking as a whole class.

Fast finishers

Ask fast finishers to decide which holiday sounds the best and why. Elicit some ideas while checking answers to exercise 3.

Answers
1 The writer seems to enjoy independent travelling because he believes it offers the most opportunities to do different things.
2 It's important to find out what the law is about young travellers in the country you're visiting, and whether the airline has any age restrictions.
3 He was able to see what daily life is like in the country he visited.
4 It's a cheap holiday.
5 You probably won't need to speak another language. It's easy and convenient as everything is organised for you.
6 You should research your holiday carefully and find something that you are specifically interested in.
7 You have to pay your travel expenses and contribute towards training costs.
8 You can get a real taste of a different culture.

Talking points

Students should discuss these questions in pairs. Ask students to think about whether the situation or type of holiday makes a difference to their answer to the first question. If they are struggling for ideas, you could ask them to think about the teenager's personality, the legal situation, the potential dangers of going on holiday without adults, the skills that could be learnt by holidaying without adults, and whether the holiday is in the teenager's own country or abroad.

Cooler

Ask students to work in small groups and discuss whether they think experiences, such as holidays, or possessions which they can keep make them happier and why. In general, research says that experiences make people happier than possessions. Ask one or two groups to feed back to the class.

GRAMMAR   Reported speech

1 Give students a few minutes to read the sentences. Then ask them to discuss which ones have changed and which haven't, and why they think this is the case. Then ask students to read the rules to check whether their reasons were right or not. For rule b, ask students to identify which example sentence is a general truth or opinion (1) and which relates to an event which is not in the past (3). Finally, ask them to match each example sentence to the relevant rule.

Answers
1 b   2 a   3 c

→ Grammar reference Student's Book page 161

2 Ask students to do this task individually, and encourage them to think about the reason for the correct answer in each case. They should look at the tense of the reporting verb to give them a clue. Check answers and reasons with the whole class.

Answers
1 hadn't (a)   2 it's (b)   3 learn (c)   4 must (b)   5 will (c)
6 they were (a)

Corpus challenge

Ask students to correct the sentence and to explain the error (we use an indirect object like *me* after *tell*, but not after *say*. We also need to change the tense when reporting this sentence as this refers to the past and is not a general truth or opinion.)

Answer
Last week he told me that you were working very hard.

3 Do the first sentence as an example on the board and remind students of the basic tense changes with reported speech (e.g. present simple to past simple, as in question 2), then ask students to complete the exercise in pairs. Check answers as a whole class.

Extension activity

Tell students to write three sentences in direct speech about travel, e.g. about a problem they've experienced or somewhere they'd like to visit. Then ask them to say these to a partner. Students should then switch partners and report what their first partner said, using reported speech.

Answers
1 the hotel won't take guests under 18.
2 she wanted to take a year off before university.
3 her mum is a better driver than her brother.
4 he'd been travelling through Europe in the holidays.
5 they've been waiting for over an hour.

VOCABULARY   Reporting verbs

1 Books closed. Write *My brother agreed to give me his pen* on the board. Elicit the reporting verb here (*agree*) and ask students to come up with any other reporting verbs they know, in addition to *say*, *tell* and *ask*. Books open. Students work individually and make a note of any in the exercise or from the board which they didn't already know. Check answers.

Answers
a agreed   **b** insisted   **c** persuaded   **d** criticised
e enquired   **f** pointed out   **g** recommended   **h** confessed

2 ▶2.22 Ask students to predict with a partner what they think was actually said for each sentence in exercise 1. Ask them to write down a sentence for each one and then play the recording to compare their predictions.

Audioscript

Narrator:	One
Speaker 1:	Listen, you really must get going now. It's getting close to five.
Speaker 2:	Yes, things will get really busy if you leave it much longer.
Narrator:	Two
Speaker 1:	Yes, it's here. I always have it with me. Here you are.
Speaker 2:	Thank you, sir. Are you aware that this is out of date?
Speaker 1:	What?
Narrator:	Three
Speaker 1:	I really wish you wouldn't drive like this. We're in no hurry.
Speaker 2:	Sorry! Yes, you're right. We don't need to go so fast. I'm just looking forward to getting there. Switch on some music, can you? Maybe that'll help me relax.
Narrator:	Four
Speaker 1:	OK. A nice straight road. Now's the perfect opportunity. Go on! You'll never get a better chance! We don't want to be stuck behind this forever.
Speaker 2:	Here goes! Mirrors, indicators, and we're off.
Narrator:	Five
Speaker 1:	If I were you, I would wait until after seven before you leave. The buses are very crowded around six o'clock when everyone's coming home from work.
Speaker 2:	OK. I'll wait till a bit later and leave at about seven then.
Narrator:	Six
Speaker 1:	Is everything back on time or are there still delays on certain lines?
Speaker 2:	I'm afraid there are still delays on some routes.
Narrator:	Seven
Speaker 1:	Good evening, sir. Do you have your licence on you?
Speaker 2:	No, no, I don't, but I know I was going a bit fast back there. I'm sorry.
Narrator:	Eight
Speaker:	Right, just go straight on here. You're doing well but you really shouldn't keep slowing down so much. Try to keep a steady speed.

Answers
1 b   2 f   3 a   4 c   5 g   5 e   7 h   8 d

◖ Prepare for First for Schools
Reading and Use of English Part 4

Task description

This key word transformation task focuses on grammar, vocabulary and collocation. Students are given six separate items, each with a lead-in sentence, and a gapped second sentence to be completed in two to five words, one of which is a given 'key' word.

Tip

Remind students to make a note of the different forms of words when recording new vocabulary, e.g. *important*, *importance*, as learning these will help them to deal with this task.

3 ◖ Tell students that they cannot change the form of the word given, and ask them to complete the exercise individually. Tell them that they should use their knowledge of affixes to help them with this type of exercise. If your students are taking the First For Schools exam, then set a strict time limit of ten minutes. Remind them that sometimes more than one answer is possible. Check answers as a whole class.

Answers
1 receptionist recommended leaving their
2 criticised David for never remembering
3 confessed to losing / confessed that she had lost
4 dad agreed to give her
5 insisted that he'd locked
6 enquired if the campsite accepted / accepts
7 persuaded Kurt to go
8 pointed out that sharing

LISTENING

1 Books closed. Ask students to work in pairs and make a list of problems they might have whilst travelling. Elicit some examples from different pairs. Books open. Ask students to look at the photos and to work with a partner to explain what they think each travel problem is. Find out if anyone has experienced any of the problems shown.

2 ▶2.23 Tell students that they are going to hear five people talk about bad experiences when travelling. Play the recording and ask students to match each speaker to one of the photos. Check answers as a whole class.

Audioscript

Narrator: One

Speaker: It was our first family holiday abroad, but we almost got no further than the local airport. For my kid brother and me, it was all a big adventure and we were so excited. While we were waiting to be called to the gate, he suggested playing hide and seek. I thought it'd help pass the time, so, I counted and he hid. <u>The trouble was he hid a bit too well. Nobody could find him and we ended up missing the last call for our flight.</u> That's typical of him. Being older, of course, it was me who got told off when we nearly missed the flight – that was so unfair!

Narrator: Two

Speaker: Going abroad for the first time at the age of seven, I remember being amazed because everyone was speaking in a way I couldn't understand. Unfortunately that's pretty much the only memory I have of it. We'd barely left the hotel on the first day when <u>I tripped on a crack in the pavement and broke my wrist.</u> My mum says she knew that something terrible was going to happen – but she's always saying things like that! She says we spent the next forty-eight hours in hospital before heading straight back home. <u>My dad claims he stayed and enjoyed the rest of the holiday, but he's only joking.</u>

Narrator: Three

Speaker: We did an exchange with a French school a few years ago. You know, you visit them for a week and then they stay with you. I didn't know much about my partner in advance. I couldn't find him on any social networking sites and I only had his parents' email. So, the first time we met was in France. He looked about 12! And he still watched cartoons – though he did have a younger brother, I suppose. <u>But the absolute worst was that after a few days, I went down with some virus and spent the rest of the week in bed.</u> It was a disaster. I didn't even learn any French!

Narrator: Four

Speaker: Last summer, my parents finally said I could go to a music festival. Even better, my friend Lauren – she can already drive – persuaded her dad to lend us his car. We were really organised – tents, sleeping bags and stuff, and set off really early. <u>But halfway there, the car just died! We ended up being taken to a nearby garage, but they couldn't fix it. There we were in the middle of nowhere with no choice but to wait for Lauren's mum to come to our rescue. She came as quickly as she could, but by then, we'd missed half the festival.</u> We were *so* miserable!

Narrator: Five

Speaker: <u>I should've realised that I needed to leave a lot earlier than I did, but I thought I'd left enough time.</u> I knew Arsenal were playing at home that night and it's always busy near the stadium on those days. The police had closed down several roads, so I ended up catching four different buses to get to the cinema. I must have broken some kind of record – a journey that normally takes fifteen minutes took well over an hour! By the time I arrived, everyone had already gone in and I'd missed half the film.

Answers

1 c **2** d **3** no photo **4** a **5** b

Listening part 3

Task description

The focus of this part is on identifying attitude, opinion, gist, purpose, feeling, main points and detail. Students hear five short related monologues. There are five questions, which require the selection of the correct option from a list of eight.

Tip

Encourage students to make brief notes on the main topics as they listen. This will give them a reference if they are not sure immediately, and may help them to answer the question by a process of elimination.

3 ● ▶2.23 Ask students to read the sentences and to underline the key information they are listening for. Remind them that they will not hear the exact sentences from the book and that they will not need three of the letters. Play the recording. Ask students to compare their answers with a partner before whole-class feedback. Invite students to say which words in the script told them the answer. If they have difficulty with the distraction, read the words from the script and discuss as a class why this could not be the correct answer.

Answers

Speaker 1: H
Speaker 2: E
Speaker 3: D
Speaker 4: F
Speaker 5: C

SPEAKING   Making decisions

1 ▶2.24 Before students listen to the dialogue, ask them to look at the photo and describe some of the things they can see. They should work with a partner to think of different problems there might be with going on a camping holiday. Play the recording and ask students to compare their ideas with the dialogue. Did anyone think of the same problem experienced by Dan and Ahmed (*how to travel*)? Then set the task in the book and check the answer together.

Audioscript

Ahmed: OK. I think we know what we're taking. <u>What do you reckon about</u> getting there?

Dan: <u>It makes sense if we</u> drive, doesn't it? Carrying all this stuff will be a nightmare.

Ahmed: Well, that's true but I don't actually have a car!

Dan: What about your mum's? Haven't you asked her yet?

Ahmed: Um, no. <u>The trouble with</u> driving <u>is</u> the traffic. We'll have to leave really early to avoid the rush hour.

Dan: <u>Do you think it's best to</u> go by train then?

Ahmed: Possibly. It'll be more expensive, but we can relax. Plus I'm not a very confident driver yet. <u>What about this for an idea</u>? We go by coach!

Dan:	No way. That will take ages!
Ahmed:	Oh, OK. So <u>are we agreed</u>?
Dan:	Well, I think <u>what we've decided is</u> we're not going by car or coach …
Ahmed:	So <u>that means the train</u>.
Dan:	<u>Right</u>. Let's go through the stuff again. We need to cut it down a bit.

Answer

by train

2 ▶2.24 Give students time to read through the speaking profile and then play the recording for them to number the phrases. Ask students to compare answers with a partner before checking as a whole class. Ask if they can add one or two more phrases for each function and write these on the board (e.g. presenting an argument: *I really think we should*; giving a counter argument: *Well, the only problem with that is…*; asking somebody's opinion: *What about if we*; making a decision: *So, we're clear that we…*).

Extension activity

Tell students to imagine they are going to spend six months travelling. Write *backpacking*, *volunteer work* and *internship* on the board. Ask students to discuss the advantages and disadvantages of each option with a partner, and decide which one they would both like to do. Tell students the aim is to use as many of the expressions from the *Prepare* box as possible during a two to three minute conversation. Ask one or two pairs to perform their conversation to the class.

Answers

1 What do you reckon about …?
2 It makes sense if we …
3 The trouble with … is …
4 Do you think it's best to … ?
5 What about this for an idea?
6 Are we agreed?
7 what we've decided is …

3 Books closed. Ask students to suggest places to go for a day out to celebrate something and write suggestions on the board. Books open. They look at the list in the box and see if there are any which they haven't already suggested. Books open. Ask students to work in groups of four and to discuss the advantages and disadvantages of each destination. Elicit ideas from students and then hold a class vote on the best and worst destinations amongst those on the board and in the book.

4 Give students a strict time limit of four minutes if they are preparing for the First For Schools exam. Afterwards, ask one or two pairs to act out their dialogue for the class. The rest of the class should listen and write the student's initial against each function in the *Prepare* box if they use that function. At the end, gather feedback on whether every student used every function or not, and if not, how they could have worked it into their conversation.

Mixed ability

If some of your students struggle with interaction, demonstrate its importance by asking a student to think of an advantage of one of the holidays. When you respond, ignore what they said and just give your own idea. Ask students what was weak about your response. You could also record a dialogue where the two speakers do not respond to or build on each other's statements. Ask students to listen and identify what is wrong and then ask them how they could improve the dialogue. Ask one or two stronger pairs to model their improved dialogue.

EP Word profile

Ask students to work with a partner to write an example sentence using each expression. Discuss their ideas. Then set the exercise on page 136.

Answers

1 c   2 d   3 g   4 f   5 b   6 e   7 a

Cooler

Tell students to write a summary of the discussion with their partner from exercise 4. They should then work with another partner to compare their summaries. Ask students whether they think they could have used any of their partner's ideas in their own discussion.

Project

Ask students to research a volunteer holiday scheme online. In the following class, they should report back in small groups about the details of the scheme and whether they would take part or not and why.

Teacher's resources

Student's Book
Grammar reference and practice page 161
Vocabulary list page 144
Video
Travelling
Speaking Part 2
Workbook
Unit 14, pages 56–59
Go online for
- Pronunciation
- Progress test
- Video extra worksheet
- Speaking test video worksheets
- Corpus tasks

Culture
Cultural highways

Learning objectives

- The students learn about the history of the Silk Road and its impact on a range of cultures.
- In the project stage, students design a cultural route for visitors to their own country.

Warmer

1 Ask students to work in pairs to brainstorm what they think their country is famous for in other countries. Elicit some ideas from the class.

2 Write the areas from exercise 1 on the board and ask students to say what they know about them.

3 Ask students to work with their partner again to think of different products that each area is famous for, and discuss as a class.

1 Tell students that they are going to read a text about the Silk Road. Ask students if they have ever heard of the Silk Road and, if so, to describe its route. Ask them to estimate the length of the Silk Road with a partner and then suggest what it was used for.

Answers

The Silk Road was over 4,000 miles (6,437 km) long. It was used for trade: primarily silk cloth, but also tea, salt, sugar, porcelain and spices.

2 Ask students to discuss the question in pairs before reading Part B. Then tell them to read Part B to check their answer. Check the answer as a whole class asking them to share where they found the answer and why they decided to look in the part of the text.

Extension activity

Ask students to discuss if trade in their country has changed over the years. Ask them to spend a few minutes brainstorming changes and reasons for the changes, e.g. the production of goods in another country, the closure of mines, political changes, aviation for transport of goods.

Answer

Traders started travelling by sea, as shipping goods was faster and easier.

3 Ask students to read the text quickly to find the answers. Tell them to rewrite any false sentences so that they are correct. Ask students to compare their answers with a partner before whole-class feedback. As an alternative, you could put students in pairs at the start of the activity and give them two sentences each to find out about before looking for the final answer together.

Answers

1 False. It also went south to different parts of the world.
2 False. It was also used to transport other luxury goods and exotic food.
3 False. They travelled in all directions.
4 True. The roads were poor or non-existent and and merchants risked being attacked by robbers.
5 False. It is less busy with trade, but some parts are popular with tourists.

4 Put students into small groups and ask them to discuss the questions. Monitor and give positive feedback for interesting ideas. Elicit ideas for each one in a whole-class discussion.

Fast finishers

Ask fast finishers to discuss these questions:
1 What are the benefits of being influenced by other cultures?
2 Do you think the world will have only one culture in the future? Why / Why not?
3 Do you think traditional ways of life and cultures should be protected?
Invite one or two students to share their ideas with the class during feedback for Question 4.

5 ▶2.25 Give students a couple of minutes to look through the table and then play the recording for students to complete it. Play the recording again, pausing after each speaker to check answers as a whole class. Ask students which of the two routes they would most like to travel.

Mixed ability

Ask weaker students to listen as a pair. Student A should complete the column for Jenny and student B should complete the column for Michael. They can then work together to complete the whole table. Stronger students can complete both columns.

Audioscript

Narrator: Jenny

Jenny: I think the most interesting route that I ever took was during an adventure tour across Central Asia. I took the trip with a friend of mine two years ago. <u>We started off in Istanbul, Turkey</u>, and then we travelled east, along the old Silk Road across Asia, travelling by <u>bicycle</u> almost all of the time. We took <u>buses</u> and <u>ferries</u> a couple of times, and <u>once we had to take a short flight by aeroplane</u>, but everything else was done by leg-power! It was a good thing we trained before starting our journey! <u>We finally ended our trip a year later in northern India, after cycling more than ten thousand kilometres!</u> In total, we visited ten different countries, including Azerbaijan, Uzbekistan and China, and we travelled through all different kinds of landscapes, from <u>snowy mountains</u>, to <u>green hills</u>, to <u>dry deserts</u> and even through <u>tropical rainforests</u>. It was the most fascinating journey of my life, definitely. As far as the highlights of our trip, I think <u>what I enjoyed the most was meeting people from so many different cultures</u> along the Silk Road, and people were so friendly. We often stayed in people's homes, and so we got to try lots of local dishes. We also learned a lot about folk music, and I even made recordings of some traditional musical instruments. It was fascinating! It was also interesting to cycle along the Silk Road, and think that people travelled all that way in the past, when there weren't any roads. I'd really recommend a trip like this to everyone, but you really need to be in good shape. It's a very long trip!

Narrator: Michael

Michael: The most interesting journey that I've ever taken was probably the South American Challenge last autumn. <u>It was a fifteen thousand kilometre trip</u> that I took around South America with two friends. <u>We started in Río de Janeiro</u>, and went west, through Brazil, Bolivia, and Peru. Then we went south, through Chile and Argentina. Oh! And the South American Challenge is a <u>car</u> rally, and we drove the whole way in a 1957 Mercedes Benz! There were twenty nine other cars, and we came in nineteenth place, which wasn't too bad! The whole journey took us <u>six weeks</u>, and we saw some amazing countryside along the way – we saw <u>rainforests</u> in Brazil, and then the Iguazu Falls. After that, we headed to Bolivia, and <u>the capital city of La Paz</u>. It's the highest capital city in the world! In Peru, we saw Lake Titicaca and Machu Picchu, before turning south into Chile, through the <u>Atacama Desert</u>, which is one of the hottest and driest places on the planet. It was an incredible experience! After that, we entered Patagonia, in Argentina, and continued <u>south to Tierra del Fuego</u> – the southernmost tip of the continent, <u>where the rally ended</u>.

For me, <u>the Andes Mountains were probably the highlight of the trip</u>, and we followed them for most of the journey south. Along the way, there are so many different climates and cultures, as well as traditions for things like food, music and clothing. But one thing we noticed in many places was *yerba mate* tea. People prepare it in a special gourd cup, and drinking *mate* is a very social activity, so we did it a lot! And that's another highlight of the trip – we met wonderful people everywhere we went, and I was really sorry to see the journey end, even though I was exhausted!

Answers

Route 1
Starting point: Istanbul, Turkey
Finishing point: northern India
Distance travelled: more than 10,000 km
Length of time: a year
Form(s) of transport: bicycle, ferries, buses, one flight
Types of landscape: all different kinds – snowy mountains, green hills, dry deserts and tropical rainforests.
Highlights: meeting people from so many different cultures
Route 2
Starting point: Rio De Janeiro
Finishing point: Tierra del Fuego
Distance travelled: 15,000 km
Length of time: six weeks
Form(s) of transport: car
Types of landscape: rainforests, deserts, cities, mountains
Highlights: the Andes Mountains

Cooler

Ask students to think of a journey, either one they have been on, one a friend has been on, or one they have read about. Give them a few minutes to note down any details of the journey and then ask them to work in small groups to describe and talk about the journey. Ask each group to tell the class about one journey.

Project

This will need to be set as homework for students to be able to do their research, unless there are particularly well-known routes students will know. Ask students to produce a poster with a map, including pictures and information about any points of interest. In the following class, students can display their posters around the room and ask each other questions about the planned routes.

Unit profile

Vocabulary: Global issues: nouns and verbs; Phrases with *in*

Reading: Youth parliament

Grammar: Modals (3): Deduction

Writing: An essay (3)

Warmer

1 Write *Global issues* on the board and put students into groups of four. Ask them to make a list of the issues facing the world today. If they need more direction, give them some ideas, e.g. natural resources, food, health, pollution, etc.

2 After a few minutes, ask students to choose the five most important issues on their list and to rank them from 1 (most important) to 5 (least important).

3 Ask one group to give their most important issue. Find out if the rest of the class agrees and hold a class discussion based on students' ranking. Did any group think of an issue that was different from all the other groups'?

4 Ask students who should be responsible for solving each issue and how it might be done. Is it up to individuals or governments?

Your profile

If you have done the Warmer, simply hold a class vote to choose the three most concerning issues. If not, you could include some ideas from the Warmer here to expand the students' discussion.

VOCABULARY   Global issues: nouns and verbs

1 Before students do the exercise, ask them to explain to a partner the meaning of the words in bold. Model the pronunciation of *cooperating* /kəʊˈɒp.ər.eɪt.ɪŋ/ and explain that this can also be written with a hyphen (*co-operating*). Then ask students to work individually to match the sentences. Don't check answers at this stage, as students will do this in exercise 2.

Fast finishers

Ask fast finishers to write a sentence saying what things they would like to ban and which charities they think should be supported. When checking answers to exercise 1, ask a fast finisher to add their sentence to the point being made.

Answers

1 cooperating – working together
2 collected – brought together
3 banned – forbidden
4 criticised – complained about
5 support – agree with
6 elected – chosen

2 ▶ 2.26 Tell students that they will hear six people talking about their concerns. Play the recording for students to check their answers to exercise 1.

Audioscript

Narrator: One
Speaker: A powerful tornado which passed through northern Oklahoma has destroyed thousands of properties and injured hundreds of people. <u>Aid agencies are cooperating with the state government</u> to get emergency supplies to the worst-affected areas. Unfortunately, cooperation between the two has been made more difficult because of problems with cell phone coverage.

Narrator: Two
Speaker: <u>We've collected one hundred pounds for an anti-poverty charity</u> called Chance4All. They do lots of work with long-term unemployed people and people on low wages. I think it's really important to help people in society who are less fortunate. Sometimes we organise a food collection for a local homeless hostel.

Narrator: Three
Speaker: Cars in this city cause terrible congestion and drivers are either standing still or going much too fast! The traffic and parking is dreadful. <u>Cars should be banned from busy city streets.</u> City centres should be quiet, safe environments for pedestrians and cyclists – and public transport. A ban on private cars would make a huge difference in the city centre.

Narrator: Four
Speaker: <u>The local council has been criticised for not dealing with litter in the city.</u> The number of people employed to pick up litter in the city has been reduced, and people are starting to complain that rubbish is lying around in the streets. There has been further criticism of the local council for the way it is cutting spending on other necessary services.

Narrator: Five
Speaker: I just want to explain my position because I think we're in agreement here! To start with, <u>you seem to think I don't support your views on animal rights</u>. In fact, that's not true. I'm a great supporter of animal rights, and I certainly think we should do more to protect animals.

Narrator: Six
Speaker: <u>It's great that Ann's been elected as the student representative</u> for our year. It means she'll be going to monthly meetings with the head teacher and the board of governors. The election was for student representatives from the other years too and they'll be at the meetings with her. I can't believe it! It's a massive responsibility. I'm so proud of her!

3 ▶2.26 Books closed. Ask students to write down the noun form of the words from exercise 1. Then ask students to open their books and compare their answers with the nouns in the box. Tell students to complete the gaps and then play the recording for them to check their answers.

Answers

1 cooperation   2 collection   3 ban   4 criticism
5 supporter   6 election

READING

1 Ask students if they are interested in, or involved in, politics. Do they think politics is important or relevant to young people? Tell them to look at the photo and ask them if they know what this building is. Big Ben may be familiar to them but elicit what the rest of the building is called (Houses of Parliament). Make sure they understand that they are not supposed to read the text at this stage – they should just look at the photo, the title and the big quotes in grey. If they are struggling with Question 2, tell them that MP stands for 'Member of Parliament', then elicit that MYP stands for 'Member of Youth Parliament'. From there, they should be able to work out what 'UKYP' means. Then give them two minutes to try to answer the three questions. Afterwards give the students time to read the text to check their answers. They should read the text quickly at this stage, just to find the information they need and not worry about words that they do not know the meaning of. Check answers as a class. You could give them information from the Cultural background.

Cultural background

UK voters elect 650 **Members of Parliament (MPs)** to represent their interests in the House of Commons. MPs assess and propose new laws, and examine government policies.

The **UK Parliament** is the supreme legislative body in the United Kingdom. Its head is the Sovereign of the United Kingdom (currently Queen Elizabeth II) and its home is the Palace of Westminster in London.

The **House of Commons** is the lower house of the UK Parliament, and is where MPs meet. The **House of Lords** is the second house. Together, these are called the 'Houses of Parliament'.

The **West Midlands** is a region of England, and home to the second most populous city, Birmingham.

Answers

1 A young person's experience of the UK Youth Parliament
2 Member of Youth Parliament, United Kingdom Youth Parliament
3 Yes

2 Tell students to read the summaries and to then read the text again to choose the best one. Emphasise that it is not necessary to understand every word to understand the overall meaning of the text. Ask students to compare their choice with a partner and check answers together.

Answer

2

3 Ask students to complete the gaps individually, and check answers. Alternatively, you could ask pairs of students to complete three sentences each and the last one together before checking answers as a class.

Answers

1 aspect   2 debates   3 ensure   4 organise   5 position
6 run   7 speeches

4 Ask students to read the sentences. Then ask them to work with a partner to explain the meaning of each sentence. Ask different pairs to explain the meaning of each one to the class and describe how they worked out the meaning. For example, in sentence 1, there is a clue to the meaning in the previous sentence where Charity suggests people don't need to give up their social lives in order to be involved.

Extension activity

Ask students to work in small groups to discuss whether they agree or disagree with these statements and why:
Work is more important than family life.
Luck is more important than hard work.
You can work hard but if you don't have natural talent you will never be successful.
Your work should always focus on the needs of others and not yourself.
Ask one or two groups to share their ideas with the class.

Possible answers

1 It's important to have time and energy for hobbies and friends as well as for work.
2 The more effort you make, the more rewarding it will be.
3 Something very important happened during the time I was involved in the UKYP.
4 To get results, you need to be able to negotiate and express yourself well.
5 Don't turn down offers to do new things.
6 It may be hard at the time, but it will be enjoyable and you will achieve good results eventually.

EP **Word profile**

Write the word *key* on the board and ask students what it means. Elicit a couple of example sentences using the word *key*. Then ask them to read the sentences on page 87. Did they come up with the same meanings? Set the exercises on page 137. Discuss their responses to exercise 2 as a class.

Talking points

Students should discuss these questions in pairs. Ask students to think about whether young people should be involved in all aspects of parliament or only limited areas. For the second question, if they are struggling, encourage students to think about what they could do at school, in their community, at home or online.

Cooler

Tell students that they are applying to be members of a youth parliament. Ask them to consider the key things they would like to work on whilst in power, and to prepare a brief speech. Put students into groups of five or six. Students should deliver their speeches in their groups and each group should elect its MYP. In feedback, ask each group who they chose and why.

GRAMMAR Modals (3): Deduction

1 Ask students to read the sentences and decide whether each one is about the past, present or future. Tell them to compare their ideas with a partner before checking answers together. Draw their attention in particular to the use of *could* in sentence 2 for the future.

Answers

1 present 2 future 3 past 4 past 5 past

2 Tell students to do this exercise individually and check answers with the whole class. Remind them that when we are using *must* to express certainty in the present (e.g. *he must be cold – it's freezing outside*) the opposite is *can't* (e.g. *he can't be cold – he's wearing a hat, coat and gloves*). Remind them also that to talk about certainty and possibility in the past, we use *must/can't* etc. + *have* + past participle, e.g. *There's a note from George. He must have written it before he left.*

Answers

a must b can't, couldn't c could, may, might
d may not, might not

→ Grammar reference Student's Book **page 162**

3 Do the first sentence as an example on the board, emphasising that it is important that they look at the tenses in both sentences to know whether the present, past or future is being referred to. Time phrases (e.g. *today* in sentence 2 and *last week* in sentence 4) will also help them to make correct choices. Then ask students to complete the exercise individually. Monitor and provide support as necessary. Tell them to compare answers with a partner before whole-class feedback.

As you check answers, ask students to explain their choice each time. If you feel that students are still not clear about the meaning, you could adapt sentences from the exercise and ask for them to complete gaps, e.g. sentence 5: *Kids from that school* [must have] *damaged the car. The tall man saw a group of them by the car just before it happened.*

Answers

1 must have stuck 2 can't be 3 must
4 might have delayed 5 couldn't have damaged
6 might not have 7 may 8 can't have lost

4 Ask students to look at the photos and in pairs try to guess what is happening or has happened. Elicit ideas for each photo from different pairs. Focus on the students use of modals of deduction and encourage them to use a range of modals. Monitor and give positive feedback for accurate use. It may be useful to teach your students the phrase *There must have been* if they are not able to work this out for themselves.

Possible answers

1 They might be delivering food after a natural disaster.
2 They must be having a student election.
3 She must be collecting money for charity.
4 There could have been an accident.

Corpus challenge

Ask students to correct the sentence and to explain the error (we say *should have* rather than *should* to talk about something that was supposed to have happened at a point in the past).

Answer

The show should have started at half past seven but nothing happened.

Mixed ability

For further, fun practice of this area, tell stronger students to draw three pictures showing something that has just happened. In mixed-ability groups, they should share their pictures for other students to guess what has happened. Ask groups to share their favourite pictures and the best/funniest guesses with the rest of the class.

VOCABULARY Phrases with *in*

1 Books closed. Write *You will get loads back in return* on the board and underline *in return*. Ask students to explain what it means and then refer students to the explanation in exercise 1. Tell students to complete the task individually and then check answers together.

Answers

1 e 2 c 3 a 4 f 5 d 6 b

2 Ask students to complete the sentences individually. Allow them to compare their answers with a partner before checking as a whole class.

Fast finishers

Ask fast finishers to write their own example sentences using the phrases. When checking answers to exercise 2, elicit these example sentences.

Answers

1 in public 2 in secret 3 in all 4 in turn 5 in progress
6 in general

WRITING   An essay (3)

1 Ask students what the last essay they wrote was about, and how they usually plan their essays. Then tell them to look at the diagram and check that students understand all of the words and phrases on it. Ask students to work in pairs to create a diagram for two more topics. They should aim to have five subtopics for each. For example: education: qualifications, future career, leaving age, free access to all, social aspects, etc. In feedback, you could group students who chose the same topics together to discuss and share ideas.

2 Ask students to quickly read the essay and decide whether it's about employment or education. Tell them to underline any employment-related vocabulary and to brainstorm more employment vocabulary with a partner. Elicit a word pool from the class, and tell them that such a strategy can be useful when generating ideas for an essay in an exam.

Answer
both

3 Explain that the sentences numbered 1–3 are different possible essay questions and that students need to match one to the essay they read in exercise 2.

Answer
3

4 Give students a few minutes to read the *Prepare* box and then ask them to find examples of linking words in the essay. Check answers as a class.

Answers
Once teenagers leave school …
… **provided** they already have some experience …
… have the opportunity to travel **now** that there are …
… **considering** the job market is difficult at the moment …

5 Ask students to work in pairs to complete the sentences with words from the box. Check answers as a whole class. Write *considering* and *provided* on the board and elicit one more example sentence for each from the

class, then write these on the board. This will provide extra help for weaker students when they come to write their essay in exercise 7.

Extension activity

Write *Issues facing my generation* on the board. Ask students to write sentences on this topic using the linking words from the box, e.g. *My generation should have a good standard of living provided that we deal with the environmental issues our society is facing.* Tell students to discuss their ideas with a partner, before whole-class feedback.

Answers
1 or 2 once 3 now 4 provided 5 considering

6 Ask students to read the information and to brainstorm their ideas on the topic. Tell them to create a word pool of ten to fifteen words on the topic. Ask students to share their ideas with a partner and to write three example sentences using words from their partner's word pool and some of the linking phrases from the *Prepare* box.

⬤ Prepare for First for Schools
Writing Part 1

Task description
This part is a compulsory task. Students are required to write an essay giving their opinion on the essay title using the ideas given and providing an idea of their own. Students should write 140–190 words.

Tip
Give students some advice on writing an effective introduction. For example, the first sentence should get the reader's interest. The introduction should start with general points and move to more specific information.

7 ⬤ Give students time to do the task, and set a strict time limit of 40 minutes if students are preparing for the First For Schools exam. Then ask pairs to share their essays with each other. When reading their partner's essay, they should underline any linking expressions from this lesson. They should also circle any sentences they think could be linked together.

Extension activity

Tell students to read a partner's essay and discuss the different ideas that they included. Then ask them to work together to suggest solutions to the problems they wrote about. In feedback, ask two or three pairs to present their solutions to the class.

Sample answer

Our world has many environmental problems, which have been mainly caused by man. However, most governments recognise these issues, and scientists are trying to find solutions.

The number of people sharing the planet is rising rapidly and this could lead to food shortages, unless the situation is carefully managed. Farmers may have to use different methods to increase the amount of food they produce, which could present new problems for the countryside.

Some species such as bees are already endangered, due to the use of certain pesticides. We must protect bees if we are to survive ourselves, for they are essential to the growth of crops, and other insects provide food for birds.

Pollution remains perhaps the biggest problem we have to deal with, in spite of attempts by world leaders to reduce the amount of emissions from homes, factories and power stations. Considering our love of travel, cars and planes will need to be even cleaner than today, perhaps powered by other forms of energy instead of petrol.

To sum up, although things could get worse in the future, there could be some improvements too. It is in our hands.

Cooler

Ask students to work in small groups and to discuss questions 1 and 2 from exercise 3. Tell them to brainstorm their ideas and produce a mind map to plan their essay. If you would like to give your students more practice, ask them to write the essay for homework.

Project

Ask students to research one of the topics from exercise 1 on page 89. Tell them to focus on their own country and find out:

1   What problems currently exist in that area?
2   What is being done to deal with these problems?

In the following class, ask them to find other people who looked into the same area and compare their research. Ask each group to choose a spokesperson to summarise their group's discussion for the class.

Teacher's resources

Student's Book
Grammar reference and practice page 162
Vocabulary list page 145
Video
The big picture
Workbook
Unit 15, pages 60–63
Go online for
- Video extra worksheet
- Corpus tasks

16 New and improved!

Warmer

Bring in five adverts from magazines, but remove the product and company name. Ask students to work with a partner to make sentences about what the adverts could be for, using *could*, *might*, *can't* and *must*. For example, *It must be for a mobile phone*. Discuss some ideas as a class.

Your profile

In pairs, students discuss the questions. If they prefer, they can discuss adverts which they have seen on the internet, rather than the TV. After the discussion, you could play clips of popular adverts and ask students for their reaction.

VOCABULARY Advertising: nouns and verbs

1 ▶3.02 Ask students to look at the adverts and say what is being advertised. Play the recording and ask students to make notes for each question. You may need to play the recording twice. Ask students to compare their notes with a partner before checking answers together.

Answers

1 the cola ad
2 Emma prefers the shampoo ad. She thinks it's sophisticated, and already likes the product. Dan prefers the car ad, as he finds out the company are launching a new model.
3 Students' own answers.
4 He realises that he is also a consumer, and that he likes being informed about new products.

2 ▶3.02 Ask students to complete the sentences individually. Play the recording for them to check their answers.

Audioscript

Man:	So join us after the break for the second half and see if West Bromwich Albion can hang on to their three nil lead over Premier League leaders, Chelsea.
Dan:	Who's got the remote? Can you turn down the volume?
Emma:	No way. The commercials are the best bit!
Dan:	Give me the remote, please! Phew! I can't stand the commercial breaks!
Emma:	Hey! Turn that back on. It's the football that's boring!
Girl:	Hi!

Boy:	Hello!
Girl:	Oh!
Boy:	Hel-lo-o?
Girl:	Agh!
Man:	Have you ever dropped your phone and damaged it? Have you lost your phone or had a phone stolen? Can you afford not to have phone insurance? For a small sum every month, protect your phone against accidental damage, loss and theft. Free same-day replacement on most phones. Keep talking. Go to PhoneGuard.com.
Emma:	Hmm. Boring! Not all advertising is good!
Dan:	I bet it's really expensive, but I could do with some kind of phone insurance. I'm always dropping mine.
Woman:	Cleaner. Smoother. Fresher. Hmm. That's better! For really beautiful hair, use La Catch Total Shine.
Dan:	Honestly! Who cares? Shampoo is shampoo! This is just meaningless publicity.
Emma:	Well, that ad wasn't for you, was it? It was aimed at a more sophisticated audience – people like me! I do like that brand of shampoo, actually. I've got a sample at home.
Dan:	Ha! You'd buy any brand that had a nice advert.
Emma:	Not at all. I don't buy things just because they're advertised. I only tried that shampoo because it came as a free sample on the cover of a magazine.
Dan:	Anyway, what's the big deal about adverts? Why do you like them so much?
Emma:	It's just good to be informed, that's all, you know, about cool products and new brands. It's the same as being interested in news about DJs or movie celebrities or current affairs. Or football transfers!
Dan:	Rubbish!
Emma:	The reason adverts are good is they help you to see what's available. You'd never know what new products were on offer if they weren't advertised. Wait a minute. What's this? I haven't seen this one before.
Man:	Take the path less travelled. Experience the freedom of the open road. Get home in time for dinner. Terms and conditions apply.
Dan:	Now I didn't mind that one! And I didn't know they were launching a new model this year.
Emma:	See? You're a consumer just as much as me or anybody else. You can't avoid being a consumer. Everyone's a consumer – everyone consumes stuff. Buying things is just a part of modern life!
Dan:	The football's back on.
Emma:	Ha, ha! See that logo?
Dan:	The bank logo? What about it?
Emma:	That's marketing.
Dan:	They're the sponsors. All football teams are sponsored by companies.
Emma:	Exactly. And why do companies sponsor certain teams? Because having their logo at matches and on football shirts is very good publicity.
Dan:	Yeah, OK. Maybe you're right. Anyway, the game's about to begin.

Answers

1 commercial breaks 2 aimed at 3 sample 4 on offer
5 launching 6 consumer 7 sponsored 8 logo

3 Ask students to discuss the questions with a partner. Monitor and give help if necessary with Question 5. In feedback, ask different pairs to answer each question.

Extension activity

Ask students to write down three characteristics of a good TV or internet advert. Ask students to compare these in groups and to try to agree on a list of five together. Ask one of the groups to come and write their list on the board. Do the other students have the same characteristics? Discuss as a class.

READING

1 Ask students if they can define *guerilla marketing* (a marketing strategy that uses cheap and unconventional methods) or give any examples of it. You may wish to tell them the meaning of the word *guerrilla* (a member of an unofficial group of soldiers fighting to achieve their political beliefs) and clarify its pronunciation /gəˈrɪl.ə/. Then give them one or two minutes to skim the text and find the answer.

Answer
2

⬤ Prepare for First for Schools
Reading and Use of English Part 2

Task description
The main focus of this task is on awareness and control of grammar with some focus on vocabulary. Students complete the eight gaps in the text with a suitable word.

Tip
Tell students to look at the sentence or clause for each gap and to think about the grammar. It can help if they can identify whether a noun, verb or adjective, for example, is needed.

2 ⬤ If you have students preparing for the First For Schools exam, set a strict time limit of ten minutes for this exercise. Ask students to compare their answers with a partner before whole-class feedback.

Answers
1 as 2 to 3 which 4 of 5 are 6 are 7 on 8 is

3 Ask students to match the words individually, Monitor and help, and allow dictionaries if necessary, whilst encouraging students to guess the meaning from context first. Check answers.

Fast finishers

Ask fast finishers to write definitions or synonyms for these adjectives from the first paragraph: *attractive* (pleasing to look at), *witty* (clever and funny), *innovative* (using new methods), *imaginative* (original and clever) and *irritating* (annoying).

Answers
1 gap 2 illegal 3 striking 4 memorable 5 clip
6 budget 7 audience 8 sophisticated

4 Give students a few minutes to answer the questions. Ask them to compare their answers with a partner and then check answers as a whole class.

Possible answers
1 Because you don't have to pay for broadcasting.
2 Because it relies on individual viewers to share it.
3 Because it cleans things rather than damages them, and there are no laws against cleaning.
4 Because it can look very strange, so not many people are willing to wear it.
5 Because if people recognised the actors, they would realise the conversation wasn't real and the marketing campaign would fail.
6 If people realise that the conversation isn't genuine, they might start to strongly dislike the company.

EP Word profile

Ask students to write their own sentences using each of the phrases with *no*. Then set the exercise on page 137.

Answers
1 no matter what 2 no good 3 no need 4 no wonder
5 no matter what 6 No wonder 7 no good 8 no need

Talking points

In pairs, students discuss these questions. Encourage them to add examples and justify their opinions. Elicit some ideas after a few minutes. Give positive feedback for interesting ideas and comments during class feedback.

Cooler

Put students into small groups. Tell them to use the vocabulary from this unit to describe an advert, product or company. They should not mention it by name. The rest of the group should try to guess what they are describing. Alternatively, bring in an example of one of the advertising techniques mentioned in the text. Ask students to work in small groups and discuss how successful they think the advert was and why. Share some ideas as a class.

GRAMMAR Conditionals (1): Review

1 Ask students to work with a partner to complete this exercise. Check answers.

Answers

1 possible   2 No; no   3 a true statement   4 No

2 Give students a few minutes to read the information, and complete the rule box as a class. Ask students to match the examples in exercise 1 to a rule in the box (*1 b, 2 d, 3 a, 4 c*).

Answers

a general   b present   c future   d past

→ Grammar reference Student's Book **page 163**

3 Tell students to match the sentence halves and to check answers with a partner before whole-class feedback. Ask them to underline the verbs in each half of the sentence and note which tense is used in each half.

Answers

1 c   2 e   3 b   4 a   5 d

4 Ask students to complete the sentences individually and to then compare their answers with a partner. Once they have agreed on the correct form of the question, they ask and answer the questions in pairs. In feedback, elicit an answer for each question from different pairs.

Extension activity

Ask students to write the start of three conditional sentences, e.g. *If I were the teacher … , If I had a car … .* Then ask them to swap sentences with a partner and complete each other's sentences. Elicit some examples from the class.

Answers

1 lost   2 would you have done   3 do you wear   4 pass
5 would you go

Corpus challenge

Ask students to correct the sentence and to explain the error. Explain that the sentence should be in the third conditional as it speculates about a past event, and about how something that happened (*they made a mistake*) affected other things (*they lost*).

Answer
We would have won if I hadn't made a mistake.

VOCABULARY   Adverb + adjective collocations

1 Remind students that collocations are two or more words that often go together. Tell students that these adverbs modify (i.e. give extra information about) the adjectives that follow, and point out that, apart from *well*, they end -*ly*. Ask them to complete the exercise individually and then check answers.

Fast finishers

Ask fast finishers to write sentences using three of the adverb + adjective collocations and to share these during feedback to exercise 1.

Answers

1 environmentally   2 scientifically; well   3 constantly
4 globally   5 financially   6 ecologically; incredibly

2 Tell students they will need to use an adjective modified by an adverb, as in exercise 1, formed from the words in bold. They should complete the exercise individually, and to compare answers with a partner before whole-class feedback.

Answers

1 nicely dressed   2 automatically generated
3 actively involved   4 conveniently-located
5 naturally-talented   6 finely-chopped

LISTENING

1 Ask students if they have been involved in any viral marketing campaigns. Tell them that they are going to hear about Anita's experience. Remind them of the useful strategy of underlining key words before listening, and do the first two as an example. Explain that this will help them focus on what they need to listen for. Ask students to underline the key words individually. When checking each answer, ask students to predict the type of information they are listening for (e.g. noun, pronoun, adjective, etc.).

Possible answers

1 Anita, recently, role   2 thought, parcel, received
3 favourite item   4 The Emissary, aims, appeal
5 Advertisers, believe, best, advertising, age group
6 uses, describe, tactics   7 tickets, concert   8 invited, London
9 asked, take part in, advertising
10 excited, meet, well-known, event

● Prepare for First for Schools
Listening Part 2

Task description
Students are required to complete ten sentences with information they hear in a 3–4 minute monologue. This part focuses on detail, identifying specific information and stated opinion.

Tip
Highlight to students that spelling is important and check spelling as you check answers.

2 ▶3.03 ● Play the recording for students to complete the sentences. Remind them that they need to write a word or short phrase which is the same as they hear in the recording. Play it again so they can check their answers.

Audioscript

My name's Anita Lloyd and I study at Keyworth Girls' school. I'd like to tell you about an unusual advertising campaign I was involved in thanks to a new role I've been given at school. At the beginning of last term, I was made Head Girl. That means I'm the official link between the teachers and students – representing the students' point of view on the school council, attending parents' evenings, and so on.

Anyway, the advertising story all started when I received a huge parcel one day at school. It was a great laugh opening it with my friends. We assumed it was going to be publicity from a bookshop or something, but it turned out to be from a record company. The box was full of stuff linked to a band called The Emissary. There were the usual posters, caps, that kind of thing, and a diary – that was special because it had my name on it in gold. They also supplied a link to some free downloads. Someone in my class had seen a video of the band and reckoned they were OK, so we put up the posters in the common room and I shared the link to the downloads.

From the internet, I found out that these parcels had been sent to 130 school students – all girls like me! The band's target audience is fifteen to nineteen-year-old girls, and *somehow* the recording label had decided we, these 130 schoolgirls, were *particularly* cool. If we liked The Emissary, others would like them too, was the theory. I wasn't so sure. I might have some influence on the twelve to fourteen-year-olds at school, but everyone in my year's fairly independent-minded. Though that's not how advertisers see things when it comes to teenage girls. For them, a personal recommendation is often much more effective than a glossy advertisement. And it's worth even more if that person is influential, like me!

Well, if they wanted to send me free stuff, I wasn't going to complain. But this is how their tactic was clever – manipulative, you could say. The posters were on the wall, everyone was wearing the caps, and we played The Emissary in the common room quite a lot. We were becoming fans whether we liked it or not!

Next I was sent a box of T-shirts to hand out because they wanted to use them to launch the band's first album. They were quite cool, actually! They also sent five tickets for the band's next live tour. I kept one for myself and offered the other four on Twitter. Some of the gigs were held in concert halls in other parts of the country, but my tickets were for one in a stadium not far from here.

The gig was unbelievable and the whole experience was fun. I didn't think about it too much until three weeks later, when I got a call from a London-based publicity agency. They had worked with The Emissary's label and wanted to talk about a new campaign. I was keen, but I discussed it with my parents before I said yes. With the record label promotion, everyone at school had known about it. That wasn't a problem, in fact from the label's point of view the campaign was a huge success, but now the ad agency want us to promote this clothing brand in secret. It's called 'undercover' advertising. We aren't even supposed to tell our closest friends. Now I'm not sure what to do. Part of me feels it's dishonest. But then they're offering a lot of money. They invited us to a launch event in London. I went with my mum and it was great watching the famous models walking up and down – though we didn't get to meet them. I did speak to lots of famous journalists though, which was very exciting. I must admit I'm tempted. What would you do if you were offered money to work in the glamorous world of advertising at my age?

Answers

1 head girl   2 record company   3 leather diary   4 15–19
5 a personal recommendation   6 manipulative
7 (fairly) large stadium   8 ad agency   9 undercover
10 journalists

3 In groups, students discuss the questions. In feedback, ask for a show of hands to find out who would or wouldn't work for the ad agency, and ask why.

SPEAKING   Opinions

🔵 Prepare for First for Schools

Speaking Part 2

Task description
This involves an individual 1-minute 'long turn' for each student with a brief 30-second response from the second student. In turn, students are given two photographs to talk about.

Tip
Make sure each student knows what is expected from them in each role, and for how long they must speak. It's important for students to listen actively to their partner and think of something to respond to.

1 🔵 Ask students to compare the photographs in pairs. Monitor as students do the task and then review any problem areas with the comparative as necessary. The Student Bs should then talk for around 30 seconds about their preferred shoes.

2 Set the task and monitor students as they talk about the photos. Check that each student is given the full time. Offer feedback as a class. You may want to ask selected pairs of students to model their answers to the class.

3 ▶ 3.04 Give students a couple of minutes to read the task, then tell students to listen to the discussion and answer the question. Play the recording and then check answers together. Do your students agree with Emma and Dan?

Audioscript

Emma: Where shall we start?

Dan: Let's start with TV commercials. I imagine that they're the most expensive way to advertise. You have to make the commercial, which means paying the actors and a film crew, a producer and an editor, plus the music and so on. Then you have to pay every time the commercial is broadcast.

Emma: I agree, but TV commercials can have a big impact. They can be very memorable.

Dan: Only if the audience watches TV. If you think about it, TV commercials are either for really valuable products – like cars – or something that people will buy a lot of.

Emma: That's true. What do you reckon about posters in the street?

Dan: I assume that they're cheaper to produce than TV ads and the good thing about posters is they last for a long time. So a poster might stay in the street for a month or two, and every time you walk past it you're reminded of the product.

Emma:	That's a good point. And a magazine ad's the same, because it seems to me that every time you flick through the magazine, you might see the ad. A magazine ad is quite permanent, and more personal too because you have it in your hands or in your home.
Dan:	What about online pop up ads?
Emma:	Well, as I see it, pop-up ads are a nuisance because they always appear when you're busy trying do something else.
Dan:	Yes, I get that. Suddenly you hear a voice and you're like, what's that? Then you realise it's the audio on a pop-up ad!
Emma:	Exactly. From the point of view of the company that's advertising, I guess they must work otherwise they wouldn't exist. Maybe they're a cheap option for advertisers?
Dan:	Maybe. What do you think of guerrilla marketing?
Emma:	It depends. To be honest, I don't like the sound of underground marketing very much. I get the impression that it's fairly uncommon though.
Dan:	Mmm. I reckon it's a bit scary! And frankly, body advertising sounds weird.
Emma:	Yes, but viral ads are cool.
Dan:	Yes, I guess a lot of videos you see on social media are viral ads of some kind. I don't care though, if I enjoy the video, it doesn't bother me if it's some kind of publicity.
Emma:	Yes. I get the feeling that viral ads must be the best value for companies.
Dan:	But only if the video or photo goes viral. If it doesn't, it could just be an expensive mistake.

Answer
viral ads

4 ▶3.05 Play the recording so that students can hear Emma and Dan using the phrases.

Audioscript and answers
Dan:	I imagine that they're the most expensive way to advertise.
Dan:	If you think about it, TV commercials are either for really valuable products – like cars – or something that people will buy a lot of.
Dan:	… the good thing about posters is that they last for a long time.
Emma:	It seems to me that every time you flick through the magazine, you might see the ad.
Emma:	Well, as I see it, pop-up ads are a nuisance …
Emma:	From the point of view of the company that's advertising, I guess they must work
Emma:	I get the impression that it's fairly uncommon though.
Dan:	I reckon it's a bit scary.

◐ Prepare for First for Schools
Speaking Part 3

Task description

This part is a two-way conversation between the students. The focus is on expressing and justifying opinions, exchanging ideas, agreeing/disagreeing, speculation and evaluation, etc. Students should maintain the interaction and try to reach a decision through negotiation.

Tip
Active listening is as important as the actual speaking in this section. Students need to understand the importance of listening to what their partner says, and reacting to and building on this.

5 ◐ Set the task in the book and give a time limit of four minutes. Ask one or two stronger pairs to model their dialogue for the class while other students listen and tick the phrases they hear in the *Prepare* box. How many of the different forms of advertising in the task did the pairs discuss?

Mixed ability
Put the pairs from exercise 5 into mixed-ability groups of four. Ask them to role play their conversation in pairs and to provide supportive feedback to each other. Students should pay attention to the length of the other pairs' response, the *Prepare* box language used and their use of comparative language.

Cooler
Put students into A and B pairs. Ask the A students to write the adjectives from this unit onto a set of cards, and the B students to do the same with the adverbs. Ask the A and B pairs to swap their cards. Give students one minute to write the matching adjective or adverb. Check answers as a class.

Project
Ask students to find their favourite advert from a magazine. In the following class, ask them to work in small groups and explain why they chose it and how they think it influences people. This activity can also be done with video clips, if you have access to the internet.

Teacher's resources
Student's Book
Grammar reference and practice page 163
Vocabulary list page 145
Video
Speaking Part 3
Workbook
Unit 16, pages 64–67
Go online for
- Pronunciation
- Progress test
- Achievement test
- Speaking test video worksheets
- Corpus tasks

Geography
Tourism

Learning objectives

- The students learn about the impact of mass tourism and the importance of national parks in conserving the environment.
- In the project stage, students produce a presentation about a national park in their own country.

Warmer

1 Write *tourism* on the board and ask students to think of three positive effects and three negative effects of tourism.

2 Ask students to work with a partner to explain their positive and negative effects. Ask them to choose two positive and two negative effects from their joint lists. Elicit some examples from the class.

1 Ask students to read the text to find out whether the author is in favour of or against mass tourism. Ask students to underline any arguments that are similar to the ones they came up with in the Warmer.

Answer
He is against it if measures are not taken to protect the natural environment.

2 These sentences largely focus on cause and effect. If you did the Warmer, ask students to discuss whether their ideas focused on just the effects or also the causes. If they didn't include the causes, tell them to look back and add these. Then ask students to read the text again and match the sentence halves. Check answers.

Fast finishers

Ask fast finishers to read the question at the end of the article. Tell them they should imagine they have read the text and want to respond. Ask them to write a two or three line response. Ask one or two students to read their responses out after checking answers to exercise 2.

Answers
1 d 2 f 3 a 4 e 5 c 6 b

3 Ask pairs or groups to discuss the questions. You could do the first one as an example to help generate ideas. If you haven't already clarified some of the vocabulary, you might want to explain *stimulate* (encourage something to develop) and *infrastructure* (basic services that a country needs, e.g. roads).

Possible answers
1 By bringing in money and creating new jobs.
2 To create roads, bridges, airports, hotels and shopping centres for tourists.
3 Rivers are sometimes diverted to keep them green, which can have a terrible effect on the area.
4 Large ugly buildings ruin the views.
5 It can cause animals to change their eating habits.

Extension activity

Ask students to think about tourism in their own country. Tell them to work with a partner and discuss:
1 Whether it is a benefit or not.
2 Which areas of the country have benefited the most.
3 Which areas have suffered the most.
4 Whether they would place limits on international tourists or not, and why.
Discuss some ideas as a class.

4 Ask students to look at the advert. Tell them that *bonny* is a Scottish English word meaning *beautiful*. Find out what students know about Scotland (see Cultural background) and ask them to discuss the question with a partner.

Cultural background
Scotland is part of the United Kingdom. Its capital city is Edinburgh, and its population is 5.3 million. Many tourists visit Scotland's two national parks (Cairngorms and Loch Lomond & the Trossachs), famous for their beautiful scenery, amazing wildlife and fun outdoor activities.

Possible answer
walk and see wildlife

5 ▶ **3.06** Tell students that they are going to listen to a podcast about the National Park. Elicit some ideas from students about the kind of information they will hear. Give them a couple of minutes to read the questions and then play the recording. Check answers as a class.

Answers

1 2002 **2** 28% **3** more than 50 **4** four million
5 Loch Lomond and the Trossachs can look forward to a successful future

6 ▶**3.07** Play the recording and ask students to make notes on what the numbers mean. Ask students to compare their notes with a partner before checking answers as a whole class. With weaker classes, write what the numbers refer to on the board in a jumbled order. Before listening, ask students to match the number with what it refers to, and then play the recording for students to check their answers.

Audioscript

Located in central Scotland, Loch Lomond and the Trossachs National Park is one of the largest nature parks in the British Isles, with a total area of one thousand eight hundred and sixty-five square kilometres. Established in 2002, this national park includes a variety of geographical features, including high mountains, rolling hills, and lowland plains.
About twenty-eight per cent of the park is covered by forest and woodlands, including two Forest Parks: Queen Elizabeth Park and Argyll Park. Another fifty-five per cent is dedicated to farming, most especially the raising of domestic livestock, such as cows and sheep.
Water is also an essential element of the natural surroundings in Loch Lomond and the Trossachs. There are more than fifty major rivers and twenty-two large lakes, or lochs, as they're called in Scotland. By far the largest of these is Loch Lomond, which covers a total area of some seventy-one square kilometres. It's the most extensive body of fresh water in Great Britain, as well as the heart of the national park.
Loch Lomond and the Trossachs National Park is also a busy community where more than fifteen thousand people live and work, and where more than four million tourists come to enjoy the magnificent scenery, and take part in a variety of recreational activities, on both land and water.

Answers

1 There are 22 lakes.
2 55% of the park is used for farming.
3 Loch Lomond is 71 km².
4 The park's area is 1,865 km².
5 15,000 people live and work there.

7 ▶**3.08** Play the recording for students to complete the park's goals. Check answers as a whole class.

Audioscript

When Loch Lomond and the Trossachs was first declared a national park, four main goals were established for its use and protection. These four goals were as follows:
'To conserve and promote the park's natural and cultural heritage', which includes the history and traditional customs of the park's inhabitants.
'To promote responsible, sustainable use of the area's natural resources', such as its water, forests and agricultural lands.
'To promote public understanding and enjoyment of the park', including recreational activities and responsible tourism.
And finally, 'To promote the social and economic development of local communities' to ensure their continued growth and success.
If these four goals continue to be met, Loch Lomond and the Trossachs can look forward to a bright and bonny future, as one of Britain's largest and most spectacular national parks.

Answers

1 conserve, cultural **2** responsible, natural
3 public, enjoyment **4** social, communities

Cooler

Ask students to decide whether they are largely in favour of or against mass tourism. Ask those in favour to sit on one side of the classroom and those against on the other. Ask them to work together to formulate their arguments. After a few minutes, put students into smaller groups, with opposing views represented. Ask them to present their arguments to each other and hold a mini-debate.

Project

This project can either be done in a class with computer access or set as homework. Ask students to carry out the research in groups, and then prepare a PowerPoint presentation. If your country has only a few natural parks, then allow students to choose ones from around the world. This will also help make the presentations more varied. Encourage the rest of the class to ask questions after each group has finished.

17 Making headlines

Unit profile

Vocabulary: The media; Phrasal verbs
Reading: An article about citizen journalism
Grammar: Conditionals (2): Mixed
Writing: A review (2)

Warmer

1 Tell students to imagine they are famous. Ask them to write sentences about what they would want to be famous for, what they would like most about the fame and what they would like least.

2 Ask students to share their ideas in groups. Are there any similarities or differences in their attitudes to the pros and cons of being famous? Do they think it's easier to become famous now than it was in the past? Discuss some ideas as a class.

Your profile

If possible, write or display some of the news headlines from this week on the board. Try to include a mixture, e.g. some world events, some local events and some which involve celebrities. Ask students to discuss what they know about each story and the two questions from the Student's Book. You could also find out what other stories students are aware of.

VOCABULARY   The media

1 Invite students to offer definitions for any of the words and phrases in bold that they already know, and then ask students to complete the exercise individually. Emphasise that they shouldn't do the quiz themselves at this stage and that they will get a chance to do so later. Tell them to compare their answers with a partner before whole-class feedback.

Answers
1 i 2 a 3 f 4 g 5 h 6 c 7 b 8 d 9 e

2 ▶3.09 Tell students that they are going to listen to four extracts from the news. They should note down their answers using an '-ing' form as their first word, e.g. *chilling out*. Play the recording, pausing after each speaker if necessary, and then ask students to compare their answers with a partner before whole-class feedback.

Audioscript

Narrator: One
Speaker: There is growing interest tonight in reports that Alex Turner, the winner of last year's NuVoices competition, is planning a new album with the bestselling Spanish singer Elena Vilanova. There have been rumours that these two stars of R'n'B will be performing together at the Attitude Festival later in the month. Unconfirmed reports suggest that Alex and Elena are keen to work together, so we could be looking at the next great singing partnership …

Narrator: Two
Speaker 1: Hey, listen to this: 'Larsson and Dixon, at the Astoria'.
Speaker 2: Larsson and Dixon? Isn't that the DJ set you went to see last week?
Speaker 1: Exactly. 'An extraordinary return to form', it says here. 'Maddy Dixon serves up a treat for drum-and-bass fans with a breathtaking set of new material, mixed in with golden oldies dating right back to 2003. Now playing full-time with the Swedish drum-and-bass DJ Larsson, their set started off with tracks taken from the joint 2013 album 'I.R.U' before going back to their roots of ten years ago …'

Narrator: Three
Speaker: Making NBA history tonight, the Chicago Bulls beat the Detroit Pistons in a convincing one thirty-five to seventy-four victory, the Bulls' ninth win unopposed this season. The Detroit team have suffered with several key players off due to injuries, but even at full strength, nothing could have stopped the Bulls at The Palace this evening …

Narrator: Four
Speaker: Also in today's news, an eighty-year old Japanese man has become the oldest person to climb Mount Everest. Yuichiro Miura, who had already climbed Everest aged seventy and seventy-five, said he was exhausted. He described his feelings on reaching the summit of Everest at his age by saying, 'one can never be happier.' Mr Miura made the climb with his son Gota, who has represented his country twice skiing in the Olympic Games.

Answers
1 keeping you amused
2 reviewing a performance
3 keeping you up to date
4 celebrating an achievement

3 Ask students to do the quiz and to then write an additional sentence about the purpose of the media. In feedback, ask students for their additional sentences. They can rank the purposes of the media in order, according to how important they think they are.

Extension activity

Find four or five headlines from other famous news stories this year, and make a set for each group of four students. Cut the headlines into individual words and then ask students to reconstruct them. Check answers and discuss what students remember about each story.

READING

1 Ask students to look at the title and the photos. What do they understand by the term *citizen journalist*? If they have never heard it before, ask them if they can guess what it means (a member of the public who collects, distributes and comments on news, especially using the internet). They then read the whole text quickly. Give students just one minute to find the answer. Giving a short time limit is useful to get students to focus on the main idea of a text, rather than specific details, such as the meaning of individual words. Check answers as a class.

Answer

2

2 Do this exercise together as a whole class. Elicit the type of word that students think belongs in the gap and why. Remind them that their knowledge of affixes will help them greatly with this type of task and that sometimes the clue to the type of word that is missing comes 'after' the gap.

Answer

The answer needs to be a noun as it is part of a list containing other nouns (*news*, *reviews*).

● Prepare for First for Schools

Reading and Use of English Part 3

Task description

The focus of this task is word formation, in particular the use of affixation, internal changes and compounding. Students are given a text with eight gaps. Each gap corresponds to a word. Students are given the stem of the missing word which they must change to form the missing word.

Tip

Ask students to brainstorm all of the forms of the words in brackets that they know before deciding on which one would fit best.

3 ● Before setting the task, brainstorm the different forms of each word in capitals and get students to think about the type of word required for each gap. If you have students preparing for the First For Schools exam, set a strict time limit of ten minutes. Check answers.

Answers

1 continuous 2 organisations 3 professionals 4 extent
5 unbelievably 6 situation 7 variety 8 certainty

4 Invite students to read the questions first and offer answers to any that they think they already know the answers to but do not confirm yet whether they are correct or not. They then read the text and answer the questions individually and compare their answers with those that have already been offered. Tell them to discuss their answers with a partner before whole-class feedback.

Answers

1 extremely disappointed
2 He turned the disappointment of the lack of information into an opportunity to do some real-life citizen journalism.
3 He might have felt nervous about not speaking Mandinka, happy to meet his parents' friends and excited about investigating the music scene.
4 They would probably have been very impressed as it was 'unlike anything a student had prepared before'.
5 It was a very important step in starting his career as a journalist.

5 In pairs, students look at the highlighted words and offer definitions/synonyms for those they know already or those they can work out from the context. Still in their pairs, they do the exercise to check the meanings of all the words. Check answers as a whole class.

Fast finishers

Ask fast finishers to create their own sentences using three of the highlighted words. Elicit these example sentences after checking answers to exercise 5.

Extension activity

Ask students to tell a partner about their response to the article's title. Do they think they could be a citizen journalist? Why / why not? What equipment and skills would they need? Discuss some ideas as a class.

Answers

1 tricky 2 dynamic 3 overseas 4 obsessed 5 live
6 entire

EP Word profile

Ask students to write a follow-up phrase or sentence to each example to help explain the meaning, e.g. *The milk I bought yesterday was out of date.* Then set the exercise on page 137.

Answers

1 dates back 2 out of date 3 dates from 4 up to date
5 out of date 6 up to date 7 date back 8 date from

Ask students to work in small groups. Monitor and give positive feedback for interesting ideas. Tell students they need at least three advantages and three disadvantages for the first question. Bring the class together and invite two or three students to make suggestions. For each advantage, ask students to suggest a disadvantage. If they are struggling with ideas during the preparation stage, suggest some areas to think about, e.g. quality of reporting, analysis, reliability, background knowledge.

Cooler

Tell students to work in pairs and to write five questions related to music. For example, *What is the most popular form of music in your country?*, *In what ways do people listen to music these days?*, etc. When they have finished, they should ask their questions to another pair. Ask if there were any questions that students couldn't answer. If there were, ask the pairs who wrote those questions to read them aloud to the class to see if anyone can answer them.

GRAMMAR   Conditionals (2): Mixed

1 Books closed. Write the first sentence on the board, then ask the concept checking questions underneath, ask students to explain their answers rather than simply eliciting a *yes* / *no* answer. This will require them to think more deeply about the use and form of the conditionals. We can use *if it + wasn't / weren't / hadn't been + for* to show that one thing changes the situation completely, as in sentence 1 (e.g. *If it weren't for my mum, I would never have applied for the job*). Books open. Students look at the second sentence and then check answers as a class. Again, encourage them to explain their answers.

Answers
1 No; Yes 2 Yes; Yes

2 Ask students to match the answers to the rules individually and then check answers. Extend the task by asking students to write another example using each structure. Elicit an example of each and write it on the board as a model for the students (e.g. *I wouldn't play the piano now if my dad hadn't taught me as a child*; *If it weren't for my teachers, I wouldn't have passed my exam*).

Answers
1 b 2 a

→ **Grammar reference Student's Book page 164**

3 Do the first one as an example and then tell students to complete the exercise individually. Monitor and provide help as necessary, reminding students to ask themselves if each is a real or imaginary situation and whether it refers to the past or the present. With weaker students, you may like to give them the first half of the sentence for them to complete, or perhaps read out the entire sentences with the books closed before students begin this exercise. Ask students to compare their answers with a partner before whole-class feedback.

Answers
1 wouldn't have understood; didn't speak
2 wasn't; would have locked
3 'd brought; wouldn't be
4 wouldn't have passed; weren't
5 would be; hadn't missed

4 Books closed. Model the example question on the board. Tell students to open their books and to complete the exercise with a partner. You could offer more support for weaker students by giving them the first few words of each sentence in the correct order. Check answers.

Answers
1 if they hadn't invented it, how would life be different?
2 where would you have gone on holiday last summer if you were (a millionaire)?
3 if you had already left, where would you live?
4 how would you communicate with your friends if they hadn't become popular?

5 In pairs, students discuss these questions. Elicit some responses for each one from different students.

Fast finishers

Ask fast finishers to write two more questions similar to those in exercise 4. Monitor and help with grammar and vocabulary as needed. Students can ask and answer their questions with their partner. When checking answers to exercise 5, ask two or three students to report back on their questions and answers.

Corpus challenge

Ask students to correct the sentence and to explain the error (the third conditional is needed here as the sentence speculates about past events).

Answer
The book's OK, but if you had seen it on television you would like it much more.

VOCABULARY Phrasal verbs

1 Match the first sentence as an example and then ask students to complete the exercise individually. Check answers. Extend the task by asking students to define the phrasal verbs with a partner (see Answers). Elicit a definition for each one and check whether all students agree with each definition.

Answers
1 b (make someone understand something)
2 a (take further action) 3 e (raise) 4 h (learn about)
5 c (not include) 6 f (support) 7 g (solve) 8 d (examine)

2 If you have already looked at the definitions of the phrasal verbs, this exercise should be straightforward. Do the first one together as an example and then set the rest as an individual task. Check answers. If students haven't defined the phrasal verbs, take the opportunity to define any that they struggle with.

Answers
1 catching up on 2 brought up 3 get across 4 leave out
5 clear up 6 look into 7 back you up 8 follow up

3 Ask students to work in pairs and to write eight sentences using the eight phrasal verbs. Tell students at least three of the sentences should be questions. Monitor and help as needed. Elicit some example sentences, and then ask pairs to work with another pair to ask and answer their questions.

Extension activity
Ask students to read their sentences aloud to another pair, but without saying the phrasal verb. The other pair should guess what the missing phrasal verb is. Share any challenging ones as a class.

WRITING   A review (2)

1 Give students a minute to read the text under the photo and then ask them to discuss the questions in pairs. Ask them to think about the age of people the review is aimed at. Elicit ideas from different pairs.

Answers
1 teenagers who are into writing, art and photography
2 The style is lively. *Are you into, tired of, check out, full of, interesting, amazing*

2 Ask students to think about what they already know about reviews from their work in Unit 13, and then ask them to read the texts and discuss the questions with their partner. Elicit ideas from different pairs.

Answers
1 B
2 B. This style is more appealing to readers.

3 Ask students to read the *Prepare* box and then, as a whole class, underline one example of each feature in review B. Tell students to complete the exercise individually. Check answers.

Answers
a stuffed full of, makes a nice change, love its style, And the best thing is, look out for it
b Do publishers really think we only want to read trivial gossip? Who wants to read poems aimed at children?
c get across, let down, stand out, look out for
d As we know, I know you'll, use of 'we' and 'us'

4 Ask students to think of their favourite news website. Monitor and help with ideas, organisation and vocabulary. They should make short notes based on each of the bullet points in the task. Ask one or two students to share their plans with the rest of the class. Alternatively, students could compare their ideas in small groups. Then ask individual students to make sure they have notes for each of the four bullet points.

Mixed ability
Put students in mixed-ability pairs or small groups to brainstorm ideas, before asking them to work on their plan individually.

⬤ Prepare for First for Schools
Writing Part 2
Task description
In Part 2, students have a choice of task. They may be asked to write an article, an email or letter, a review or a story. They are given a clear context, topic, purpose and target reader. Students should write 140–190 words.

Tip
Make sure students are aware that who they are writing for is important in terms of register, and that this will affect their choice of grammar and vocabulary.

5 ⬤ If you have students preparing for the First For Schools exam, set a strict time limit of 40 minutes. Ask students to look at their partner's review and to check it against the instructions in the Student's Book. They should check it for informal phrases, friendly tone, direct questions and phrasal verbs, as well as for all the listed bullet points.

Extension activity
Ask students to read each other's reviews and to find a website they do not know well. For homework, ask them to visit the website and decide whether they think their partner's review was accurate or not.

Sample answer

CAN'T COOK? SURE YOU CAN!

I came across the website *Cooking 4 Teens* by chance a month ago and I immediately bookmarked it as one of my favourites. It's aimed at teenagers who have very little experience of cooking and it introduces you to life in the kitchen in a fun way. The website has loads of useful information about the basics of cooking and tips on how to use different ingredients. What's more, new recipes are posted every week, with several vegetarian dishes featured. All of the recipes are presented in a really cool way, with great photos and even video clips showing the dishes being made.

If you're interested in finding out about different styles of cooking, such as Italian, Asian, and Mexican, you'll pick up lots of new ideas here. There are also interesting articles by top chefs and cookery writers, and a careers section for anyone who is thinking of training as a chef.

Check it out soon – you won't regret it!

Cooler

Ask students to work in small groups to discuss ideas for a website. What kind of website would they like to design? Each group should choose one idea to present to the class. Take a class vote on the most interesting one.

Project

Tell students to sketch out ideas for their own website, including what they would have on each page. Ask them to produce a poster to showcase it. In the following class, ask students to display their posters around the room for other students to read. Students could then choose one of these websites to review.

Teacher's resources

Student's Book

Grammar reference and practice page 164

Vocabulary list page 146

Video

The news

Workbook

Unit 17, pages 68–71

Go online for

- Pronunciation
- Video extra worksheet
- Corpus tasks

18 Start-up

Unit profile

Vocabulary: The world of work; Word pairs
Reading: A blog post
Grammar: Uses of verb + -ing
Listening: An interview
Speaking: Agreeing and disagreeing

Warmer

1 Write these jobs on the board: *astronaut*, *lawyer*, *beautician*, *plumber*, *web designer.*

2 Ask students to work in pairs. Tell them to discuss what it would be like to do each of these jobs and which they would like to do, and why. Elicit ideas from different pairs.

Your profile

Ask students to discuss the questions in pairs and elicit ideas for each question. If a number of students have had summer jobs, ask them to describe their jobs to the class. Then hold a vote on which ones sound like the best and worst jobs.

Cultural background

In the UK, many students undertake a short period of work experience as part of the school curriculum, when they are aged 16–18. Their schools help them organise work experience for a week or more with a local employer. This could be in an office, school, warehouse, hospital, etc. Students are encouraged to apply for work placements in areas which may interest them in their future career. The benefits of the work experience are to improve students' employability and their key skills, in particular with regard to risk assessment, working with others and ICT skills, and to develop their personal and social development, for example their maturity, motivation, interpersonal skills and self-confidence.

VOCABULARY   The world of work

1 Before students do the exercise, put them into pairs and give them one minute to think of as many jobs as possible. Alternatively, give them more time and the challenge of completing an A–Z of jobs (e.g. *astronaut*, *builder*, *cab driver*). Then ask students to complete the exercise in pairs and elicit ideas for each one.

Possible answers
a make up artist **b** diplomat **c** entrepreneur **d** teacher
e designer **f** banker **g** artist **h** nurse **i** accountant
j builder

2 In pairs, students discuss what jobs they think are being shown in each picture. Tell students to think about the qualities needed for the jobs pictured. Accept any answers with a logical explanation.

Possible answers
a design/advertising – they seem to be discussing some artwork (creative)
b building site (manual work)
c travel agent (opportunities for foreign travel)
d teacher/lecturer (personally rewarding)
e doctor (professional)
f artist (being your own boss)

3 ▶ 3.10 Ask students what kind of job they would like to do when they leave school. Tell them they will hear three people talking about their plans, and ask them to take notes. Play the recording and discuss students' answers, which may vary. If necessary, pause the recording after each speaker to give students time to write notes.

Audioscript
Narrator: One. Sara.
Sara: I don't mind deadlines, but I want a balance between work and my social life. Life outside work will always be important to me so I'd like a job with flexible working hours. I don't want a job that means working shifts or anything that might mean I can never see my friends. I don't really see myself working in a boring office or anything like that. I want to be my own boss. I'd like to have my own company, something to do with design, something creative that's also personally rewarding.
Narrator: Two. Dan.
Dan: I'd like something that involves working with my hands, something manual, in a way. I don't mean something repetitive – I'd get bored very quickly doing the same thing over and over again. I definitely can't imagine doing lots of paperwork – I hate that kind of thing. And I don't want to feel stressed. I wouldn't enjoy anything that involved meeting deadlines. That would start to stress me out. I'd also like to have a job where I can take lots of time off.
Narrator: Three. Emma.
Emma: I really want something that challenges me. So, my dream job needs to be demanding, something professional, you know, like a lawyer, doctor or something like that. It needs to be well-paid too, and I'm a sociable person, so I think I'd be good at dealing with people, and sorting out their problems. That's the kind of stuff I'm good at. I'd also like a job that gives me opportunities for foreign travel. That would be cool.

Possible answers

Sara: jewellery making. She doesn't want to work shifts and she doesn't want to work in an office. She would like to do something creative, with flexible working hours.
Dan: construction. He wants to work with his hands and doesn't want to do a lot of paperwork or work to deadlines.
Emma: medicine. She wants a demanding and well-paid job, that involves helping other people.

4 ▶ **3.10** Play the recording again for students to make a list of the different aspects. Tell them to compare their answers with a partner before checking as a class.

Answers

Sara: flexible working hours, working shifts, have my own company, personally rewarding
Dan: working with my hands, manual, feel stressed, meeting deadlines, take lots of time off
Emma: well-paid, professional, opportunities for foreign travel

5 Take a class vote to find out which person most students are like. Discuss the question as a class. Students could rank the aspects which are important for them in order from most to least important.

READING

● Prepare for First for Schools
Reading and Use of English Part 5

Task description
Part 5 is a multiple-choice task. The text is followed by six four-option multiple-choice questions. It focuses on detail, opinion, attitude, tone, purpose, main idea, gist, meaning from context, implication and text organisation features (e.g. exemplification and reference).

Tip
Encourage students to read the options quickly first and then the text to help them identify the information.

1 ● Tell students that Thelma's blog post is about her future career plans. Ask them to scan it to find the answers to the questions. If you have students preparing for the First for Schools exam, then set a strict time limit of ten minutes. Students should identify the key words in the questions before scanning the text. They may like to find their own answer to the question before looking at the options and then choosing the one closest to their own answer. Ask students to compare their answers in pairs before checking together.

Fast finishers

Ask fast finishers to underline any new vocabulary in the text and to look it up in a dictionary. After checking answers to exercise 1, ask fast finishers to read the definitions out loud to the class, but tell them not to name the word. The rest of the class should try to find the words in the text.

Mixed ability

You could set additional reading tasks for this text for different students, depending on their ability. Tell weaker students that they are student A, and ask them to read the text again and to underline anything they find interesting. Tell slightly stronger students that they are student B, and ask them to use their dictionaries to find the meaning of any new words. Tell the strongest students that they are student C, and ask them to write a short summary of the text. For feedback, put one student from each group together to share their tasks.

Answers

1 C – Thelma raises lots of questions about her future in the first paragraph and says that *the only thing that's clear to me…*, which supports C and rules out A. Options B and D, though plausible, are not suggested in the paragraph.
2 A – The phrase *make it* means *be successful*.
3 C – Although Thelma recognises that investment banking offers a high salary, it would not satisfy her need for a job with flexible working hours and she would not find it rewarding. A is wrong as we know she is good at economics and maths; B is not supported by the text in terms of being *physically* demanding; and D is not suggested in the text.
4 D – Thelma's father *talks about being passionate about whatever you do* and her mother *holds the same view*. Although qualifications are mentioned, A is wrong as they are not stated in relation to Thelma; B is not suggested; and C is ruled out because her father has no regrets about his career choices.
5 D – The answer is supported by the last two sentences of the fifth paragraph. A is tempting because of the reference to *six months ago we might have laughed at them* but it is wrong because Thelma states she is now *jealous* of her friends' plans; B is not suggested by the text; and C is wrong because she clearly does understand both professions.
6 B – A is wrong because she has not been offered any work experience yet; C is wrong because she recognises she would have to borrow money to fund a course; and D is wrong because although she is considering journalism and has been *researching courses*, she hasn't applied for anything.

EP **Word profile**

Books closed. Write *balance* on the board and tell students to write an example sentence using it. Books open. Ask students to compare their sentence with the ones in the book, and to identify any with a similar meaning and use. Then set the exercise on page 138.

Answers

1 c   2 e   3 a   4 b   5 d

Cooler

Ask students to discuss these questions with a partner: *Do you have a career plan? What are your best subjects at school and what jobs do they lead to? What do your parents think is the most important thing about your career?* Elicit some ideas from each pair and open the discussion up to the whole class.

GRAMMAR Uses of verb + -ing

1 Books closed. Write 'I enjoy swimming in the sea on holiday' on the board. Ask students why you have used the form *swimming* (verb + -ing follows certain verbs such as *admit, avoid, deny, enjoy, miss, recommend, suggest*, etc.). Books open. Ask them to look at sentence 1 and then match it to the correct rule (c). Students then do the rest of the matching individually. Then check answers as a whole class. Elicit a further example for each rule and write it on the board.

Answers
1 c 2 e 3 d 4 b 5 a 6 f

→ **Grammar reference Student's Book page 165**

2 Do this exercise as a whole class. Ask students to spell each word to make it more challenging. Remind them that verbs ending in e usually drop the e when -ing is added.

Answers
1 changing 2 creating 3 Cooking 4 tasting 5 working
6 being

3 Ask students to work in pairs to find and correct the mistakes. Check answers.

Answers
1 test → testing
2 receive → receiving
3 sell → selling
4 do → doing
5 see → seeing
6 be → being
7 hope → hoping
8 given → giving
9 contained → containing

4 Ask students to complete the sentences individually. Then ask them to read them aloud in small groups. The other group members should ask follow-up questions. Encourage them in particular to ask 'Why' questions and to ask other students to justify their opinions, where appropriate. Ask students to feed back any particularly interesting discussion points.

Extension activity

Ask students to write questions based on the sentence stems in exercise 4. For example, *Why can't you stand eating in fast food restaurants?* Then tell them to work in different groups to the previous task and ask and answer each other's questions.

Corpus challenge

Ask students to correct the sentence and to explain the error. (We use verb + -ing after *recommend*.)

Answer
I would strongly recommend visiting our annual festival.

VOCABULARY Word pairs

1 Write the first example on the board to demonstrate the word pairs. Then ask students to complete the exercise individually. Check answers.

Answers
1 d 2 e 3 b 4 c 5 a

2 Tell students to complete the exercise individually and then ask students to compare their answers with a partner before whole-class feedback. Invite students to think of more word pairs they know and write these on the board (e.g. *body and soul, nice and easy, pros and cons, rise and fall*).

Fast finishers

Ask fast finishers to write three sentences about themselves using the word pairs. Tell them to share their sentences with their partner and ask questions to find out more information about each one.

Answers
1 now, then 2 round, round 3 Sooner, later 4 more, less
5 up, down 6 more, more 7 one, two 8 over, over

LISTENING

1 Ask students to briefly discuss in pairs what kind of business they would have if they could set up their own company. Then give students just one minute to do the exercise to simulate exam conditions. Remind them that underlining key words in exam questions is a very useful exam strategy, as it helps them to concentrate on the key information needed.

Possible answers
1 Aiden, idea, T-shirt business, parents, neighbours, selling T-shirts, profitable
2 problem, ran out of space, weren't enough good T-shirts, too long to repair

3 now, brother, designs, imports, other countries, original designs
4 paperwork, looking for someone, wishes he were better, does it himself
5 hardest, school, work, doesn't do his best, business more interesting, school, flexible
6 friends, useful suggestions, fed up, don't take much notice
7 summer jobs, hard work, success, deal with people, money

● Prepare for First for Schools

Listening Part 4

Task description

The focus of this multiple-choice task is on identifying opinion, attitude, detail, gist, main idea and specific information. Students hear an interview or exchange between two speakers, and answer seven three-option multiple-choice questions.

Tip

Remind students of the importance of synonyms or near synonyms in this task type.

2 ▶ 3.11 ● Play the recording for students to answer the questions, but do not check answers at this stage.

Audioscript

Interviewer: Our guest today is Aiden Cass, the seventeen-year-old behind Unique Tees, an online T-shirt business that's made quite an impact in just a few years. So how did it all start, Aiden?

Aiden: At fifteen, I desperately wanted a new computer – a pretty expensive one, so I started up a business collecting stuff from neighbours, things they were going to throw out, and then selling it online. There was no shortage of stuff, but one thing I noticed was that <u>cool T-shirts attracted a lot of interest and often sold for good prices</u>. Chatting to my dad, I mentioned if I could just sell T-shirts, I'd be earning a fortune. He agreed and offered to help.

Interviewer: But now you sell new T-shirts. What happened?

Aiden: Well, at first I started advertising for unwanted T-shirts. I soon had hundreds of them – at one point our garage was completely full. But quality was an issue. Stains that couldn't be removed, holes that were impossible to fix. People tend to keep their favourite – and often coolest – T-shirts until they fall apart. <u>But above all, the majority were just boring. I'd spend hours sorting through them and only find a few I could actually sell</u>. I'd also end up with piles of T-shirts I couldn't get rid of.

Interviewer: So, you changed your approach? What happens now?

Aiden: Yes, at first we tried importing old T-shirts from abroad. We had some success, but getting them delivered wasn't cheap. Then my brother pointed out that thousands of people are designing cool logos and putting them on the web. So why not

use those? On new T-shirts, of course. He's into design, so he found some great sources online. <u>I contacted various designers and they agreed, for a share of the profit, to let us use their designs.</u>

Interviewer: Does that involve a lot of paperwork? Contracts, for example?

Aiden: Sometimes. I used to spend every Friday night catching up with paperwork and I found it quite hard by myself. Nowadays my parents help me out a lot, especially with the financial side of the business. <u>I'm advertising for an assistant though, as my parents have jobs too and they'd like their weekends back!</u>

Interviewer: How do you balance your business with other priorities? School, for example.

Aiden: I go to an online school, which means I can take lessons at almost any time, even when I'm travelling. <u>But I won't pretend that the business hasn't had an impact on my education. It has. Sometimes I've missed a few homework deadlines, just because I've been too tired or I haven't been able to get interested in the subject.</u> It's more difficult to ignore work. If I do, I end up with hundreds of emails from dissatisfied customers!

Interviewer: How have people around you reacted to your success?

Aiden: My teachers are happy as long as my schoolwork is OK. <u>To be honest, I try not to talk about it with my friends much. Those that know aren't actually that interested, really.</u> Though they sometimes complain about it when I can't go out because I'm too busy. My family are a different matter of course. They're always giving me helpful ideas.

Interviewer: Had you had any experience of business before you started your company? A summer job, for example?

Aiden: From a young age, I always had summer jobs. They weren't necessarily interesting and often involved a lot of hard work for not much money! I was happy with anything then! But <u>interacting with adults gave me a lot of 'people' skills.</u> I was always persuading people to let me cut their lawn or clean their car. That kind of thing's been really useful with the business now.

Answers

Refer also to the underlined parts of the script above.

1 C – A is wrong because although he chatted to his dad about selling T-shirts, it was Aiden who had the idea; B is ruled out as he says there *was no shortage of stuff.*
2 B – A is wrong because although he admits that *at one point, our garage was completely full*, there is no suggestion that he ran out of space; C is wrong because the mention is of T-shirts being *impossible to fix.*
3 C – A is incorrect because the brother only pointed out cool designs on the web; B is wrong because although Aiden used to import T-shirts, he no longer does this.
4 A – B is not suggested and C is wrong because his parents *help me out a lot.*
5 A – B is not suggested and C is wrong because the online school he attends is very flexible.

6 C – A is wrong because it is his family who give him useful suggestions and B is ruled out because it is only *sometimes* that Aiden can't see his friends, when he is busy.

7 B – A is not stated and C is ruled out because the jobs he did were for *not much money*.

3 ▶3.11 Play the recording again for students to check their answers. Then check answers as a whole class. If necessary, explain why answers are correct and why the distraction is not correct.

SPEAKING Agreeing and disagreeing

1 In pairs, students decide what job each photo illustrates and discuss the questions. Elicit some advantages and disadvantages for each job. Then take a vote to find out the most and least popular jobs.

2 ▶3.12 Play the recording and ask students to answer the three questions. Remind them of the importance of turn-taking and asking opinions in both general communication and in speaking exams.

Audioscript

Paul: The best thing about working in a fast food restaurant is that you might get some free food!

Ana: I'm not sure about that! A friend of mine did it for a summer. She says that by the end of the first week, she didn't want to see another chip in her life again. And that her clothes always smelled of greasy fried food.

Paul: Ugh! That's horrible.

Ana: Stacking shelves is pretty repetitive, but you might be able to listen to music while you're doing it.

Paul: I bet they wouldn't let you do that. Personally, I can't really see the point of doing this kind of work. You're hardly learning anything.

Ana: I'm with you on that.

Paul: Working in a shop is probably quite well-paid for a summer job and it isn't particularly demanding. One of the best jobs here, I reckon. What do you think?

Ana: I'm not convinced. Firstly, you'd have to dress smartly every day and you'd spend most of the day folding clothes.

Paul: And you'd have to look happy while you were doing it!

Ana: Yes!

Paul: To me, babysitting feels like the least demanding job. As long as you don't get disturbed by the children, you can just watch TV! What do you reckon?

Ana: Absolutely! The bad thing is, you'll usually be working in the evenings. And that means, no going out.

Paul: That's a good point. Maybe …

Ana: I reckon that being a waiter is quite hard work, especially when the restaurant's busy. And you probably get difficult customers sometimes, which wouldn't be much fun.

Paul: I agree up to a point but it's also good to get some experience of working under pressure.

Ana: Fair enough. I guess lots of us will have to deal with pressure at work at some stage.

Answers

1 All of them except the cleaner.

2 Yes, they do.

3 Paul asks 'What do you think?' and 'What do you reckon?'

3 ▶3.12 Set the task in the book and then play the recording for students to check their answers.

Answer
P: That's a good point, I can't really see the point of, I agree up to a point, but
A: I'm with you on that, Absolutely, Fair enough, I'm not so sure about that, I'm not convinced

4 ⬤ If you have students preparing for the First for Schools exam, set a four-minute time limit for this task. Afterwards ask one or two pairs to model their dialogues to the class. Remind students to take turns, ask each other's opinions and use the phrases from the *Prepare* box.

Extension activity
Put students into groups of six. Ask them to discuss the questions in exercise 4 again, but this time each person should talk for no longer than twenty seconds at a time. The person to their right should respond or ask a question within five seconds of the person finishing. If a person speaks for too long or reacts too slowly, then they are eliminated until one person is left.

Cooler
Tell students to imagine that they will never have to work. Put them into small groups and ask them to discuss how this would make them feel and what the advantages and disadvantages would be. Elicit some ideas from each group.

Project
Students should use the internet to research the job they would like to do in the future. Ask them to find out what qualifications they need, what skills and qualities are required, what the average salary is, and what the advantages and disadvantages of the job are. In groups, they should present their findings in the following class.

Teacher's resources
Student's Book
Grammar reference and practice page 165
Vocabulary list page 146
Video
Jobs
Speaking Part 4
Workbook
Unit 18, pages 72–75
Go online for
- Pronunciation
- Progress test
- Video extra worksheet
- Speaking test video worksheets
- Corpus tasks

Culture
Fair play

Warmer

1 Read out the following situations and ask students to write notes about their reaction to each one:

Someone scores a goal with their hand in a football match.
Someone dives to win a penalty.
Someone takes performance-enhancing drugs.
Someone uses illegal equipment to make their racing car faster.

2 Ask students to discuss their reactions in small groups before discussing as a whole class.

3 Tell students to discuss this question with a partner: *Is it ever OK to cheat? Why / why not?*

1 Ask different students to describe what is happening in each photo. Then ask students to discuss with a partner whether the people are behaving appropriately or not. Find out in which pictures students think the people are behaving inappropriately and why.

2 Ask students to scan the text to find the two rules. Then ask them to discuss with a partner what they think each rule means.

Extension activity

1 Ask students if they think it's right or wrong to argue with a referee. Then ask them why they think so many footballers argue with the referee.

2 Give students the following strategies for dealing with conflict and ask them to put them into the categories of *stop*, *listen* and *respond*.
Stop
Stay open-minded, intending to make the situation better.
Don't argue, accuse, or tell them to calm down.
Listen
Receive other people's comments without interruption. Show empathy and use statements carefully.
Respond
Remain calm and keep your language short and simple.
It is better to say: *I need* or *We need* rather than *You must* or *You have to*.

3 Ask students to discuss what they think is the best advice and to add two more pieces of advice to the list. Discuss ideas with the whole class.

Answers
Respect others and Respect the sport

3 Give students time to read the charter. Ask them to underline the most important point, and discuss their ideas as a class. Do students agree on the most important point?

Mixed ability
Put students into mixed-ability pairs. Ask one student to read numbers 1–6, and one to read numbers 7–11. They should choose the most important one in their section, and then compare and decide which one of the two they have chosen is the most important.

4 Ask students to discuss the questions in pairs or small groups. Then ask different groups to report back on their ideas for each question.

5 ▶ **3.13** Tell students they are going to listen to a conversation about two Fair Play Award winners. Give students a few minutes to read the statements and then play the recording. Tell students to correct the false sentences. Play the recording again, and check answers.

Audioscript
Boy: Have you ever heard of the Fair Play Awards?
Girl: Yes, I have. My tennis coach was talking about them last year. I think it's really important to reward people who show good sportsmanship.
Boy: I agree. Did you know that one of the first people to get one was Eugenio Monti?
Girl: That name sounds familiar. Wasn't he part of an Olympic bobsleigh team?
Boy: Yes, <u>for Italy</u>, at the 1964 Winter Olympics, in Austria.
Girl: And why did he get an award? For winning a gold medal?
Boy: No. Actually, <u>he got a Fair Play Award for helping other teams to win</u>.
Girl: How's that? I mean, what did he do?
Boy: Well, the British two-man team was missing a part for their bobsleigh, so they were going to drop out.
Girl: And what did Monti do?
Boy: <u>He lent them a spare part, and then they won the gold!</u> <u>Monti's own team came in third place</u>.
Girl: That was generous! I mean, his own team could have won the silver!
Boy: It's hard to believe, isn't it! And <u>then Monti helped the Canadian team in the four-man competition</u>. Their bobsleigh was damaged, and he helped them to repair it.

Girl: And did the Canadians win a medal too?

Boy: Yep, they won the gold! And Monti's team came in third place again.

Girl: Well, I can see why he won a Fair Play Award. It's a shame more people aren't like that now.

Boy: I don't know about that. There are lots of honourable athletes out there now. What about Miguel Indurain, for example?

Girl: The Spanish cyclist? Why? Has he won a Fair Play Award too?

Boy: Yes, but it wasn't for just one thing he did. He got a Fair Play award in 2004, but it was for his entire career in cycling.

Girl: Didn't he win the Tour de France, like three or four times?

Boy: Five times, actually, and in a row, from 1991 to 1995.

Girl: Oh, so why did he get an award then, if it wasn't for something special, like Monti?

Boy: Well, they say Indurain was famous for always being really respectful to other people, like his teammates and coaches, and even the people that he competed against.

Girl: Even when he lost?

Boy: Especially when he lost, apparently. He was just a good sport, all round, it seems.

Girl: Well, I suppose that's hard to do. I know I'm not a very good sport when I lose. I'm just too competitive!

Boy: I know! Believe me, I know!

Answers

1 False. He was competing for Italy.
2 True
3 False. His team came third.
4 False. He won it in 2004 but it was for his entire career.
5 False. He won it five times.
6 True

Extension activity

Ask students to work in small groups and discuss:
1 Which person they think was more deserving of the award and why?
2 How they feel about losing?
3 Whether they would help a competitor?

Discuss some ideas as a class.

6 ▶ **3.14** Tell students to complete the text individually. Ask students to compare their answers with a partner and then play the recording for them to check their answers.

Audioscript

In 2006, a Turkish girl named Hilal Coşkuner won a Fair Play Award for generosity towards a rival. Hilal was competing in a championship that she had a good chance of winning. However, when another girl fell down during the race, Hilal stopped to help her get up. In doing so, Hilal lost the race, but became a symbol of fair play.

For the Euro 2008 finals, the Union of European Football Associations (UEFA) launched the RESPECT campaign against racism. The campaign won a Fair Play Award for encouraging tolerance and for promoting respect for ethnic and cultural diversity. Since then, the campaign has continued to expand and grow in popularity.

Answers

1 generosity   2 championship   3 fell down   4 lost
5 symbol   6 launched   7 racism   8 encouraging
9 diversity   10 expand

Cooler

Ask students to work in small groups. Tell them to discuss these situations and what they would do:
1 The goalkeeper is on the floor injured and the goal is empty. Do you stop playing or do you score?
2 The umpire doesn't say you are out, but you know you should be. Do you stop playing or carry on?
3 You are the manager of a football team. Your team wins by a controversial goal. Do you say nothing and take the points or offer to play it again?
4 A player hears a whistle and picks up the ball thinking the game is over. The whistle was in the crowd and a penalty is given for handball. Do you score the penalty or miss it?

Ask each group to feed back to the class on a different situation.

Project

This will need to be set as homework for students to be able to do their research, unless you have access to the internet in your classroom. Ask students to research a person who demonstrates fair play. They should write up their biographies including the information asked for on page 107. In the following class, put students into small groups and tell them to read each other's biographies. Then ask them to decide who should win an award for fair play. Ask them to tell the rest of the class who they chose and why.

19 Points of view

Warmer

1 Write these sentence stems on the board:

  1 *I can't stand …*
  2 *I spend a lot of time …*
  3 *I don't think it's worth …*
  4 *I'm thinking of … one day.*

  and these topics: *vegetarianism, salaries of sports stars, banning mobile phones at school*

  Tell students to write sentences giving their opinion on the topics using the sentence stems.

2 Ask students to discuss their opinions in small groups. Elicit some views from the class and hold a brief whole-class discussion on the topics.

Your profile

In groups, students continue their discussion from the Warmer and lead into this discussion. In feedback, focus on issues that currently concern students.

VOCABULARY Opinions and beliefs

1 3.15 Ask students to work with a partner to take turns to describe what they can see in each picture. Then elicit a description for each picture from a different pair. Play the recording and ask students to match each extract to a picture. Check answers.

Audioscript

Narrator: One
Speaker 1: I really think that professional sportspeople are paid too much.
Speaker 2: I'm not sure. <u>You have to bear in mind that their careers are short</u>. Only the best are still involved at a competitive level by their mid-thirties.
Speaker 1: <u>I've never been convinced by that argument</u>. I mean, at the top, many of them earn more in six months than most people earn in their life. <u>They could, to my mind, easily get another job after playing</u>. Lots of people change jobs in their thirties.
Narrator: Two
Speaker 1: <u>Are you in favour of allowing mobile phones in schools</u>? I'm not!

Speaker 2: I think you have to keep an open mind about this. A ban isn't necessarily the best thing.
Speaker 1: <u>I'm totally against students using their phones at school</u>. Some people can't help checking them every five minutes. It can be really distracting for everyone.
Speaker 2: <u>I'd go along with that view</u>. But I'm still not sure a ban is the answer.
Narrator: Three
Speaker 1: So, <u>what are your views on vegetarianism</u>?
Speaker 2: <u>It's hard to deny that it must be better for you</u>. Some meat products are really bad for you – they've got so much fat in them. What about you? What do you think?
Speaker 1: <u>As far as I'm concerned, people just need to eat less meat</u>. Then their diets would be just as healthy.
Narrator: Four
Speaker 1: A lot of people say that being an adult is better than being a teenager.
Speaker 2: <u>I suspect this is true, to be honest</u>. As you grow up, there's so much more freedom.
Speaker 1: I agree up to a point. I mean, <u>there's no doubt that you're more independent when you're older</u>. But in many ways that means more responsibility, too. Work, money, things like that. <u>I firmly believe in enjoying yourself while you've got the chance</u>.

Answers
1 b 2 c 3 d 4 a

2 Match the first two sentences as an example and then ask students to complete the exercise individually. Do not check answers at this stage.

3 ▶3.15 Play the recording again for students to check their answers.

Answers
1 c 2 a 3 f 4 b 5 d 6 e 7 j 8 k
9 i 10 l 11 g 12 h

4 In pairs, students discuss the topics using the phrases from exercise 2. To make this exercise more fun, you could tell students to put the phrases onto cards. Students collect a card each time they use a phrase. The winner is the one with the most cards.

Extension activity

Give students some or all of these sentences. You could put them onto cards and cut them up, or write them on the board. Put students into small groups and ask them to discuss which ones they agree with and why. In feedback, elicit some ideas from the whole class.

a Animals shouldn't be used in medical research.
b Being an adult is better than being a teenager.
c It would be better for the planet if more people were vegetarians.
d Most people are not influenced by advertising.
e Students should have a right to use their mobile phones in class.
f Some professional sportspeople are paid too much.
g Young people care about the environment more than older people do.

EP Word profile

Ask students to write example sentences using each meaning of *mind*. Then set the exercises on page 138.

Answers

Exercise 1
1 to my mind 2 cross your mind 3 bear in mind
4 keep an open mind 5 put your mind to something
6 be in two minds
Exercise 2
1 bear in mind 2 to my mind 3 is in two minds
4 put my mind to 5 keeping an open mind
6 crossed my mind

READING

1 Before students read the text, ask them to discuss whether they think the statements in exercise 1 are true or false. Elicit which sentence students think is most likely to be true, and discuss why. Tell them to read the article and check their answer.

Answer

2

◐ Prepare for First for Schools

Reading and Use of English Part 6

Task description
Part 6 is a text from which six sentences have been removed and placed in jumbled order, together with an additional sentence, after the text. Students must decide from which part of the text the sentences have been removed. In this part, there is an emphasis on cohesion, coherence, and text structure.

Tip
This part typically tests understanding of structure and organisation, so encourage students to focus on synonyms and other referents.

2 ◑ Tell students to complete the exercise individually, and to then compare their answers with a partner. In feedback, ask students to explain their reason for choosing each sentence. Generally this should be due to the use of pronouns or synonyms.

Answers

1 G – the sentence following the gap reinforces the idea of teenage brains being *unique*.
2 E – the missing sentence outlines the experiment, with *Everyone* referring back to *teenagers and adults*, and the sentence after the gap gives the results of the study.
3 A – the word *area* in the missing sentence refers back to the part of the brain known as the frontal cortex.
4 F – the missing sentence refers to the researchers and what they *concluded*, which links to the sentence following the gap: *And that this might explain…*
5 B – the missing sentence links to the example of a *dramatic conclusion*, that playing video games or watching too much TV is *biologically unhealthy*.
6 D – the word *It* in the missing sentence refers back to *The brain* in the previous sentence.
Extra sentence: C

3 Ask students to work in pairs, and check answers as a whole class.

Fast finishers

Tell any fast finishers to look back at the text and underline any sentences they don't agree with. Then ask them to rewrite the sentences, changing the parts they don't agree with to statements that they do agree with. Elicit some examples after checking answers to exercise 3.

Answers

1 instant 2 controversial 3 complex 4 conflict
5 pattern 6 phase 7 go through 8 stress 9 observe

Talking points

In pairs, students discuss the questions. Ask them to think of three ways adults expect too much from teenagers, and discuss these as a class.

Cooler

Ask students to work in pairs and discuss what they think the phrase *Use it or lose it* means (if you don't practise a skill, you lose the ability to be able to do it). Then ask them to match this phrase to part of the text (*it matches best to the last paragraph*). Then get them to discuss what they do that they think helps to develop their brain, and in what areas they might be losing some of their skills or potential. Ask one or two pairs to feed back to the class.

GRAMMAR Subject-verb agreement

1 Set this as an individual task and then check answers as a whole class. In feedback, ask students to explain their answers. They can then confirm or refine their understanding in exercise 2.

Answers
1 have 2 knows 3 was 4 is 5 has

2 Ask students to complete the rules in pairs before checking answers as a whole class.

Answers
1 e 2 c 3 d 4 a 5 b

→ Grammar reference Student's Book page 166

3 Complete the first one as an example and then tell students to complete the task individually. Ask students to compare their answers with a partner before whole-class feedback.

Answers
1 agree 2 feels 3 do 4 tells 5 comes 6 has

⊙ Corpus challenge

Ask students to correct the sentence and to explain the error (*each one* is followed by a verb in the singular).

Answer
Each one of these has its advantages and its disadvantages.

4 Ask students to read through the text and at first just underline the parts they think contain an error. Then ask them to compare the sections they underlined with a partner and work together to correct the mistakes. Check answers as a whole class.

Answers
1 If we think someone looks …
2 a number of people were shown …
3 all the people were told …
4 the process of scoring the faces was …
5 one of the researcher's conclusions was …
6 following the opinion of a larger group leads …

5 In groups, students should discuss each one and find an example. Monitor and help with ideas as necessary. Elicit two or three examples for each from different groups.

Fast finishers
Ask fast finishers to write four sentences that can be used as model answers on the board during feedback.

Extension activity
Ask students to make a list of different influences on their opinion, e.g. friends, the media, parents. Get them to rate each one with a score from 1–5 where 1 is a 'little influence' and 5 is a 'strong influence'. Tell students to compare their ideas in small groups. Ask each group what are the biggest influences on their opinions and why.

VOCABULARY Plural nouns

1 Ask students to look at the examples. Then give them one minute to work with a partner to make a list of nouns that are always in the plural form. After one minute, ask them to count their words, and ask the pair with the longest list to read it aloud. Ask other pairs to add any plural nouns not included on this list.

Possible answers
glasses, jeans, scissors, sunglasses, trousers, shorts

2 Do the first one as an example and then ask students to identify which word they think should be plural. Check answers before moving onto the matching task. Check answers.

Extension activity
Ask students to write three sentences about themselves using the words from exercise 2. Two sentences should be true and one should be false. Tell students to read their sentences aloud to a partner who should guess which one is false. Ask students to share any funny examples in feedback.

Answers
1 e lyrics 2 a contents 3 d refreshments 4 f belongings
5 b surroundings

WRITING An essay (4)

1 Ask students to discuss this question in pairs. They should think of at least two reasons for their answer, and write these on the board for use in exercise 5.

2 Ask students to make notes on their own opinion. Then ask them to briefly discuss and compare their ideas in small groups. Ask one or two groups to feed back to the class.

Mixed ability

Ask weaker students to read the essay title in exercise 2. Then give them this list of advantages and disadvantages:

1 It could cause transport problems for some students.
2 It would be safer, as fewer students would be travelling to school at the same time.
3 Teenagers would simply end up going to bed later.
4 Teachers would end up working longer days.
5 Fewer students would be studying on an empty stomach.
6 There would be less time for after-school activities.
7 Students would be in a better mood during school hours.
8 Fewer students would be absent from school in the mornings.

Tell students to decide which ones are advantages and which ones are disadvantages. Then ask them to discuss their ideas with a partner, before doing exercise 2.

3 Ask students to read the essay and to identify the opinions included that are similar to their own, or those in the Mixed ability exercise.

4 Ask students to highlight the linking words from the *Prepare* box that are used in the essay, and check answers as a whole class.

Answers
in order to, consequently, therefore, despite

5 Ask students to complete the exercise individually before comparing their answers with a partner. Check answers. Ask students to write example sentences to demonstrate contrast, purpose, reason and result using the ideas on the board from exercise 1.

Answers
1 so 2 Even though 3 consequently 4 as 5 despite
6 whereas 7 as 8 In order that

6 Ask students to add notes individually and to then compare their ideas with a partner. Allow only a short amount of time, e.g. five minutes, to make this reflect realistic exam conditions.

Prepare for First for Schools
Writing Part 1

Task description
This part is a compulsory task. Students are required to write an essay giving their opinion on the essay title using the ideas given and providing an idea of their own. Students should write 140–190 words.

Tip
Highlight that students also need to give reasons for their opinion and not just simply state their opinion.

7 Tell students to write their essay. If you have students preparing for the First For Schools exam, set a strict time limit of 40 minutes for this task and provide less support. If not, you can be more flexible with the timing and give more help. In pairs, students exchange their essays and provide feedback on the task. They should highlight any linking words and suggest other ones that could have been used.

Sample answer
Homework is a necessary part of learning, which allows teachers to spend more time in class explaining their subjects to us. Of course, nobody wants to have a huge amount of studying and essay-writing to do, especially at the weekends, but most students in my school manage to keep up their social life and hand their homework in on time. It is all about balancing the various things you have to do with what you actually want to do. Homework is beneficial as it allows you to reflect in your own time on what was done in class. You can also catch up on aspects that you may have missed, or not understood properly. If you have to spend a couple of hours each night completing homework tasks, this is only reasonable, especially as you get older and start to prepare for exams. Any student who intends to go on to university knows the value of home study. For me, it would only be discouraging if the homework set was too hard or unclear. However, my teachers always explain the homework to us in advance, so we are properly prepared.

Cooler

In groups, ask students to make a list of other changes they would make to their school. Encourage students to think of the reasons for these changes and what the result might be. Write their ideas on the board and then hold a class vote to find out the most popular suggestion.

Project

Tell students to research a school system from a different country, or an alternative system used in your country. Ask them to make a note of the differences and whether they would like to study in this type of school. If students are struggling for ideas of schools to research, give them one of these ideas:

- The Finnish school system (often considered one of the best)
- The Montessori school system
- A school system from an English-speaking country

In the following class, ask students to present their research in small groups. You could extend this activity by asking students who have researched the same school system to work together. Tell them to create a PowerPoint presentation, and to present this to the whole class. Encourage other students to ask questions, and say whether or not they like the approach of the school system being presented.

Teacher's resources

Student's Book
Grammar reference and practice page 166
Vocabulary list page 147
Workbook
Unit 19, pages 76–79
Go online for
- Pronunciation
- Corpus tasks

20 Speak up

Unit profile

Vocabulary: Idioms; Commonly confused words
Reading: An article about language
Grammar: Determiners
Listening: Different situations
Speaking: Taking turns and negotiating

Warmer

1 Write this opinion on the board:

Your use of your own language shows how intelligent you are.

Then ask students to discuss whether they agree or disagree with this statement, and why.

2 Elicit students' reasons and hold a class vote to see if students generally agree or disagree.

Your profile

In pairs, students should brainstorm idioms in their own language and in English. Elicit examples of both. If possible, provide translations of some of the idioms or teach students the equivalent idiom.

VOCABULARY Idioms

1 In pairs, students look at the idioms and guess the likely meaning. Do not check answers at this stage.

2 ▶3.16 Play the recording for students to check their answers. Were there any they found surprising and if so, why?

Audioscript

Narrator:	One
Man:	There was a tense atmosphere when I arrived for the rehearsal. No one likes being the first to talk, so I decided to tell a joke, which helped to break the ice. Soon, everyone was chatting quite happily.
Narrator:	Two
Girl:	Don't turn over to Channel Four!
Boy:	Why not?
Girl:	There's a documentary about the dairy industry, and I don't want to watch it. I saw the ad for it, and it broke my heart to see all the cows in little sheds.
Boy:	But you aren't a vegetarian!
Girl:	I know. But I still have feelings!
Narrator:	Three
Woman:	Our plane landed at ten pm in Zürich and from there we had a two-hour coach journey to Tirol. When I woke up the next morning, I opened the hotel window and the view really took my breath away. I'd never been to the Alps before, and I simply hadn't expected the landscape to be so perfect – so impressive and so beautiful!

Narrator:	Four
Boy:	Have you written your essay yet?
Girl:	Do you mean the history homework?
Boy:	Yes. Was it hard?
Girl:	Not at all! It was a piece of cake. I did it in less than half an hour.
Boy:	Wow! Will you help me with mine?
Narrator:	Five
Girl:	When I got home late last weekend, my mum asked me where I'd been and who I'd been with. I thought she was annoyed because I'm always late. Then I realised that she had tears in her eyes and she just held my hand and smiled. It had never crossed my mind that she was actually just worried. I felt really guilty and promised to keep in touch in future by texting more often.
Narrator:	Six
Boy:	How come you're so good at drawing? Have you had drawing classes or something?
Girl:	No. I've always loved drawing though.
Boy:	So this one, did you do it from memory or did you actually go down to the city centre with a notepad?
Girl:	Well, I did a quick sketch while I was there. Then I filled in the rest from memory.
Boy:	You have a very good eye for detail. There are so many little bits you've remembered, it's really amazing!
Narrator:	Seven
Boy:	My best friend lives on the fifteenth floor. If I'm visiting, it can be a real pain if we need to pop out to the shops or something. One time we had to go out four times in one afternoon. Waiting for the lift every time drove me mad!
Narrator:	Eight
Man:	When I'm on holiday, I love doing absolutely nothing. I can lie on a beach for days and days, and I never get bored. It's great to lose track of time and feel completely relaxed, in my own little world.

Answers

1 a 2 b 3 b 4 b 5 a 6 b 7 b 8 a

3 Ask students to discuss the questions in small groups. Get each group to report back on a different question.

Fast finishers

Ask fast finishers to write more questions using the idioms. They should then ask and answer their questions in their groups. Elicit some examples during feedback to exercise 3.

4 Give students five minutes to write their paragraph. Monitor and give help to weaker students if necessary. Then ask students to raise their hand to show how many idioms they have used by asking, e.g. *Who has fewer than three idioms? More than four? More than five?* Ask the student with the highest number to read their paragraph aloud.

READING

1 Do this exercise as a whole class. Ask students to look at the picture and then elicit one or two ideas from the group. (The characters in the pictures appear to be stamping on / wrestling with the words *bad*, *wicked* and *sick*. Students may guess that some people object to the use of these words / how these words have changed their meaning.) However, don't tell the students this yet as they are going to read the text to check whether their guesses are correct.

2 Give students just one minute to read the article to see if their guesses were correct. Then give them more time to answer the questions. Ask students to compare their answers with a partner before whole-class feedback. Alternatively, you may like to pair weaker students and stronger students together to look for the answers in pairs in the first place.

Answers
1 They change standard grammar and vocabulary to mark the difference between them and the older generation.
2 Changes of meaning (e.g. *wicked*) and the use of *innit* as a question tag.
3 **a** didn't you; **b** don't you
4 It uses shortened words and emoticons.
5 Texting helps people's reading and writing.
6 The phrase means that language changes constantly.

3 Ask students to complete the exercise individually and then check answers. Remind them that they should be using the context of the rest of the sentence to work out the meaning of the highlighted words.

Answers
1 linguistic   2 literacy   3 pick up   4 slang   5 substitute

4 Ask students to discuss the questions in pairs, then feed back as a class.

Extension activity
Set a quiz for the students on the origin of words. Put students into teams of four to six. Tell them that you will read ten words aloud and they should write down the language they think the word comes from. You can use any words, but here are some suggestions: *kangaroo* (*Aboriginal*), *aubergine* (*Arabic*), *ketchup* (*Chinese*), *angst* (*German*), *biology* (*Greek*), *bangle* (*Hindi*), *karaoke* (*Japanese*), *mammoth* (*Russian*), *macho* (*Spanish*), *Dad* (*Welsh*). You could help students by giving them multiple-choice options.

EP Word profile
Ask students to explain each use of the phrases with *standard* to their partner. Discuss ideas as a class. Then set the exercise on page 138. Check answers.

Answers
1 quality   2 usual   3 behaviour

Talking points
In pairs, students discuss this question and give examples. You could give students some common text spellings to try to work out, e.g. *c u l8r* (*see you later*), *afaik* (*as far as I know*), *b4* (*before*), *gr8* (*great*), *atm* (*at the moment*), *lol* (*laugh out loud*), *thx* (*thanks*).

Cooler
Ask students to work in pairs and to write a text conversation using short forms. Get one or two pairs to write their conversations on the board.

GRAMMAR   Determiners

1 Set this as an individual task. Check students' understanding of the rules by asking them to give you another example sentence for each one.

Answers
1 –, the, a   2 Plenty of   3 a lot of   4 many   5 a

→ Grammar reference Student's Book **page 167**

2 Ask students to read the sentences, and go through each one as a class. Emphasise the importance of getting the determiners exactly right when writing, as not doing so can greatly affect the meaning of what you are trying to convey.

Answers
1 **a** Not much help was given.
  b Some help was given.
2 **a** Not many people can speak Chinese.
  b Some people can speak Chinese.
3 **a** Most of the French has been forgotten.
  b Some French is still spoken.
4 **a** There is some rain.
  b There isn't much rain.
5 **a** Not many schools offer Latin.
  b Some schools offer Latin.

Corpus challenge
Ask students to correct the sentence and to explain the error (we use *a few* before plural countable nouns and *little* before uncountable nouns, like *experience*).

Answer
I am keen on singing but I have very little experience.

3 Do the first one as an example, and then ask students to complete the exercise individually. Check answers.

Mixed ability
To provide further practice for weaker students, write five sentences with typical determiner mistakes that your students make. Read them aloud and ask students to write down the correction for each one.

VOCABULARY Commonly confused words

1 Ask students to complete the exercise individually and then check answers as a whole class.
Other words that are commonly confused are 'false friends', i.e. words that look similar to words in the students' language, but which have a different meaning. For example, *sensible* in French means *sensitive*, but it means *using good judgment* in English. Other words are commonly confused because an English-sounding word is used in the local language, for example, *handy* in German means *mobile phone* but it means *useful* in English. If you know of any similar problems students have because of their own language, use these to extend the exercise.

Fast finishers

Ask fast finishers to look at question 2 and to write three sentences describing the best way to practise English. Elicit some ideas when checking answers to exercise 1.

Answers

1 means 2 way 3 journey 4 way 5 opportunities
6 a possibility 7 fun 8 funny

2 Ask students to complete the sentences individually and then check answers. If they are confused about the uses of *opportunity* and *possibility*, tell them that we use *opportunity* to talk about a situation in which we can do something that we want to do: *I had the opportunity to go to university when I was younger but I didn't. Now I wish I had gone.* We use *possibility* to talk about something that may happen or be true: *The possibility that there is life on other planets has always inspired scientists.* We don't say *have THE possibility: I would love to have the opportunity to meet the Prime Minister* NOT *... have the possibility to meet ...*

Answers

1 journey 2 opportunity 3 funny 4 way 5 possibility
6 fun

3 Ask students to work with a partner to explain the meaning of the words in the box. Which words do they think are commonly confused with one another? (e.g. *damage* and *injure*). Feed back as a class and then tell students to complete the exercise. Check answers.

Extension activity

In pairs, students should write five questions using the vocabulary from exercise 3. Monitor and help students. Then put them into groups of four and ask them to ask and answer their questions. Ask one or two groups to report back to the class.

LISTENING

● Prepare for First for Schools
Listening Part 1

Task description

The focus of this part is on genre, identifying speaker feeling, attitude, topic, opinion, purpose, agreement between speakers, gist and detail. Students hear a series of short unrelated extracts from monologues or exchanges between interacting speakers. There is one multiple-choice question per text, each with three options.

Tip

Students will need to pay attention to synonyms and phrases with similar meanings to identify the points they are listening for.

1 ● ▶3.17 Tell students that they are going to hear eight short extracts. Tell them to read through the questions and to think about what information they are listening for each time. Remind them that underlining key words is a useful strategy, and give them time to do this. Play the recording. Then play the recording again, pausing after each extract to check answers. If your students are preparing for First for Schools, do this task under exam conditions.

Audioscript

Narrator: One. You hear two friends talking about their college library.

Boy: I had to go to the library to renew my books again this morning.

Girl: You can renew them online, you know.

Boy: Yes, I realise that, but after you've done that twice you have to actually take them in to the library if you want to renew them for a third time.

Girl: Well, I guess the staff have to make sure you haven't lost them?

Boy: Or stolen them! But it's not helpful, is it? <u>And in any case, borrowing books should be fully automated these days. You should be able to order things online and get them sent to you.</u> And return them in the post if you want.

Girl: Mmm, that seems unlikely to me!

Narrator:	Two. You hear a girl start a presentation about endangered languages.
Girl:	Did you know that half of the world's languages are endangered? There are currently about six thousand languages spoken on the planet and we might well lose up to three thousand of them. This is very worrying, because little is known about many of these languages, and if they disappear, they will be lost forever. <u>Each endangered language can teach us a lot about the abilities and limits of our own minds, and about the cultures and natural systems of the regions they come from.</u> There are few better sources of historical evidence.
Narrator:	Three. You hear two friends talking about a novel they read for their English class.
Girl 1:	I've finished *Kes*. Thanks for lending it to me!
Girl 2:	What did you think?
Girl 1:	Yeah. It was really well written, I thought.
Girl 2:	You think so? I didn't think it was exactly a work of art, but I felt like I had a really good idea of what it must have been like to live in a northern English town fifty years ago.
Girl 1:	That's true. <u>It gave you a really clear picture of life in Barnsley in the 1960s.</u> And what about the main character? He was brilliant.
Girl 2:	Billy? I don't know. Were kids really so different back then? I found it hard to believe in him.
Narrator:	Four. You hear a teacher talking about the holidays.
Woman:	At this time of year, of course you're all thinking about the holidays and looking forward to spending time with your families and friends. By all means, relax, and forget about your schoolwork and studying. That's what the holidays are for. <u>But I do need to ask one thing of you. Please make an effort each week to keep a diary, so that you can share your experiences with each other next term.</u> I don't need to remind you to have a great time these holidays, but do take care all of you. Have a good break.
Narrator:	Five. You hear two friends talking about the advantage of speaking two languages.
Boy:	I saw this really interesting programme about being bilingual. You know, speaking two languages fluently. So, what do you think is the main advantage of speaking two or more languages?
Girl:	Well, you can speak to a lot more people around the world, obviously. And you can appreciate different cultures.
Boy:	That may be true, but did you know that speakers of two or three languages may actually be more intelligent than people who just speak one?
Girl:	Really?
Boy:	<u>Being bilingual seems to have an effect on the brain that has nothing to do with language. Bilingual people are faster at solving problems and puzzles, they're better at planning and at concentrating.</u> It's quite surprising.
Narrator:	Six. You hear part of an interview with a university lecturer.
Woman:	Thinking about teenagers who might be starting at university in the next year or two, can you tell us a little bit about what they can expect?

Man:	Well, I always think it's best for students starting out at university to be aware of what lies ahead. They probably won't have any concern about moving to another city, especially if it's one where there's lots to do! <u>The biggest change is the amount of research that students are expected to do. Studying at school level tends to be fairly classroom-based, whereas at university, even though students attend lectures, the vast majority of their time will be spent in libraries or sitting at their computer.</u>
Narrator:	Seven. You overhear a conversation about a long-distance running race.
Boy:	So, have you been training for Saturday?
Girl:	Yes, I've been out every day after school, so I should be OK. I was a bit worried that my shoes were rubbing, but I bought some new socks and the shoes feel fine now. Imagine if I'd dropped out of the race just because of my shoes!
Boy:	That would be bad luck! So you're not too nervous then?
Girl:	Well, I wouldn't say that! Actually, <u>I think I'm more bothered about the spectators than the actual race.</u> I mean, all my friends and family will be there, cheering and stuff. <u>It adds a bit of pressure.</u>
Boy:	Well, try to forget about that, try to think of the finish …
Narrator:	Eight. You overhear a boy telling a friend about his blog.
Girl:	How long have you been doing your blog?
Boy:	It must be about five years now. It's incredible really, it doesn't feel that long. At first, I thought it'd be really hard thinking of something to say each week, but in fact, I usually have more to say than I have space for – I mean, <u>I try to limit each post to about two hundred and fifty words. That's the key thing, because if you write longer posts, people stop reading.</u> I write what I write because I enjoy it, I don't just try to keep my readers happy. But I do have over a thousand followers now, so that's pretty cool.

Answers
For confirmation of answers, refer to the underlined parts of the script above.

1 A **2** C **3** C **4** C **5** B **6** A **7** C **8** A

Extension activity
Ask students to discuss these questions in pairs:
- *How would you feel if the language you speak was endangered?*
- *Have you ever read a novel in English? What was it about?*
- *What do you think are the advantages of speaking two languages?*
- *What kind of blogs do you enjoy reading?*

Discuss ideas as a class.

SPEAKING Taking turns and negotiating

1 Ask students to work in groups and to think of at least five ways to learn vocabulary, e.g. writing example sentences. Elicit ideas and write them on the board.

2 ▶3.18 Play the recording for students to answer the questions. When checking answers, ask if the techniques are different to those mentioned in exercise 1, and explain any new techniques to the students.

Audioscript

Sara: You always seem to find Spanish so easy! How do you remember all that vocabulary?

Dan: That's a good question. Um. I have a vocabulary notebook, but it isn't very well organised. I've been meaning to get a bit more organised with my vocabulary learning, actually. I saw a list online somewhere recently. Wait a second …

Sara: Let's have a look.

Dan: Here: writing sentences, categorising words, mind maps, vocabulary cards, and translation.

Sara: That's not a bad list. Let's choose one technique and use it next term for learning vocabulary.

Dan: Good idea.

Sara: Right! You go first. <u>What would be your top techniques</u>?

Dan: <u>For me, the ones that make the most sense are</u> <u>categorising words</u> and <u>mind maps</u>.

Sara: Yes, I'd agree with that.

Dan: OK. <u>It's your turn now</u>.

Sara: <u>Well, personally, I'd choose categorising words</u> and <u>writing sentences</u>. I'd leave out vocabulary cards because they seem a bit tedious – and a bit young, they remind me of primary school!

Dan: That's a good point.

Sara: And I'd leave out translation, because translation on its own isn't enough.

Dan: Absolutely!

Sara: <u>So if you had to choose just one, what would it be</u>?

Dan: <u>I think I'd go for</u> mind maps. What about you?

Sara: I'm not so sure about that. Mind maps <u>are all very well</u> if you have a photographic memory, <u>but they're</u> a bit time-consuming to do all the time, aren't they? <u>I think I'd go for categorising words</u>.

Dan: Fair enough, <u>I'm happy with categorising words as well</u>.

Sara: Great. Let's try that next term and see how much difference it makes.

Answers

1 writing sentences, categorising words, mind maps
2 categorising words

3 ▶3.18 Play the recording again for students to note who uses each phrase. Check answers.

Answers

Dan: For me, the ones that make most sense are …
It's your turn now.
I think I'd go for …
I'm happy with … as well.

Sara: What would be your top …?
Well, personally, I'd choose …
So if you had to choose just one, what would it be?
… are all very well if … but they …

4 In pairs, ask students to rank these methods from the most to the least effective. Encourage students to use phrases from the *Prepare* box by setting a competition to see who can use the most phrases during the discussion.

5 In pairs, ask students to rank these ideas from the most to the least effective/enjoyable, and to add one or two more ideas to the list. In feedback, ask students to explain the reason behind their ranking. Invite one or two strong pairs to perform their dialogue in front of the whole class.

Cooler

Ask students to work in small groups and give them one minute to recall the five ways of recording vocabulary from exercise 4. Then tell each group to provide an example of each method, using the word *language*. For feedback, ask each group to provide one example for each method, e.g. *writing sentences: We are learning the English language*.

Project

If you have come to the end of term or academic year, ask students to write an action plan for their English studies during the break. What do they need to prioritise and how will they do it? Ask them to share their ideas in small groups and then feed back as a class.

Teacher's resources

Student's Book
Grammar reference and practice page 167
Vocabulary list page 147
Workbook
Unit 20, pages 80–83
Go online for
- Pronunciation
- Progress test
- Achievement test
- Corpus tasks

Economics
A school business

Learning objectives
- The students learn about entrepreneurship and school projects around the world.
- In the project stage, students design and plan their own school business.

Warmer

1 Tell students they have been given £100,000 (or an equivalent amount) to start a business. Tell them to discuss with a partner what type of business they would start and why.

2 Ask students to discuss what they think the role of their business is:
   1 to improve society as a whole.
   2 to provide jobs and make a profit.
   3 any other ideas.

3 Ask students to discuss how their business might benefit society. Discuss some ideas as a class.

1 Ask students if their school runs a business or campaigns for charity. Tell them to read the text to find the answer to the question. Elicit ideas and ask students which programme they think sounds the best and why.

Answer
Tanzania – by raising funds for needy pupils and building beehives to help local people who need jobs
Nicaragua – by supporting the school financially, and enabling students to develop artistic skills and learn business and life lessons

2 Give students time to read the questions and choose the best word to complete each one. Check answers before asking students to answer the questions in pairs. Check answers.

Fast finishers
Ask fast finishers to write one more question about the text and to exchange it with another fast finisher. They should answer each other's question. Elicit their questions and answers after checking answers to exercise 2.

Answers
1 earn – honey and beeswax candles
2 raise – by making and selling craft products
3 set – a socially responsible, environmentally friendly, long-term project
4 make – improve school buildings, donate money to charity, buy classroom equipment, help needy classmates, help other schools
5 win – cameras and laptops

3 Encourage students to not only use information from the text to answer these questions, but also their own ideas. Tell students to work in groups for this task and encourage discussion about possible ideas. Discuss answers as a class.

Mixed ability
Ask weaker students to answer the questions in pairs, before discussing them in groups of four. Stronger students could answer them individually before discussing them in groups.

Answers
1 The first step helps to develop ideas and knowledge, and the second helps to develop practical skills and raise money.
2 Students' own answers.
3 Students' own answers.
4 Tanzania – they help schoolchildren and other people in the local community. They reinvest some of their profit in the business. They use recycled wood.
Nicaragua – it teaches people artistic and business skills. The profit helps support the school. They use natural and recycled products.
Arguably, the Tanzania project is better, as it helps local people, as well as school children.

4 Tell pairs that they have to think of at least three alternative ideas of what to do with the money. Then put students into groups of four to assess and compare their ideas. Ask groups to choose their favourite idea and present it to the class.

Extension activity
Ask students to think about how their business idea from the Warmer matches the three P's – people, profit and planet. Ask them to talk about how they could change their business to be better for the planet.

5 ▶3.19 Tell students that they are going to listen to two students presenting plans for their 'Bags to Books' business idea. Give them a couple of minutes to read about the project and then play the recording. Ask students to make notes on the main points as they listen. Take a vote on whether students think the business will be successful or not.

Audioscript

Boy: Good morning everyone! Today, we're here to present our business plan for a new school enterprise. It's going to be called 'Bags to Books'. So, 'what does that mean?', you're probably asking yourselves.

Girl: Well, it means that we're going to make and sell homemade cotton bags for people to use when they go shopping for food at the market.

Boy: Firstly, we think this is a good idea because it's environmentally-friendly. Everyone knows that plastic bags are bad for the environment, and our plan will help to stop that problem!

Girl: Secondly, the plan will also be good for our school, because we'll make money to buy books for the school library and our classrooms. In addition, we'll use some of the money to offer free reading lessons for people in our community, including older people who never learned to read.

Boy: And thirdly, this project will be good for students, because they'll learn about sewing, about economics, and about how important books are for education.

Girl: Now, you probably want to know how this enterprise will work. Well, first of all, we'll need to make some preparations. We'll visit local companies that can supply us with cotton, and we'll compare their prices, to get the best deal. Then, we'll ask for donations to rent sewing machines, at least for the first year, because we won't have a lot of money.

Boy: We're also going to find a local company that can print logos on the bags. When that's finished, <u>we'll calculate our production costs, and decide the final price</u> for our bags, to make a profit.

Girl: When that's all done, we'll get started with the project. We'll order cotton cloth from the company that has the best price, and we'll organise an art contest to design the best logo for our business. <u>We'll also need to set up some basic sewing classes</u> for people who don't know how to sew.

Boy: After that, we can start production. <u>The students will form teams to sew the bags</u> after school. And we'll offer a prize to the team that produces the most bags every week. And when we have enough bags ready, <u>we'll take them to the printer</u>, to have our official company logo printed on them.

Girl: Finally, we come to promotion and sales. <u>We're going to sell most of the bags to supermarkets and other shops</u> in town, and we'll sell some bags on the street, too.

Boy: And to advertise our business, we'll talk to the local newspaper. We could buy an advert, but maybe the newspaper will also interview us, for a news article. That would be great publicity for us.

Girl: And of course, <u>we'd like to offer a grand prize to the person who sells the most bags</u>, or to the class that sells the most. That might be a better idea, to encourage people to work together.

Boy: Well, that's our plan for the Bags to Books enterprise. Are there any questions?

6 ▶3.19 Ask students to insert steps a to g into the plan. Then play the recording for them to check their answers.

Answers

4 g **7** b **8** d **10** f **11** a **13** e

Cooler

Ask students to brainstorm characteristics of successful entrepreneurs. Discuss the characteristics as a class, and take a vote on the most important one. You could ask students to take this quiz to find out whether they have the personality of an entrepreneur or not: http://www.entrepreneur.com/personalityquiz

Project

Give students a few minutes to read the instructions and to brainstorm some possible ideas with a partner. Then ask them to find other people who are interested in a similar type of business, and ask them to work in groups to develop their business plan. Groups should be between three and six people. Tell students to answer all of the questions and present their plan to the class. Ask the class to vote on the best project.

Exam profile 1

Warmer

1 Tell students to work with a partner and ask them to discuss:

   a what sports they like doing and why.

   b how they try to keep fit.

   c what advice they would give someone who wanted to get fit.

2 Read the following tips aloud and ask students to discuss whether they find them helpful.

   a Run in bare feet.

   b Shout motivational phrases while exercising.

   c Focus more on your diet than exercise.

   d Exercise first thing in the morning.

READING AND USE OF ENGLISH PART 7
Multiple matching

1 Remind students of the format of Part 7. This is also practised in the Student's Book on page 10 and in the Workbook on pages 4, 28 and 68. Ask students to read the questions and tick the one they think asks for an opinion. Ask students to compare their answers after reading the highlighted parts.

> **Answer**
> Question 2 asks for an opinion. The word *disapproves* shows that you need to look for a negative opinion.
> 1 Tomas 2 Mats

2 Ask students to underline the distraction on their own and then compare with a partner before checking the answer as a whole class.

> **Answer**
> 'Swimming and long-distance running suit me better than arranging extra matches …'
> The words *arrange* and *matches* appear in both the question and in Text A, although this is not actually the answer to the question.

3 Ask students to work in pairs to highlight the phrases in the text that enabled them to answer questions 3 to 5.

> **Answers**
> 3 Tomas – I expect to see some benefit from that soon.
> 4 Tomas – I need to watch out there …
> 5 Mats – … comes up with really smart suggestions about what to eat when.

READING AND USE OF ENGLISH PART 4
Key word transformations

1 Remind students of the format of Part 4. This is also practised in the Student's Book on page 26 and in the Workbook on pages 14 and 54. Read the information on Part 4 as a class. Then ask students to read the rubric to exercise 1 and highlight what they must remember to do, i.e. *use four words including the word given, use a phrasal verb and a modal*.

> **Answer**
> 1 should cut down on

2 Ask students to answer the two questions on their own. Encourage them to check their own spelling and grammar. They could also check a partner's spelling and grammar as well. Check answers.

> **Answers**
> 2 voted for Jackie than
> 3 unless I really have
> (1 tests a collocation.)

LISTENING PART 3
Multiple matching

1 ▶ 3.20 Remind students of the format of Part 3. This is also practised in the Student's Book on pages 27 and 83 and in the Workbook on pages 19 and 59. Ask students to read through the information on Part 3 and the tips in the box. Tell them to underline the key words in options A and B, and play the recording for students to choose the correct option for Speaker 1. Play it again for them to check their answer. Then check as a whole class.

> **Answer**
> A. Speaker 1 doesn't mention different natural environments.

2 Ask students to highlight the part of the Audioscript that gives them the answer, and to check their answer with a partner.

Answer
… A – it was very rewarding, especially when I realised that without my efforts, the animal I was looking after would've died.

Narrator:	One
Speaker 1:	I was working in a rescue centre in South Africa for a month, looking after animals and birds that were hurt or young ones that'd been found wandering about alone – mainly monkeys. It was quite demanding work, with long days, but <u>it was very rewarding, especially when I realised that without my efforts, the animal I was looking after would've died</u>. It was tiring though. Luckily we all slept on site so we didn't have far to travel to our accommodation at the end of the day.

3 ▶ **3.21** Give students time to underline the key words in options C to H and feed back as a class. Then play the recording for students to choose which ones match to the speakers. When checking answers, ask students why the other options didn't quite match.

Answers
Refer to underlining in Audioscript in ex. 1.
Speaker 2 – F
Speaker 3 – H
Speaker 4 – D
Speaker 5 – E

Audioscript

Narrator:	Two
Speaker 2:	I'd always wanted to see Costa Rica so I was so happy to get the chance to help as a volunteer on a research project there. My work involved trekking through the rainforest with a group of researchers, helping them as they collected data on the various birds we came across. When they interviewed me, they'd made it clear that I'd need some local knowledge – you know, like being able to recognise different birds from their song – stuff like that. <u>So I'd spent three weeks going through all the websites. It was time well spent, because applying that knowledge was the highlight of the trip for me.</u>
Narrator:	Three
Speaker 3:	My trip to a Caribbean island was supposed to be a working holiday, but at the beginning it was all work and not much holiday! I wasn't prepared for that. I did everything from planting vegetables to repairing buildings, and I ended up with a bad back as a result. Still, I made some nice friends, and when more volunteers arrived, we got more free time to go exploring. <u>That was the thing that made the trip for me, having time to take in the amazing scenery.</u> We'd hoped to see several rare species out in the rainforest, and although that never happened, it didn't spoil it for us.

Narrator:	Four
Speaker 4:	I had a memorable time working in Mexico. I was on the Yucatan Peninsula, helping on a jaguar conservation project. Jaguars are a kind of very big cat, and they're seriously endangered, so I knew I probably wouldn't actually see any during my stay. But as my job was to install and repair the remote cameras in the jungle, to record their behaviour, <u>I did manage to capture them on video, and it was truly amazing to think they were somewhere nearby</u>. Now I'm passionate about preventing this beautiful creature from dying out altogether and I'll be returning to the same camp as soon as I can afford it.
Narrator:	Five
Speaker 5:	I was involved in a project that protects the baby sea turtles born on the beaches of the Peloponnese region in Greece. The first two months were the busiest, as that's when the eggs hatch. <u>Every day, I had to do an early morning beach survey for the scientists, where I checked the nests and monitored the number of new baby turtles</u> – by looking at the tracks in the sand leading from the nest down to the sea. It wasn't difficult to do, but <u>I felt so proud to be in charge of such a key aspect of the project</u>, because not everyone gets that kind of experience as a volunteer.

Cooler
Ask students to discuss whether they have volunteered for any projects protecting animals. If so, how did they find their experience? If they haven't volunteered for any such projects, ask them to discuss what type of volunteer work they would enjoy and what they would hope to gain from it.

Exam profile 2

Warmer

1 Ask students to think about a book they have read recently and enjoyed. Ask them to write a basic summary of what happens in the story.

2 In pairs, ask students to swap their summaries. They should read each other's summaries to find out about the story and what makes it so good.

3 Ask the class if anyone has found a book they would now like to read. Ask one or two students to share the reasons why they would like to read the story with the class.

READING AND USE OF ENGLISH PART 5
Multiple choice (fiction)

1 Remind students of the format of Reading and Use of English Part 5. This is also practised in the Student's Book on page 42 and in the Workbook on pages 36 and 76. Make sure students understand the difference between fiction (about imaginary characters and events) and non-fiction (about real facts and events). Then give them one minute to read the text to find the boy's name.

Answer
Shay

2 Ask students to highlight the key words in each of the sentences. Then give them one or two minutes to think of synonyms or similar expressions. Tell them to compare the options with the highlighted part of the text. Ask students which synonym helps them to answer the question (*suggested* is similar to *recommendation*).

3 Ask students to work with a partner to answer the question. Check answers as a class.

Answers
A We know this is incorrect as he says 'I'd never thought anything of it.'
B We do not know where the characters live.
D We know that Curtis is there 'to hear me play.'

4 Ask students to underline the key words in each option and then read the text to answer the questions. Check answers as a whole class.

Extension activity

Ask students to work with a partner to discuss these questions:
1 Do you think Shay's parents' reaction is fair? Why / why not?
2 How would your parents react in such a situation?
3 How much of success in music and sport do you think is due to a) luck, b) natural talent and c) hard work?
After students have discussed the questions, elicit responses from different pairs.

Answers
2 B. Curtis needed the agreement of Shay's parents. A and C are incorrect as 'According to Curtis, I was just the kind of thing they were looking for'. D is incorrect as Curtis 'thought I had something special – raw talent, awesome songs'.
3 D. The injury 'was enough to wipe out Ben's chances of a premier-league career'. A is wrong as the injury 'wasn't that serious'. B and C are not mentioned in the text.

READING AND USE OF ENGLISH PART 1
Multiple-choice cloze

1 Remind students of the format of Reading and Use of English Part 1. This is also practised in the Student's Book on page 36 and in the Workbook on page 60. Ask students to read the information on Part 1 and the rubric in exercise 1. Ask students to quickly read the text and to ignore the gaps. Elicit a few possible titles from the class.

Possible answer
City life

2 Ask students to identify the word form they would need in gap zero (a verb, as it follows the word *to*) and to try to guess the word they might need. Then ask them to look at the options in exercise 2. Ask a volunteer to explain why A is correct.

Answer
Because the verb *rise* collocates with the noun *percentage*.

3 Ask students to identify the part of speech in pairs.

Answer
The four options are all nouns here.

4 Ask students to complete this exercise individually. Then tell them to compare their answers with a partner before checking as a whole class. Remind students of the importance of learning collocations as set phrases, e.g. *make the most of something*.

Extension activity

Ask students to work with a partner to think of more advantages and disadvantages of living in a city. Then ask students to work individually to write sentences describing these advantages and disadvantages, using the collocations or fixed phrases from the gaps in exercise 1. Elicit a sentence for each fixed phrase or collocation.

Answers
2 B 3 C 4 D

LISTENING PART 1 Short extracts

1 ▶3.22 Remind students of the format of Listening Part 1. This is also practised in the Student's Book on page 39 and in the Workbook on pages 27, 51 and 83. Ask students to read through the information on Part 1 and elicit any tips to help with this task. Tell students to read through the options and then play the recording. Check answer as a whole class.

Audioscript
Narrator: One. You hear two friends discussing a novel.
Girl: I've just finished that novel you lent me. I'm really glad I read it, but I must admit I found the plot a bit difficult to follow at times.
Boy: Did you? That wasn't an issue for me. I'd read it again, too. What about the main character, Jake? He was really true to life somehow, and I thought that was brilliant.
Girl: Good point. And his friends behaved just like we do at times, didn't they?
Boy: Mmm. One thing I was less keen on were the descriptions of Liverpool and Manchester. I mean, I've been to those cities and for me they didn't feel right.
Girl: Oh? That didn't bother me.

Answer
A. B is incorrect as the plot is describes as 'a bit difficult to follow'. C is incorrect as the boy says the descriptions 'didn't feel right'.

2 ▶3.22 Ask students to listen again to answer the question.

Answer
They don't agree that the plot was difficult to follow (the girl says, 'I found the plot a bit difficult to follow at times,' whereas the boy says, 'That wasn't an issue for me') or that the descriptions of the cities wasn't right (the boy says, 'One thing I was less keen on were the descriptions of Liverpool and Manchester,' whereas the girl says, 'That didn't bother me'). They agree that Jake's character and his friends' behaviour were true to life (the boy says, 'He was really true to life somehow, and I thought that was brilliant,' and the girl says, 'Good point … his friends behaved just like we do at times, didn't they?').

3 ▶3.23 Give students time to underline the key words in the question, and feed back as a class. Then play the recording for students to answer the question. When checking answers, ask students why the other options didn't quite match.

Audioscript
Narrator: Two. You overhear a boy talking on the phone about his homework.
Harry: Hi, it's Harry here. Er, I just wanted to chat about our geography homework, have you got a moment? Great! Well, I'm really rather nervous about it, actually. I know there're a couple more days before it's due, so that's not a worry for me. <u>But I've read the right chapter in the textbook loads of times, and I still can't come up with many things to say about the topic. And the essay's two thousand words, right?</u> Are you having the same problem?

Answer
C. A is incorrect as he says he has 'read the right chapter in the textbook'. B is incorrect as he says 'there're a couple more days before it's due, so that's not a worry for me.'

Cooler

Ask students to discuss in groups the best homework they were ever given. What was the subject of the homework and what did they have to do?

Exam profile 3

Warmer

1 Ask students to think about their own personality and to write down a few adjectives or sentences to describe themselves.

2 Ask students to swap their descriptions with someone they know quite well. Tell them to read each other's descriptions and see if they agree with them. Encourage students to tell each other what they would change or add to the description. Share some ideas as a class.

READING AND USE OF ENGLISH PART 3
Word formation

1 Remind students of the format of Reading and Use of English Part 3. This is also practised in the Student's Book on page 56 and in the Workbook on page 45. Then ask students to read the description of Part 3. Tell them to complete the first four gaps and to check their answers against the explanation.

2 Refer students to question 5 and ask students to decide on the answer in pairs.

Answers
adjective – *various*

3 Ask students to discuss with a partner the type of word they think they will need in each gap. Then ask them to try to complete the gaps together. Remind students that it's useful to make a note of different forms of a word when recording vocabulary.

Extension activity

Ask students to brainstorm the various word forms of the words in exercise 1. Then tell them to use these words to write three sentences about themselves. Monitor and check before eliciting an example for each word.

Answers
6 friendly **7** behaviour **8** membership

WRITING PART 2   An article

1 Remind students of the format of the Writing paper. This is also practised in the Student's Book on pages 35 and 67 and in the Workbook on pages 23 and 39. Ask students to read through the information on Part 2 and brainstorm with a partner what they should include when writing an article. Elicit some ideas and write some on the board. Then give students five minutes to answer the question together. Feed back as a class.

Analyse the question in more detail and discuss what the specific expectations of this task are. Tell students to choose an event from their lists and to spend a few minutes planning the structure of their article. Give them 20 minutes to write their article. Then ask them to exchange their articles with a partner and to underline any examples of lively and engaging language.

Sample answer
AN UNEXPECTED MEETING
Last month I went to a concert with some friends, but there was a problem with our tickets and we weren't able to sit together. Luckily, I was given a seat in the front row and so I was really close to the stage.
There were two bands playing that evening and after the first one had finished, I went to find my friends during the break. When I came back to my seat, I just couldn't believe my eyes – sitting next to me was Alexis Sánchez, the Chilean footballer! I recognised him immediately and we started chatting, first about the music and then about football. To begin with, I felt a bit shy talking to such a famous person, but he was really friendly. I have to admit I don't remember much about the second band!
When I got home, I told my brother about my experience, but of course, he didn't believe me. I didn't care about that, though – I knew that it was true. I'll never forget meeting such a famous and talented footballer.
(177 words)

WRITING PART 1   Essay

1 Remind students of the format of the Writing paper. This is also practised in the Student's Book on pages 13, 57, 89 and 111 and in the Workbook on pages 7, 47 and 71. Ask students to read through the information and elicit any tips on essay writing they remember from previous lessons. Tell them to work in pairs to answer the question.

Answer
A and C

2 Tell students to complete the list of do's and don'ts individually. Then ask them to compare their answers with a partner before whole-class feedback. Finally, ask students to write one more tip and then share some of these with the class.

Answers

1 plan **2** introduction **3** paragraphs **5** grammar; spelling
6 conclusion **7** language

Ask students to spend a few minutes brainstorming and organising their ideas. Monitor and check, and then ask students to compare their plans with a partner. Give students 40 minutes to write their essay. Then ask them to swap with a partner and to check each other's essays using the do's and don'ts list from exercise 2.

Sample answer

Sport is very important in most people's lives, so in general, I agree with the statement. Combined with a good diet, regular sport ensures that people stay fit and healthy.

By providing free access, everyone can take part in some kind of physical exercise without worrying about whether they or their parents can afford it. However, some sports are only available in private clubs and it isn't realistic for young people to expect to gain free entry to these places.

What is equally important to my mind is that sports clubs help to develop obvious talent in teenagers. There are many football coaching programmes available, but fewer opportunities exist in other sports such as tennis or rugby. Some children miss out on playing their chosen sport because of financial hardship, and this may prevent them from becoming the sports stars of the future.

All in all, every effort should be made to provide sport to young people for free. If this is done, public money will be saved on healthcare and gifted players will get the support they need to do well.

(182 words)

Cooler

Ask students to discuss in groups what other things they think should be free for young people to use in a city. Ask them to write a list of three to five things and to put them in order of priority. Discuss their ideas as a class. If students are struggling, tell them to rank: *public transport*, *taxis*, *wifi*, *cinemas* and *bikes*.

Exam profile 4

Warmer

1 Ask students to discuss the different ways in which perfume, trainers and medicine are usually advertised. What are the differences and the similarities?

2 In pairs, ask them to choose one of the three products and think of a poster or TV advert they would create to sell it. Ask students to think about who they are trying to sell it to, what their main message will be and which celebrities they would use in their advert.

3 Ask two or three pairs to describe their advert to the rest of the class.

READING AND USE OF ENGLISH PART 6
Gapped text

1 Remind students of the format of Reading and Use of English Part 6. This is also practised in the Student's Book on pages 58 and 101 and in the Workbook on pages 12, 52 and 80. Then ask students to read the information about Part 6. Give them one minute to read the title and the first paragraph, and ask them to predict what they think they will read in the rest of the text.

2 Ask students to read paragraphs two and three to decide where the sentences should go. Check answers as a whole class.

Answers
1 C. It gives an example of an advert appealing to your positive emotions.
2 B. 'Commercials like this one' refers back to the commercial described in the previous sentence.

3 Set this as an individual task and then check answers as a whole class.

Extension activity

1 Ask students to work with a partner and to think of one advert that uses an emotional appeal, one that shows pain and suffering and another that uses scientific evidence.

2 Then ask them to work with another pair and describe the adverts. In their groups they should decide which technique they think is the most effective and why. Ask one or two groups to share their ideas with the class.

Answer
3 E. It gives an example of the statistics mentioned in the previous sentence.

LISTENING PART 2   Sentence completion

1 Remind students of the format of Listening Part 2. This is also practised in the Student's Book on pages 49 and 71 and in the Workbook on pages 35 and 75. Ask students to read through the information on Part 2. Then give them 30 seconds to read the text and make their prediction. Elicit some ideas from the students.

2 ▶3.24 Ask students to listen and identify how many words are needed. One word is needed if the answer is given as 'foxes', two if the answer is given as 'urban wildlife'. Play the recording again, if necessary, for them to find the answer. Check as a class.

Audioscript
Jamal Edwards started his own online broadcast music channel SBTV a few years ago at the age of sixteen. He had been given a video camera as a present and took it outside to film the urban wildlife where he was living in London. He focused on some foxes and uploaded a short video of them that anyone who was interested could see. Jamal couldn't believe it when he got one thousand views for this single clip, and decided to try something else.
At the time, grime, that unique mix of hip-hop and garage music, was just becoming really popular, but you couldn't find it on the main TV channels. Jamal immediately saw an opportunity to make this kind of music more widely available. He filmed rappers doing their thing in London, went backstage at gigs and even captured any live music that was happening in the back of cars – that setting was especially liked, as it was so original. These performances, delivered straight to camera and without any editing, were posted online within days and became an instant hit.

Answers
1 foxes (one word) / urban wildlife (two words)

3 ▶3.25 Ask students to look at gaps 2, 3 and 4, and to predict what information they might hear for each gap. Play the recording for them to complete the gaps. Check answers.

Audioscript

Jamal Edwards started his own online broadcast music channel SBTV a few years ago at the age of sixteen. He had been given a video camera as a present and <u>took it outside to film the urban wildlife</u> where he was living in London. <u>He focused on some foxes and uploaded a short video of them</u> that anyone who was interested could see. Jamal couldn't believe it when he got one thousand views for this single clip, and decided to try something else.

At the time, grime, that unique mix of hip-hop and garage music, was just becoming really popular, but you couldn't find it on the main TV channels. Jamal immediately saw an opportunity to make this kind of music more widely available. He filmed rappers doing their thing in London, went backstage at gigs <u>and even captured any live music that was happening in the back of cars</u> – that setting was especially liked, as it was so original. These performances, delivered straight to camera and without any editing, were posted online within days and became an instant hit.

But he didn't stop there. <u>SBTV, which makes its money from advertising, has already had over thirty-nine million visits</u> and Jamal now has a team of eight assistants, who are out filming the music scene in and around London and uploading their videos to <u>the SBTV website, which also features many interviews with the latest musicians.</u>

Answers

2 back of cars **3** 39 million **4** interviews

READING AND USE OF ENGLISH PART 2
Open cloze

1 Remind students of the format of Reading and Use of English Part 2. This is also practised in the Student's Book on pages 32 and 90 and in the Workbook on page 20. Ask students to read through the information on Part 2 and then give them 30 seconds to skim read the text. Ask students to tell you what the text is about.

Answer
Different varieties of crocodiles

2 Before doing the exercise, elicit an example of each word type a to f from students. Then ask them to work with a partner to work out what type of word is needed in each gap. Check answers as a whole class.

Answers
1 a **2** a **3** b **4** f

3 Ask students to complete the gaps individually and then check answers as a whole class.

Answers
1 as **2** or **3** the **4** some

Cooler
Ask students to write a short text about an animal. Then tell them to blank out four words (using the word types in exercise 2). Students should then exchange their texts with a partner and try to complete it. Monitor and help where necessary.

Exam profile 5

WRITING PART 2 A story

1 Remind students of the format of the Writing paper. This is also practised in the Student's Book on page 45 and in the Workbook on page 31. Ask students to read the information about writing a story. Students can either answer the questions individually, or you could do this as a discussion task.

Set the writing task for students to do. Then ask them to work in groups of four and to read their stories to each other. Each group must choose the story they think is the best and why. Ask each group to read their best story out loud and to explain the reasons for their choice.

Sample answer

Sofie was so furious that she stood up and ran out of the room, slamming the door behind her. How could her best friend Lulu have done this? She had always trusted Lulu to keep a secret, and yet this time, she had let her down badly – or so it seemed. Sofie headed towards the park and as she walked, she began to calm down a little, realising how important her friendship with Lulu was to her. Then her phone rang and, sure enough, it was Lulu, wanting to give her side of the story. It was a complete misunderstanding and Lulu hadn't given away Sofie's secret after all. Sofie was so relieved!
The two girls arranged to meet up in the park immediately. Sofie gave Lulu a big hug and apologised for being so mad at Lulu earlier. They ended up laughing about it and got back to doing what best friends do – sharing secrets with each other.
(159 words)

LISTENING PART 4 Multiple choice

1 Remind students of the format of Listening Part 4. This is also practised in the Student's Book on pages 39, 61, 105 and 115 and in the Workbook on pages 43 and 67. Ask students to read the information on Part 4. Ask students to underline the key words in the question, and to then find the answer in the Audioscript. Ask students to find the expressions that show whether something was easy (*no trouble*, *straightforward*) or difficult (*trickiest*) and feed back as a class.

Answer

1 C. Option A is incorrect as she says she 'had no trouble'. B is incorrect as she describes analysing the results as 'quite straightforward'.

2 ▶3.26 Ask students to underline the key words. Ask one or two volunteers to tell the class what they underlined. Play the recording twice, and check answers as a whole class.

Audioscript

Narrator: You will hear an interview with a teenager called Maria Gonzalez, who is talking about her generation's views on the future.

Interviewer: My studio guest today is seventeen-year-old Maria Gonzalez, who has just completed an internet survey on attitudes to the future among students of her own age. Maria, I know this was a college project for you. What was the most challenging part of the work you had to do?

Maria: Well, none of it was easy! First of all, I had to design the survey, improving my questions so that they were clear and asked for the right information. I guess that was the trickiest thing. In terms of finding enough people to take part, I had no trouble with all my social media connections. Analysing all the results took a fair bit of time, though it was quite straightforward, really.

Interviewer: And what have you found out? Is your generation any different from previous ones, in terms of how they see the future?

Maria: Yes, I think we are, in several ways. It's interesting, I've got a brother who's seven years older and his opinions don't generally match my survey results. For example, he's already in work, so he's much more optimistic about where his career will take him. Typically, seventeen-year-olds like me are extremely nervous about finding the type of employment they believe is appropriate. Additionally, quite a few expressed concern about the impact the economy could have on their future way of life. Around forty per cent are worried they won't get into the right university, either, and think that this will affect their job prospects.

Interviewer: Let's hope they're wrong. And what did you find out about attitudes to technology?

Maria: That's another difference, actually. My brother's generation had less technology available to them when they were growing up, whereas it has surrounded us from birth. So we just take everything for granted, from Facebook to the apps on our smartphones. The survey suggests we feel more in control than my brother's generation, and we definitely regard it as central to our future lives. Surprisingly, though, over eighty per cent of students expressed at least one negative comment about this and would prefer to be less dependent on technology. Sometimes I wish I could take a break from it once in a while, although I'd be lost without it.

Interviewer: Yes, I'm sure. Maria, how are you going to use these survey results …

Answers

2 B 3 A

SPEAKING PARTS 2, 3 AND 4
Long turn, shared task and related discussion

1 Remind students of the format of the Speaking paper. This is also practised in the Student's Book on page 117. Ask students to read through the information on Part 2. Tell them to read the question and look at the photos. Give students one minute to think of ideas and then give them five minutes to compare the photos in pairs. Ask one pair to perform their dialogue to the class.

2 ▶ **3.27** Play the recording and ask students, in pairs, to compare their ideas with Ludmila's. You may want to repeat the recording if students are finding it difficult to pick out her ideas. Draw students' attention to the explanations of Parts 3 and 4 before moving on to exercise 3.

Audioscript

Examiner: Here are your photographs. They show teenagers doing activities in their free time. I'd like you to compare the photographs, and say what you think are the advantages and disadvantages of doing these activities.

Ludmila: Well, they're very different, aren't they! The girls sitting on the floor in a bedroom are playing a game on PlayStation or some other device, and they're wearing casual clothes. The climbers, on the other hand, are dressed for extreme conditions. So that's probably one disadvantage of rock climbing, that you have to buy or hire special clothes and safety equipment.
But I think the big advantage of any outdoor activity is that it's good for your health, you're out in the fresh air and you feel great afterwards. I think this is probably especially true of rock climbing, because it's a very difficult challenge – when you reach the top, you must feel so satisfied!
Computer games, on the other hand, don't give you much exercise! But then again, the girls are having fun and they're able to chat, while up on a rock it's going to be a lot more serious.

Examiner: Thank you.

3 ▶ **3.28** Direct students' attention to the two boxes and make sure that they understand that Ludmila and Oleg are discussing their options. Then play the recording and ask students to compare their answers in pairs. You may want to play the recording a second time before feeding back as a class.

Answers
online access in the café
films in English once a month

Examiner: I'd like you to imagine that a town is deciding how it might attract more teenage visitors to its museum. Here are some ideas that are being considered and a question for you to discuss. First you have some time to look at the task. Now, talk to each other about what a museum might provide to attract more teenagers.

Ludmila: OK, shall I start?

Oleg: Sure, go ahead.

Ludmila: I think museums can be pretty boring places, so it seems good to introduce some extra things, to persuade young people like us to go inside them. Actually, I think live concerts might be quite a good idea, something a bit different. Do you agree?

Oleg: Well, it depends what sort of music is on offer! If it's only classical, then I'm not sure about it, really. I'm not into classical music. And besides, that's probably not something we could afford to go to. Mmm. What about organising English films regularly, say once a month? There could be a link with something in the museum's collection, maybe – I don't know, show the film *Gravity* with something on astronauts.

Ludmila: Yes, that's quite an interesting idea I suppose, though I wonder how popular that kind of event would be after a while?

Oleg: Better than going to lectures about the museum objects, I guess! I can't see many teenagers sitting through something like that.

Ludmila: Absolutely not. Erm … Let's think about the shop and the café now.

Oleg: OK … Speaking personally, I don't ever spend money in shops like that – you know, on postcards and books and things –

Ludmila: Neither do I!

Oleg: So having discounts in the shop isn't going to attract many young visitors, is it? It might work with little kids and their parents, but …

Ludmila: I agree. And what about the café? If there was free internet, that might encourage teenagers to buy a cup of coffee, or lunch or something.

Oleg: Yes, that would attract a lot of people of our age, wouldn't it?

Examiner: Thank you. Now you have about a minute to decide which two ideas would be the most attractive to teenagers.

Ludmila: Well, let's see. We didn't think many teenagers would go for boring lectures or films …

Oleg: Actually, I disagreed with you about the films, and I still quite like that suggestion.

Ludmila: Uh huh. We'll come back to that one, then. What about the other ideas? We said no to the shop, but we both liked the idea of having free online access in the café?

Oleg: Yes, that's definitely worth doing, I'd say.

Ludmila: OK. So internet in the café is number one, and for our second idea, it's either live music or films in English? You thought the music could be too expensive and I agree with you. Let's go with your other choice then.

Oleg: Good. It's a useful way of practising our English!

Examiner: Thank you.

4 ▶ **3.29** Ask students to read the questions. Point out that the questions also ask *Why? / Why not?* and so students should aim to expand on their answer in the exam (Ludmila and Oleg both do this). Play the recording and ask students to check in pairs. Then play the recording a second time (if necessary) and feed back as a class.

Answers

Oleg quite likes visiting museums, especially when there are temporary exhibitions from other countries; Ludmila is less interested in museums.

Ludmila thinks museums are less important than they used to be because there are now other ways of finding out about history and beautiful objects; Oleg thinks they are still important because they give the opportunity to see the real objects face to face.

Ludmila thinks that it is easier to find out about history online, especially because museums charge for admission; Oleg thinks that the problem with the internet is that you can never rely on the information, though he agrees with Ludmila on the convenience of the internet.

Ludmila thinks that museums should be free for students, though not for everyone because that would mean that the government would have to pay; Oleg agrees with Ludmila, and adds that adults should be willing to pay if there's an exhibition that they want to see.

Audioscript

Examiner: Do you enjoy visiting museums, Oleg?

Oleg: Well, it's not my favourite activity, but yes, I quite like going to museums, especially when they have temporary exhibitions from other countries. Those kinds of exhibitions tend to be better presented and you have the chance to see something really unusual, for example ancient gold objects from Colombia or the Chinese terracotta warriors.

Examiner: And you?

Ludmila: I'm not that keen on museums, to be honest. They're such dark places and I prefer to be outside in the fresh air! I don't think I've been inside a museum since I was about thirteen, in fact!

Examiner: How important are museums in the twenty-first century?

Ludmila: They're definitely less important than they used to be, in my opinion. We have other ways now of finding out about history and we can see programmes on television about rare and beautiful things …

Oleg: But that's not quite the same as being face to face with the real objects, is it? Going back to that Chinese warriors exhibition I mentioned, that was really amazing, seeing the actual objects all lined up in front of you, very impressive. And it wouldn't have been as good on television, I'm sure. So, for me it's still important to see the real thing whenever you have the opportunity.

Examiner: Is it easier to learn about history by visiting a museum or by finding the information you need online?

Ludmila: Well, like I said before, we can access information in other ways now. I mean the internet provides everything you need, doesn't it, from shopping to studying. You can key your question into a search engine and get a huge number of search results instantly, which take you to sites with lots of facts, and links to pictures and video clips as well. And it's all for free, whereas you'd have to buy a ticket for most museums.

Examiner: Do you agree?

Oleg: Up to a point, yes, although the problem with the internet is that you can never be sure that the facts are correct! If you visit a museum, on the other hand, you know that you'll learn something real and factually accurate, because they have experts working there, don't they? Ludmila is right about the speed of the internet though – so that aspect is much easier – you get the required information back in an instant, in the comfort of your own home, rather than having to travel across the whole city to a museum.

Examiner: Do you think places like museums and art galleries should have free admission?

Ludmila: You mean they shouldn't charge anything for people to go in?

Examiner: Yes.

Ludmila: I'm not sure. For young people, yes, it's a good idea, and it might encourage people like me to spend more time there than I've done in the past! But at the same time, if nobody pays to enter these places then who *does* pay in the end? The government I suppose.

Examiner: What do you think?

Oleg: I think Ludmila's right about giving free entry to younger people, but when you're an adult, you can decide for yourself how to spend your money and if there's a big exhibition you'd like to go to, then you should be willing to pay for that. Otherwise, with no admission charge there will be less to see, because they won't have enough money to organise something spectacular.

Examiner: Thank you.

Cooler

Ask students to work with a partner and to work through parts 3 and 4 from this section. Ask one or two pairs to role play their speaking exam to the class.

Review answer key

REVIEW 1   Units 1–4
VOCABULARY

1 1 character 2 cast 3 lyrics 4 charts 5 compose 6 post
2 1 ~~arguement~~ argument ~~tommorrow~~ tomorrow
   2 ~~confortable~~ comfortable ~~seperate~~ separate
   3 ~~reciept~~ receipt ~~wiegh~~ weigh
   4 ~~accomodation~~ accommodation ~~oportunity~~ opportunity
3 1 A heard; B mean   2 A cautious; B do
   3 A compare; B jealous   4 A coping; B bothered
   5 A impressed; B glanced
4 1 have 2 lose 3 go 4 lose 5 have 6 get
5 1 Intelligence 2 Creativity 3 concentration 4 nature 5 luck

GRAMMAR

6 1 has called 2 started 3 posted 4 had set
   5 was attracting 6 has been running
   7 has already inspired 8 got 9 hasn't even finished
7 1 a have / 've done   b have / 've been doing
   2 a Have; been running   b Have; run
   3 a has been trying   b have / 've tried
   4 a has rung   b have / 've been ringing
8 1 came across it 2 passed out 3 hand them out
   4 came down with it 5 look after him 6 threw them away
9 1 C 2 C 3 A 4 C 5 A 6 A

10 1 ~~is~~ has been / was
   2 ~~has~~ had
   3 ~~surf~~ have / 've been surfing / have / 've [already] been surfing
   4 ✓
   5 ~~picked up them~~ picked them up
   6 ~~try~~ have / 've been trying / tried
   7 ✓
   8 ~~hadn't to~~ shouldn't / needn't / didn't have to
11 1 come down with 2 haven't / have not spoken for
   3 keep my skis under control / keep control of my skis
   4 are required to show 5 apologised for being
   6 no point (in) leaving

REVIEW 2   Units 5–8
VOCABULARY

1 1 tribe 2 decade 3 inhabitant 4 myth 5 kingdom
   6 ancestor
2 1 They can't understand him when he speaks **quickly**.
   2 He's so careless! He's **constantly** breaking things.
   3 He **eventually** got round to apologising to me ten days later.
   4 She's been ill for weeks now, so she **definitely** needs to see
     a doctor.
   5 It's lovely and sunny – why don't we have lunch **outside**?
   6 You may use the computers in the library. **Alternatively**, you
     can use the laptops in room 23.
3 1 c 2 b 3 a 4 e 5 f 6 d
4 *Possible answers* 1 rural 2 relaxing / restful 3 inner-city
   4 urban 5 close 6 welcoming
5 1 was strolling 2 leaned 3 was whistling 4 whispered
   5 rushed 6 yelled 7 was kneeling 8 tapped

GRAMMAR

6 1 was constantly getting 2 used to swim / would swim
   3 are/'re always finding 4 see 5 gets up
   6 used to play / would play
7 1 've / have finished 2 'm / am going to study 3 leaves
   4 'm / am 5 's / is leaving 6 'm / am going to arrive
   7 'll / will have 8 'm / am meeting
8 1 got used to 2 'm / am 3 was 4 got used to
9 1 was enjoying 2 was 3 had typed 4 looked
   5 had stepped 6 opened 7 took 8 was studying
   9 was working 10 knew 11 sent 12 did they find

10 1 ~~were going~~ went
   2 ~~was telling us stories died~~ who used to tell us stories had died
   3 ✓
   4 ~~have used it~~ I have got used to it
   5 ~~were playing~~ had been playing; ~~had said~~ said
   6 ~~never met~~ had never met
   7 ✓
   8 ~~you are going to see~~ you'll see
11 1 B 2 D 3 A 4 C 5 D 6 A 7 C 8 D

REVIEW 3   Units 9–12
VOCABULARY

1 1 b 2 f 3 e 4 c 5 a 6 d
2 1 by heart 2 out of fashion 3 in common 4 at fault
   5 in favour
3 1 well-built 2 last-minute 3 badly-behaved 4 short-term
   5 self-confident
4 1 letting Tom down 2 stick together 3 takes after 4 gone off
   5 falling out 6 looking down on me
5 1 d (to become an actress) 2 c
   3 e (up but he's really down)
   4 a (on his excellent exam results) 5 b
   6 f (to lend me some money)

GRAMMAR

6 1 have been given to everyone.
   2 given this computer by my brother.
   3 our house painted while we were away.
   4 have been told what to do by your teacher.
   5 phone replaced for free by the company. / phone replaced by
     the company for free.
   6 persuaded not to go by Simon?
7 1 b 2 b 3 a 4 b 5 a 6 a 7 b 8 b 9 a 10 b
   11 a 12 a
8 1 where 2 who 3 who / that 4 who 5 whose
   6 that / which 7 when 8 why

9 1 ~~have been finished~~ have finished
  2 ✓
  3 ~~should start~~ should have started
  4 ~~had been~~ would have been
  5 ~~which address~~ whose address
  6 ~~which~~ who
  7 ✓
  8 ~~been built~~ had been built
10 1 sensitive / sensible **2** consideration **3** original
  4 astonishment **5** generosity **6** judgement **7** memorable
  8 unbelievable

REVIEW 4 Units 13–16
VOCABULARY

1 1 sympathetic **2** appreciate **3** criticism **4** motivated
  5 doubtful **6** Cooperation
2 1 breaks down **2** speak up **3** pulling out **4** live up to
  5 keep up with **6** cooling (me) down
3 1 recommended getting **2** confessed to breaking
  3 criticised (me) for making **4** agreed to help
  5 pointed out that planning
4 1 launched **2** aimed **3** consumers **4** products **5** publicity
  6 sample **7** offer
5 1 d **2** a **3** f **4** b **5** c **6** e

GRAMMAR

6 *Suggested answers*
  1 Person C can't be on holiday.
  2 Person B might have stolen the bag.
  3 Person A might chase Person B.
  4 Person B might have noticed the ladder. / Person B can't have noticed the ladder.
  5 ✓
  6 Person A might have wanted to talk to Person B.
  7 ✓
  8 Person A might be angry with Person B. / Person A must be angry with Person B.
7 1 being taken out **2** to be asked **3** to be awarded
  4 be invited **5** being served **6** to be / being laughed
  7 is named **8** being given
8 1 You would have loved it if you had / you'd gone.
  2 we'll recognise him when he arrives.
  3 If I ate it regularly, I'd put on weight.
  4 If you won one, who would you take?
  5 what would you have studied if you had / you'd gone?
  6 If you heat copper, what temperature does it melt at?
9 1 's / has always loved **2** hadn't / had not seen **3** speak
  4 'll / will **5** 'd / had read **6** might not be able

10 1 ~~pay~~ paid
  2 ~~must not watched~~ must not be watched
  3 ~~officer told that~~ officer was told that
  4 ✓
  5 ~~needn't to get annoyed~~ needn't get annoyed
  6 ✓
  7 ~~died~~ would have died
  8 ~~booked~~ book
11 1 to **2** If **3** of **4** as **5** a **6** The **7** where **8** have

REVIEW 5 Units 17–20
VOCABULARY

1 1 keep **2** date **3** mind **4** comment on **5** be honest
  6 gossip **7** making fun **8** go along **9** chill out **10** keeping
2 1 bring **2** catch **3** leave **4** get **5** back **6** look
3 1 g **2** h **3** f **4** e **5** b **6** a **7** c **8** d
4 1 was a piece of cake **2** lost track **3** is a pain
  4 broke my heart **5** took your breath away
  6 cross my (your) mind

GRAMMAR

5 1 'd / would be able **2** hadn't / had not mentioned
  3 wouldn't / would not be **4** 'd / would have taken
  5 'd / had studied **6** wasn't / was not / weren't / were not
6 1 being; to do **2** learning; managed to **3** Bearing; to get
  4 being; to make **5** telling; thinking **6** Working; realise
7 1 are **2** has **3** sounds **4** works **5** Is **6** are
8 1 some **2** The **3** some / a little **4** a lot of / some
  5 a lot / a large number **6** a few / several **7** the
  8 a lot / a large number **9** several / some **10** – / some

9 1 ~~if you correct~~ if you corrected
  2 ✓
  3 ~~to shop~~ shopping
  4 ~~to go~~ going
  5 ~~are~~ is
  6 ✓
  7 ~~a few~~ some / a bit of
  8 ~~much~~ many; ~~affect~~ effect
10 1 D **2** A **3** C **4** A **5** D **6** C **7** B **8** B

Grammar reference answer key

UNIT 1

SIMPLE, CONTINUOUS OR PERFECT

1 **1** wanted, looked, had seen
  2 was, 'd/had already started
  3 've/have never seen, did you find

2 **1** d **2** f **3** b **4** e **5** a **6** c

3 **1** F **2** E **3** A **4** B **5** C **6** D

UNIT 2

PRESENT PERFECT SIMPLE AND CONTINUOUS

1 **1** Have you been waiting
  2 haven't been listening, 've been telling
  3 's/has been mending
  4 've/have been walking
  5 Have the children been playing
  6 hasn't been living

2 **1** same
  2 different (the first speaker has finished cleaning the car; in the second we don't know if the job is finished or not)
  3 same
  4 different (the first speaker has finished cooking; in the second we don't know if the lunch is ready or not)
  5 different (the first speaker has never driven the car; the second may have driven it in the past, but not recently)

3 **1** I've nearly finished **2** I've been designing **3** both
  4 I've also visited **5** both **6** both

4 (*Suggested answers*)
  1 I've been living at my present address for ten years.
  2 I've been studying English since I was eight.
  3 Francis has been supporting for six years.
  4 I've been wearing these clothes since early this morning.

UNIT 3

PHRASAL VERBS

1 **1** pay it back **2** make it up **3** looking forward to it
2 **1** broke down **2** come across **3** got me down **4** take up
  5 get into **6** have gone by **7** think about **8** pass on
3 (*Suggested answers*)
  1 insults and violence.
  2 upsetting them?
  3 your own mistakes.
  4 all kinds of people.
  5 their parents' achievements.

UNIT 4

MODALS (1) NECESSITY, OBLIGATION, PROHIBITION AND ADVICE

1 **1** had to **2** didn't have to **3** have **4** have to
  5 don't have **6** need **7** mustn't
2 **1** should I; ought I to
  2 should I; ought I to
  3 should I; should I; ought I to; ought I to

3 (*Suggested answers*)
  1 have a regular training programme.
  2 eat junk food.
  3 go to bed late very often.

4 (*Suggested answers*)
  1 you don't have to / you don't need to / you haven't got to.
  2 should / ought to talk to your teacher.
  3 mustn't bring food into the shop.
  4 have to wear uniform.
  5 Should I / Ought I to phone my brother?
  6 You must let me help you.

UNIT 5

PRESENT AND PAST HABITS

1 **1** My dad would **regularly** have a snack in the afternoon.
  2 I didn't **often** use to sleep more than six hours when I was young.
  3 Do you **usually** get enough sleep during the week?
  4 A doctor wouldn't **normally** prescribe sleeping tablets for someone as young as you.
  5 The factory workers were **frequently** short of sleep and **sometimes** injured themselves as a result.
  6 The students were **continually** yawning during lectures because they **never** went to sleep before midnight.
  7 I **normally** sleep very soundly but **from time to time** I have nightmares and wake up shouting. OR I have nightmares and wake up shouting **from time to time**.
  8 Did you use to sleep in your parents' bed **all the time** when you were little?

2 **1** 're/are always advertising special offers.
  2 was always giving her assignments in late.
  3 's/is continually shouting at his children.
  4 's/is constantly bringing mice into the house.
  5 were always promising jobs for everyone.

UNIT 6

BE / GET / BECOME USED TO

1 **1** have got used to
  2 weren't used to
  3 were used to
  4 wasn't used to
  5 had been used to
  6 am used to
  7 can't get used to

2 **1** isn't used to doing the shopping OR hasn't got/become used to doing the shopping
  2 's (is) used to staying up OR 's (has) got/become used to staying up
  3 's (is) getting/becoming used to tidying
  4 wasn't used to talking

UNIT 7

NARRATIVE TENSES

1 1 had booked 2 had been raining / had rained
  3 had been preparing 4 had already agreed 5 had texted
  6 had been wanting / had wanted

2 1 had been 2 had delayed 3 had been waiting 4 boarded
  5 were 6 had already given 7 had moved 8 heard
  9 went out 10 returned 11 got out 12 turned out
  13 had caused 14 had been completed 15 were able to
  16 had arrived 17 hadn't eaten 18 enjoyed
  19 landed 20 cheered

UNIT 8

FUTURE (1): REVIEW

1

A 1 I'm meeting 2 we'll try 3 I'm about to start 4 begins
  5 I won't be 6 comes 7 is the taxi picking 8 leaves
  9 will be 10 is 11 won't hold 12 you arrive 13 I'll see
B 1 is about to start 2 have gone 3 I'll go 4 I'll get
  5 I'll have 6 we're going to have 7 won't start 8 we're
  9 we'll be (He might say 'we're going to be fine' but he can't really
    know for sure!)

UNIT 9

THE FUTURE (2): CONTINUOUS AND PERFECT

1 1 will be closing; won't be opening
  2 will be taking
  3 Will he be playing; won't be playing

2 1 'll/will have spent
  2 'll/will have sunbathed OR 'll/will have been sunbathing
  3 won't have eaten OR won't have been eating
  4 'll/will have danced OR 'll/will have been dancing
  5 won't have missed us OR won't have been missing us
  6 'll/will have texted us

3 1 'll/will have been married for forty years.
  2 'll/will have lived / 'll/will have been living here for (over)
    ten years.
  3 'll/will have slept (for)
  4 'll/will have tidied up. (the kitchen)
  5 'll/will have been travelling

4 1 ✓ 2 ✓ 3 ✗ 4 ✗ 5 ✓ 6 ✗ 7 ✓ 8 ✓ 9 ✗ 10 ✗
  11 ✓ 12 ✗

UNIT 10

MODALS (2): MODALS IN THE PAST

1 1 shouldn't have shouted
  2 wouldn't have looked
  3 should have sent
  4 should I have given
  5 needn't have bothered
  6 Shouldn't / Should you have given
  7 needn't have worried
  8 would have sent
  9 didn't need to take
  10 would you have chosen

2 (Sample answers)
  1 have enjoyed it
  2 have changed your plan / have come with us
  3 have gone this time / have missed the concert
  4 have bought it for me

UNIT 11

RELATIVE CLAUSES

1 1 Have you ever visited the island that your grandparents came
    from? (no comma)
  2 John's bicycle, that which was stolen last week, has turned up
    in the next street.
  3 Is that the coat you wanted to buy it?
  4 This is the website who which / that I told you about it.
  5 The city where I went to university is a very lively place. (no
    commas)
  6 The singer who I like her most is from Argentina.
  7 The friend I stayed with her in Geneva is a painter.

2 (Suggested answers)
  1 have lots of car chases.
  2 you can cook at home.
  3 brother is a famous actor.
  4 there's no music.
  5 listens when you have a problem.

UNIT 12

PASSIVE (1): REVIEW

1 1 was bought 2 had been resisted 3 was made
  4 was included 5 have not been told 6 have been persuaded
  7 will be given 8 will be put 9 are being sold
  10 will be used

2 1 got the shop to replace
  2 'm/am having / 'm/am going to have it cleaned
  3 got my parents to pay
  4 got my boss to call
  5 had a bunch of flowers delivered

UNIT 13

THE PASSIVE (2): OTHER STRUCTURES

1 1 to be amused 2 being told off 3 be given
  4 to be served 5 to be awarded 6 being treated
  7 to be called 8 be chosen 9 being hugged
  10 to be asked 11 being involved 12 being stopped
  13 to be used 14 to be delivered 15 being allowed

UNIT 14

REPORTED SPEECH

1 1 they had seen Ahmed
  2 to hate / (that) he hates
  3 they went to Morocco
  4 to see
  5 where the ticket office is / was

2 1 agreed 2 denies 3 praised 4 suggested
  5 enquired 6 persuaded

UNIT 15
MODALS (3): DEDUCTION

1 1 can't be   **2** must know   **3** may/might/could be   **4** can't be
    5 can't have   **6** must be   **7** may/might/could block / be blocking
    8 may/might/could be

2 1 e   **2** c   **3** a   **4** f   **5** b   **6** d

3 1 could have been
    2 might have been
    3 can't have been
    4 could be
    5 can't be
    6 must be
    7 must have been

UNIT 16
CONDITIONALS (1): REVIEW

1 (*Suggested answers*)
    1 live   **2** get   **3** arrives

2 1 b   **2** a   **3** d   **4** c

3 1 If I were/was you, I'd take a smaller suitcase.
    2 I'd check the weight limit if I were/was you.
    3 walk along this road at night if I were/was you.
    4 were/was you, I'd take a torch with me.

4 1 have seen the band if she'd gone to the party.
    2 have won the tournament if he hadn't entered it.
    3 trained carefully, he wouldn't have felt fine at the end of the race.

5 1 wouldn't have asked   **2** find   **3** don't give
    4 would be   **5** had   **6** 'd remembered
    7 wouldn't have got   **8** didn't forget   **9** would save

UNIT 17
CONDITIONALS (2): MIXED

1 1 hadn't eaten; wouldn't be
    2 would/could go; hadn't started
    3 had told; wouldn't repeat
    4 would/could we play; hadn't installed
    5 would/might get; 'd/had studied
    6 'd/had finished; could/would relax

2 1 would/might/could have gone; had
    2 was/were; could/would have used
    3 didn't exaggerate; might have believed
    4 would/could your friends have stayed; didn't have
    5 would/could/might have given; had

3 1 hadn't worked / didn't work
    2 wouldn't be
    3 Would Rosa have
    4 might/could/would have saved
    5 could/would have
    6 weren't
    7 'd/had brought
    8 would be
    9 had never existed
    10 might/would/could have walked
    11 would/might cities be

UNIT 18
USES OF VERB + -ING

1 (*Suggested answers*)
    1 going to bed late.
    2 going out for a meal?
    3 being unhappy in a place like that.
    4 helping you.
    5 walking home.

2 1 after   **2** without   **3** by   **4** when   **5** spend time
    6 have no difficulty   **7** it's not worth   **8** pass the time
    9 get fed up with   **10** Since   **11** by

3 1 Sitting at the back of the hall, I couldn't see the show very well.
    2 Not being interested in rugby, I didn't go to the match with my cousins.
    3 My dad, wanting to know why I wasn't home, phoned the school office. / Wanting to know why I wasn't home, my dad phoned the school office.

UNIT 19
SUBJECT-VERB AGREEMENT

1 1 correct
    2 The city is very quiet because everybody **is** on holiday this week.
    3 Revising for exams **was** preventing my brother from doing any sport.
    4 correct
    5 No-one has come to see me for ages. I must have done something to upset **them**.
    6 correct
    7 A number of my friends **are** taking part in a riding competition on Saturday.
    8 My phone's dead. **Has** anyone brought their charger with them?
    9 The majority of people in this town **work** at the electronics factory.
    10 The class **were** texting their friends as they came out of the exam.
    11 correct (*The swimming club have put up their membership fees* would also be correct)
    12 Learning about other people **is** an important part of growing up.
    13 Both of my parents **work** long hours but we have plenty of fun together at weekends.

UNIT 20
DETERMINERS

1 1 a   **2** the   **3** the   **4** The   **5** the   **6** several   **7** –
    8 Some   **9** –   **10** plenty of   **11** –   **12** a   **13** The
    14 lots of   **15** the   **16** the   **17** a   **18** few   **19** very little
    20 the   **21** a   **22** number of   **23** –   **24** much
    25 a few   **26** the

Workbook answer key and audioscripts

UNIT 1 Creative minds

VOCABULARY

1 Across: 2 blog 7 review 8 series 10 compose 12 classic
13 form 14 soundtrack

 Down: 1 scene 3 lyrics 4 character 5 cast 6 bestseller
9 voice 11 post

2 1 critics 2 novelist 3 editor 4 presenter 5 director

3 1 blog (the others are people)
2 soundtrack (the others are verbs)
3 editor (the others aren't people)
4 cast (the others describe books or films; this is people in the film)
5 version (the others are connected with music)
6 charts (the others are connected with films and plays)

READING

1 Students should underline: 1 too frightening, young
2 regaining, lost 3 humour 4 journey into the past 5 may be hiding something 6 film 7 not very sociable 8 series
9 another work 10 romantic episode

2 1 D 2 B 3 A 4 E 5 E 6 C 7 A 8 B 9 D 10 C

3 Students should underline:
1 (D) While it may be a bit much for pre-teens, more mature readers will keep turning the pages ...
2 (B) ... in order to fetch back the shadows from the thieves ...
3 (A) This book is ... funny ...
4 (E) Time-travelling Sam is taken back 300 years ...
5 (E) ... Dick, who Sam suspects is not all he claims to be.
6 (C) In fact the movie rights have already been sold to a family-friendly Hollywood production company, and it is due for release next year.
7 (A) she prefers to chat with animals, trees, plants and inanimate objects, rather than other human beings
8 (B) This is the second breathtaking adventure ...
9 (D) ... she was inspired to write her children's book drawing on the *Inferno*'s rickes.
10 (C) Dark's love of tricks

Word profile

1 a 2 b 3 c 4 b 5 c

GRAMMAR

1 1 have you seen, saw
2 go, 've never been
3 are you doing, 'm doing, did
4 Did you enjoy, had finished, was
5 were you doing, was reading, 'm reading, are you enjoying, love

2 1 am writing 2 is shining 3 come 4 has been 5 moved
6 stay 7 saw 8 were walking 9 ran 10 started
11 happen 12 happened 13 were sitting 14 had just paid
15 were getting 16 came 17 started 18 didn't want
19 have just come 20 want

3 1 I <u>have taken</u> so long to write to you because I have been busy.
2 Did you <u>have</u> a good time on your holiday?
3 ✓
4 By the time I arrived, he <u>had</u> disappeared.
5 Surfing <u>has been</u> my hobby since 2010.
6 ✓

VOCABULARY

1 environment 2 successful 3 believe 4 choice
5 correct 6 although 7 until 8 correct

WRITING

1 *Students' own answers*
2 *Students' own answers*
3 1 most people agree 2 However 3 For instance
4 Furthermore
4 1 very popular
2 unrealistic ideas about the future, stop caring about schoolwork
3 very relaxing viewing, another idea of your own
4 summary of the points made, your conclusion
5 *Students' own answers*

UNIT 2 Addicted to fashion

VOCABULARY

1

about	at	by
bothered cautious decisive mean	hopeless	impressed
of	**to**	**with**
aware critical jealous	addicted loyal	adventurous

2 1 a 2 c 3 b 4 a 5 b 6 a 7 c 8 b

3 1 Meral is addicted to buying shoes.
2 Andrea isn't bothered about fashion.
3 Max is adventurous with fashion.
4 Anna is jealous of her best friend.
5 Peter is decisive about (buying) clothes.

READING

1 *Students' own answers*
2 a
3 1 twentieth 2 too expensive
3 protect their eyes from lights
4 encourage the public to wear sunglasses 5 look good
4 1 expert 2 reduce 3 luxuries 4 desirable 5 avoid
6 generates 7 comfort 8 emotions

Word profile

1 1 to a point 2 is no point (in) 3 missed the point
4 get to the 5 the point is

GRAMMAR

1 **1** been wearing **2** lost **3** been sunbathing
  4 been studying **5** sold **6** been reading **7** eaten
  8 been drinking
2 **1** have been keeping **2** has been **3** 've been sitting
  4 've already had **5** have met **6** 've been **7** 've been doing
  8 've been applying **9** has been trying **10** haven't eaten
3 **1** The football team <u>played</u> badly last year.
  2 ✓
  3 Agustina <u>has been</u> my best friend since we met in school when
    we were three years old.
  4 I <u>have been</u> playing classical guitar for three years.
  5 Yesterday I <u>was hiking / hiked</u> for five hours.
  6 ✓

VOCABULARY

1 for **2** at **3** with **4** with **5** on **6** without **7** of

LISTENING

2 **1** ✗ **2** ✓ **3** ✓ **4** ✓
3 **1** Will **2** Eddie **3** Tanya **4** Hannah **5** Hannah **6** Tanya
  7 Will
4 **1** enjoy shopping for clothes **2** into **3** look forward to **4** treat
  5 to like
1 expresses a negative attitude.
5 Suggested answers:
  1 Yes, I'm really into shopping. / No, I'm not really into shopping.
  2 It's a treat to go out for the day. / I enjoy looking at new
    fashions. / I don't particularly like shopping centres.
  3 My friends. / My brother/sister.
  4 After school. / At the weekend.
  5 Jeans and trainers. / Casual clothes for hanging out with
    friends.

▶2 Audioscript

1

Eddie: To be honest, I don't particularly enjoy shopping for
clothes, but I do like getting a good deal. That's why I
only shop when there are sales on. I buy cheap clothes.
There's something quite satisfying about paying less for
an article than it would have cost originally. Some of my
friends like to spend loads of money – I guess it makes
them feel good. But I don't understand that at all. I like to
look as good as I can with as little money as possible. To
me, that's what it's all about.

2

Tanya: Well, like all my friends, I'm really into fashion. We tend
to go shopping together, and we really enjoy seeing all
the new designs when they come out. We always look
forward to the new collection each season – but it can be
expensive to buy them there and then, so we usually wait
for a few months and then try to get a bargain. But it's
important to us to be fashionable. It makes us feel good
about ourselves – and it's important to look good, too. I'd
like to work in the industry when I leave school.

3

Will: I never have much money to spend, really, and I don't give
it away lightly! I'm careful with my money. I think I get that
from my dad. What I do like about shopping for clothes is
that it's one of the few occasions when I can make up my
own mind about things. Coming from a small family, it was
usually my parents who bought my clothes for me, and
it's only in the last year that I've been given the freedom
to make my own choices. It's quite a treat for me. Part of
growing up, I suppose.

4

Hannah: Clothes shopping? Yes! What's not to like? Shopping
for bargains, spending money, looking at yourself in the
mirror in an outfit you can't possibly afford. But most of
all, it's social for me. I never actually spend a lot, but we
always have a great laugh when we go out shopping
together – going for coffee, trying on the latest fashions.
We have a brilliant time, even if we come home empty-
handed, which, nine times out of ten, is exactly what
happens! My rich cousins don't understand me, but that's
their loss.

UNIT 3   All in the mind

VOCABULARY

1 **1** concentration **2** creativity **3** determination **4** luck
  5 success **6** development **7** agreement **8** fortune
  9 nature **10** intelligence
2 **1** intelligence **2** creativity **3** belief **4** concentration
  5 agreement **6** determination **7** success **8** nature
  9 development **10** luck, fortune
3 **1** belief **2** creativity **3** success **4** agreement
  5 concentration **6** luck **7** development **8** intelligence

READING

1 The monkeys are grooming each other to show empathy and
  affection.
2 domestic pets, monkeys, bees, whales
3 **A** <u>It</u> seemed to be willing to go hungry rather than see a fellow
    animal suffer.
  B Empathy plays a role in <u>that</u> as <u>it</u> allows us to understand our
    fellow humans better.
  C <u>This fear</u> of strangers will, we believe, protect us from personal
    danger.
  D <u>Other research</u> has shown animals displaying empathy towards
    other animals and towards humans.
  E The usual effect of <u>this</u> kind of behaviour is that <u>it</u> stops crying,
    shouting and other signs of being upset.
  F <u>We</u> assume that people are able to think themselves into the
    position of another person, even though <u>they</u> may not have
    personally experienced that person's circumstances.
  G <u>They</u> communicate this requirement by crying for attention and
    to show pain.
4 **1** F **2** D **3** A **4** G **5** B **6** C
5 **2** other research = One study
  3 it = the first monkey
  4 they = the young of all animal species
  5 that = working together, it = Empathy
  6 this fear = unknown creatures, strangers
6 **1** quality **2** citizen **3** unique **4** domestic **5** species
  6 regard

Word profile

1 c **2** b **3** c **4** a **5** b **6** a

GRAMMAR

1

without an object	show off
	break down
separable	put off
	let down
inseparable	care for
	deal with
inseparable three-part	get on with
	get out of

2 1 showing off **2** put it off **3** let you down
4 broke down **5** care for the cat **6** get on with my brother
7 get out of it **8** deal with this problem

3 1 He's let me down again.
2 Please get on with your work.
3 Can you turn the TV down? / Can you turn down the TV?
4 I'll clear up the mess in the kitchen. / I'll clear the mess in the kitchen up.
5 Mum is caring for her.

4 1 It will <u>show off</u> how healthy the students are.
2 I guess it will <u>live up to</u> your expectations.
3 She <u>has looked</u> after me since my childhood.
4 The youngest people sometimes <u>show off</u> in front of their friends.
5 ✓

VOCABULARY

1 begged Sara to help him **2** tend not to perform
3 forced me to do **4** you want me to prepare
5 reminded Ellie to hand **6** did not intend to make

WRITING

1 1 a Write soon. **2** b The thing is,…
3 d But don't forget that… **4** f To start with…
5 j It's lovely to hear from you. **6** k As far as I know…
7 h Keep in touch. **8** c To be honest, I reckon…
9 i I'm very happy to… **10** e Take care.

2 three
3 Sentences 3 and 5 shouldn't be in the response.
4 What do you think about this? – 2, 6
Are pets popular in your country? – 1
If so, which kind? – 4
5/6 *Students' own answers*

UNIT 4   Take a deep breath
VOCABULARY

1 1 mind **2** faint **3** feel **4** appetite **5** panic **6** upset
7 lose **8** bad-tempered
Word down: difficulty
2 1 going over and over … in my mind **2** an upset stomach
3 lost her temper / got bad-tempered **4** feel dizzy
5 get in a panic **6** fainted **7** having difficulty sleeping
8 lose my appetite
3 *Students' own answers*

READING

1 Suggested answers:
recording music; might be pleasant
2 Yes
3 1 a recording studio **2** because sounds mean that things
are working **3** lights can make a noise
4 because of the noises of his body **5** his time was finished
4 1 B (It isn't his family who annoy him, just noise) **2** A **3** C
4 B (I felt anxious for two reasons …) **5** A **6** C

Word profile

1 b **2** e **3** a **4** c **5** d

GRAMMAR

1 1 a **2** b **3** a **4** c **5** b **6** a **7** a **8** b
2 1 must **2** ought to **3** don't have to **4** needn't **5** can't
6 mustn't **7** should **8** have to
3 1 ✓
2 I suppose you will ~~must~~ have fun in New York.
3 ✓
4 I've been told to give my opinion about whether students
<u>should only</u> study what they enjoy.
5 You only have one life, and you <u>mustn't</u> waste it.

VOCABULARY

1 stayed up **2** cut down on **3** passed out **4** got over
5 gets me down **6** come down with

LISTENING

1 1 e **2** d **3** b **4** a **5** c
2 1 feeling calm after the run **2** learning a lot from listening
3 being with friends **4** earning money
5 feeling of achievement
3 Speaker 1 F   Speaker 2 C   Speaker 3 E   Speaker 4 D
Speaker 5 G

▶**3 Audioscript**
1
I go running every day, in the late afternoon usually. It's great after
a hard day in college, with all the concentration and mental activity.
I mean, sure, it keeps me fit – I've always been pretty sporty
anyway, but the best thing is that however I feel at the beginning of
the run, I'm always totally calm at the end of it. Ready to jump in the
shower, change into my jeans, and have a nice chilled time at home,
or maybe go out with friends. There's nothing like it!

2
I've never really been into sports or hobbies of any kind, to be
honest. When I'm stressed out about something, I like to talk it out
with a friend. Yeah, I'm a talker; people say I should get a career
in radio or something, but I'm not sure about that. I'm a believer in
the power of conversation. Not only do you feel better when you
talk something through, but you can get a lot out of just listening
to people. It's surprising how few people really listen, when other
people can be such a great source of wisdom and knowledge.
That's what I really love about it.

3

I joined the local rock choir last year during my exams because I felt I needed to do something to help me stop thinking about them. And it worked. It was the best decision I ever made. We're all amateurs – I don't think we'll ever be able to charge money for our performances – but there's a great sense of being part of a team. And you do really build a strong bond of friendship with your fellow singers. When you're singing you're really 'in the moment', but it's the opportunity to be with such lovely people that really makes it special for me.

4

The gym is where I go when I'm stressed out, which is nearly every day, I must admit! I've always been really into fitness – been a gym member since I was thirteen, and I know everyone there. If a new member comes along, I'm always the one to show them around the equipment. I do a bit of private training on the side, too, which is a useful source of income. In fact, I couldn't do without it now so that's really why I spend so much time there. Besides, it's quite satisfying to see people improving their fitness week by week.

5

Learning to play the piano was my dad's idea. I'd been under a lot of pressure and I needed something to take my mind off things. It turns out studying a musical instrument is something you can get completely absorbed in, so it did the job in that respect! I love it. It'd be great to make a living out of it, but that's a long way off. In the meantime, there's nothing like the feeling you get when you work your way successfully through a difficult piece without making any mistakes. That's what keeps me going!

UNIT 5   Past times

1 1 kingdom   2 century   3 myth   4 tribe   5 decade   6 citizen
   7 inhabitant   8 ancestor   9 launch
2 a 2   b 6   c 4   d 1   e 8   f 7   g 3   h 5   i 0   j 9
3 1 kingdom   2 myths   3 decade   4 century   5 civilisation
   6 citizen   7 ancestors   8 tribe   9 launch   10 inhabitants

READING

1 2 d   3 h   4 a   5 c   6 f   7 g   8 e
2 1 was   2 down   3 in   4 will/might   5 it   6 The   7 lot
   8 though
3 3 (Ancient Egyptians, Greeks and Romans)
4/5 1 It   2 other   3 were   4 would   5 to   6 as   7 at   8 do
6 1 Vespasian   2 people   3 sailors   4 people
7 1 artificial   2 storey   3 severely   4 major

Word profile

1 b   **2** b   **3** a   **4** b

GRAMMAR

1 1 used to   2 is eating   3 is constantly looking
   4 would go   5 feel   6 used to
2 1 I would ride a tricycle every day
   2 'm sleeping on the sofa
   3 used to hate shopping for clothes
   4 I (always) go for a run / go running
   5 I'm always/constantly forgetting my key.
   6 was constantly telling
3 1 b   2 a   3 a   4 a

VOCABULARY

1 1 seldom   2 all the time   3 once in a while   4 often
   5 from time to time
2 1 We go to a circus *every once in a while.*
   2 I *seldom* go to bed after midnight.
   3 My best friend and I meet for a chat *most weeks.*
   4 I read a newspaper *every day.*
   5 I visit an art gallery *from time to time.*
   6 I *rarely* listen to music.
   7 My family *almost never* eats in a restaurant.
   8 *Most days* I drink at least three glasses of water.
3 *Students' own answers*

WRITING

1 See answers to exercise 3.
2 4, 3, 1, 2
3 Paragraph 2 says what the writer admires about him.
   Paragraph 3 says what questions the writer would ask him.
   Paragraph 4 concludes the article.
4 *Informal*
   Not only that …
   Believe me … !
   All in all ….
   Who doesn't want that?
5 *Students' own answers*

UNIT 6   Strong emotions

VOCABULARY

1 1 h   2 f   3 b   4 c   5 e   6 g   7 a   8 d   9 i
2 1 scared   2 furious / fed up   3 over the moon
   4 fed up / furious   5 pessimistic   6 optimistic   7 relieved
   8 depressed   9 content
3 1 bright / cheerful   2 concerned / anxious   3 irritated
   4 bad-tempered   5 scared / petrified   6 down / depressed
4 1 cheerful   2 concerned   3 fed up   4 concerned   5 furious

READING

1 daydreaming / looking bored / nothing
2 have pleasant thoughts about something you would like to happen
3 2 – Alpha and Beta
4 1 True (… it may seem quite busy. Your brain is in Beta mode.)
   2 False (People who spend more time in this state …)
   3 False (He spent many productive hours being bored …)
   4 Not given   5 False (They have special rooms for encouraging daydreaming …)   6 False (If you are lucky enough … enjoy those moments of boredom.)
5 1 focus   2 crossed your mind   3 tend to   4 curiosity
   5 coming up with

GRAMMAR

1 **1** isn't used to **2** 'm not used to, 'll get used to
3 aren't used to **4** 'm not used to, 'm used to

2 **1** get used to **2** wasn't used to doing, get used to, 'm not used to **3** was used to, got used to, get used to

3 **1** used to **2** get used to **3** used to **4** am getting **5** used to **6** isn't used to

4 **1** In Sofia there are subways and trains but people <u>do not usually</u> travel on them.

2 ✓

3 I can cook very well too, because I <u>am used to doing it</u> when my mother is not at home.

4 I got used to <u>dealing</u> with people and I love cooking different kinds of dishes.

VOCABULARY

1

adverbs of time	last year, until tomorrow
frequency adverbs	seldom, from time to time
adverbs of certainty	definitely, probably
adverbs of manner	quickly, immediately
adverbs of place	in my bedroom, on the chair
connecting adverbs	however, nevertheless

2 **1** ✓

2 She enjoys going to the beach from time to time. / From time to time, she enjoys going to the beach.

3 It probably won't take you long to get used to it.

4 James ran away immediately when he saw the spider.

5 ✓

6 That's a good computer. However, it's a bit expensive. / It's a bit expensive, however.

3 **1** I don't often drink coffee.

2 The kids probably won't enjoy this film.

3 She plays the piano beautifully.

4 I'll finish my project next week. / Next week, I'll finish my project.

LISTENING

1 a 3 b 4 c 1 d 2 e 5
3 **1** B **2** B **3** C **4** A **5** C

▶4 Audioscript

1 *You hear a teenager leaving a voicemail message.*

Hi, Jason. It's Maria. Sorry you couldn't make it last night. You missed a great show! Dana and I both agreed it was the best musical we'd seen in years. She was disappointed you weren't there, by the way. She was looking forward to meeting you again. Anyway, you should really go and see it when you get the chance – you won't regret it. The music was superb and the dancing was out of this world. You could invite Dana if you don't want to go on your own – she'd be glad to sit through it again, I'm sure. Anyway, just thought I'd let you know what you missed! Speak soon, bye!

2 *You hear a boy talking to a friend about something that happened to him.*

Boy: It was a lucky escape. I was very nearly knocked off.

Girl: So the guy didn't signal? He just turned left in front of you?

Boy: I don't think he even realised I was there. I had to slam on my brakes, and stop with a foot on the pavement. My front wheel missed the back of his car by centimetres.

Girl: It could have been pretty serious.

Boy: Yes, fortunately I had my wits about me.

Girl: Honestly, cycle awareness should be part of the driving test. Too many drivers just don't have a clue.

Boy: I know – it's about time they did something about that.

3 *You hear two people talking about a school sports day.*

Boy: How was the school sports day? Sorry I couldn't help.

Woman: Don't worry about it. We had plenty of volunteers, lack of help wasn't a problem. The weather was, though. You know it started to pour down at midday and we got soaked.

Boy: Oh, no. I thought of you when I saw the rain.

Woman: It completely ruined the whole day for me. The students couldn't care less, of course. They thought it was a great laugh. And we did manage to raise the money for a new sound system for the hall, which was the whole point of it. So the head teacher was thrilled, which is the main thing.

4 *You overhear two friends in a shop talking about some trainers.*

Girl: What do you think of these? They look quite comfortable.

Boy: Well, try them on. It's the only way to find out!

Girl: Mmm. Yes, they feel good.

Boy: What about the colour? Are you sure pink'll go with all of your clothes?

Girl: Yeah! I love pink. You know that.

Boy: I do, but what about your bright red jeans? They'd look awful together.

Girl: That's your opinion. What's the price, anyway? Hmm – a hundred and fifty pounds.

Boy: Oh, no, you can't afford that, can you? It's too much.

Girl: You're telling me! Come on, let's go and get something to eat.

5 *You overhear two friends talking about comedy.*

Boy: I've just watched Mark Smith's latest comedy DVD. It's hilarious! Mark Smith is a comedy genius.

Girl: I know! I didn't know he had a new DVD out, though. Did David tell you about it?

Boy: David? Oh, your friend from the comedy club? He knows a lot of good comedians, doesn't he? But actually they featured Mark Smith's new DVD on an internet talk show, played a section of it, and I ordered a copy straight away.

Girl: Do you often read *The Comic*? You know, the monthly magazine. I get a lot of information from there.

Boy: Yes, I do actually. I'm always discovering new stuff in that.

Word profile

1 **1** good thing **2** the whole thing **3** the thing is
4 the main thing **5** a single thing **6** among other things
7 no such thing

UNIT 7 Telling stories
VOCABULARY
1

```
W H I S P E R U P H E S
V U T W I J M X N C B H
J T K A G G P M N K U A
E W U N P Z H U R N R K
T H X D T M O X L R S E
G I Y E U B F R E Z T B
S S E R Q S V T A K F R
W T L Z P P T E N N Q U
I L L M M U M B L E D S
N E O S M N O P R E P H
G Y S Q P D O X M L P R
S L A P X L C H A R G E
```

1 lean **2** tap **3** rush **4** kneel **5** slap **6** swing **7** wander **8** mumble **9** whistle **10** sigh **11** whisper **12** yell

2 1 leant **2** tapped **3** whispered **4** muttered **5** whistling **6** swung **7** burst **8** sighed **9** mumbled **10** rushed **11** shaking **12** yelled

READING
1 1 B **2** D **3** A **4** C **5** A **6** B **7** A **8** C **9** D **10** C

2 Students should underline:
  1 (B) ... her English teacher found out about her work, and contacted a literary agent on her behalf.
  2 (D) I'd be surprised if it does as well ...
  3 (A) However, she now plans to have a go at science fiction.
  4 (C) She would write a chapter and pass it on to family and school friends to see if they liked it.
  5 (A) Maths was her strongest school subject from an early age ...
  6 (B) At that time, she had over a dozen tales at various stages of completion.
  7 (A) Christine toured over a hundred schools and libraries talking about her work, all the time dressed in the clothes of her leading character.
  8 (C) After a few years of starting stories that never got finished, Flavia Bujor decided it was time she completed something. So ... she decided to write a novel.
  9 (D) 'When people praise you as 'The Voice of Youth' it can be a difficult thing to live up to.'
  10 (C) ... something she hadn't thought possible.

3 1 interfere **2** agent **3** passion **4** live up to

Word profile

1 impatient **2** patiently **3** patience **4** patient **5** impatiently **6** impatience

GRAMMAR
1 1 b **2** a **3** h **4** f **5** d **6** g **7** c **8** e

2 1 had been waiting **2** didn't believe, had passed
  3 put on, picked up, left **4** had been training, were
  5 had only been sitting, came, asked
  6 had been running, began
  7 had already started, got **8** had never met, recognised
  9 had been writing, was, offered **10** had, had all sold

3 1 The teacher was talking when the fire alarm rang.
  2 Karen had been learning Spanish for two years when she went to live in Argentina.
  3 I left home, ran for the bus and arrived at school on time.
  4 When we got home, Mum had finished preparing dinner.

4 1 a **2** b **3** a **4** b

VOCABULARY
1 1 for some time **2** before long **3** the week before last
  4 for days on end **5** in no time
  a before long **b** in no time **c** the week before last
  d for weeks on end **e** for some time

2 1 in no time **2** before long **3** for some time
  4 the week before last **5** for days on end

WRITING
1 *Students' own answers*

2 Yes, it does.

3 Who had written it? Jim, classmate from old school
  What happened next? met outside library; Jim handed over new tennis racket
  How did you feel? surprised and happy

4 1 had never been **2** lost **3** hadn't spoken **4** got **5** left **6** was shining **7** was waiting **8** took

5 In fact, …   Once, …   So …   When …

6 *Students' own answers*

UNIT 8 A great place to live
VOCABULARY
1 Across
  3 welcoming **5** residential **6** remote **7** close **8** urban
Down
  1 industrial **2** relaxed **4** diverse **6** rural

2 1 rural **2** industrial **3** diverse **4** remote

3 1 residential **2** remote **3** diverse **4** welcoming **5** industrial
  6 relaxed, inner **7** close **8** urban, rural

READING
1/2 United Arab Emirates

3 1 A **2** C **3** B **4** E **5** D **6** F

4 1 to help the world towards a greener future **2** cooling
  3 from history / the past
  4 because they were too expensive
  5 (electric) car and train

5 1 constructing **2** estimated **3** limit **4** sought out **5** massive

Word profile

1 make a difference **2** make the most of **3** make use of
4 made their way **5** makes sense

GRAMMAR

1 1 a 2 b/c 3 c 4 a/b 5 b 6 a 7 c 8 a

2 1 's going to snow 2 'll answer 3 've finished
4 's about to / going to jump 5 might get, might get 6 departs

3 1 We will pick you up from the airport when <u>you arrive</u>.
2 I am sure <u>you'll find</u> lots of interesting things to do during your visit.
3 ✓
4 It's very nice that <u>you're coming / going to come</u> to London.
5 We will discuss it when you <u>come</u> home.
6 ✓

VOCABULARY

1 Yes, he's acting as if/though he's won the lottery.
2 It looks as if/though the bus is going to be late.
3 I feel as if/though I haven't slept for days.
4 She sounded as if/though she wasn't happy about something.
5 I felt as if/though I'd never been away.
6 No, but she's acting as if/though she knows us.

LISTENING

1 a game or sport 8
a geographical feature, place 3, 9
a task 4
an ability 6
a qualification 2
a type of media 10
a food item 5
a subject / topic 1, 7

2 a conservation project on which she was a volunteer
3 1 animals 2 (university) degree 3 the beach
4 washing up 5 favourite cereal 6 data collection
7 sea life 8 card games 9 park 10 diary

▶5 **Audioscript**

Hi, and thanks for inviting me here tonight to tell you about the time I spent as a volunteer on a conservation project in Madagascar. I was looking for something to do in the year before I went to university – what they call a 'gap year'. There were various possibilities, and I had a lot of interests: ecology, sports, computer programming – but it was my long-standing love of animals which led me to become a volunteer on this conservation project.

It was a great opportunity to learn more about the wildlife of that part of the world. Not just the obvious cuddly mammals, but also fish – even the reptiles were fascinating. All good background knowledge to prepare for my university degree, which I am currently halfway through.

The project involved taking surveys of both land animals and ocean creatures. For this reason, we were based in different camps, depending on the type of data we were collecting. Mine was next to the beach, but most people slept in another camp in the forest. Conditions were pretty basic – the beds were small, and there were four of us in each tent – but they weren't actually as bad as I thought they'd be.

I had to do camp duty once every two weeks or so, which I didn't mind so much because it kept me busy. It was interesting having to cook dinner for about 30 people! The washing up wasn't exactly fun, but you just took your turn like everyone else.

The food was actually pretty good; simple and fresh with a huge variety of seafood. Seriously, I ate some strange things. I still have no idea what they were! They have amazing chocolate there, too. The only thing I really would have liked for breakfast was my favourite cereal – I couldn't find it anywhere. But I got used to fruit and coffee every morning.

One of the things that made the experience so worthwhile was all the stuff I learnt. I learnt how to scuba dive; it's so great to get up close to marine wildlife. I'm currently finishing a project at university on birds and the practice I got in data collection during my time in Madagascar has definitely helped me with that. In fact, the whole thing kept my brain working, which is handy if you're taking a gap year from studying!

If you decide to go on something like this, I'd definitely advise you to take a decent camera. It was hard trying to get photos of birds as they'd fly away most of the time, and my camera didn't have a very good zoom lens. I only had a little 35 millimetre thing, but it was completely waterproof so, although I got some reasonable shots of lizards and monkeys, the best ones were of sea life. I've had some prints made.

We didn't get much spare time, but sometimes when the weather was bad we didn't do much because the wildlife would be hiding. A few of the volunteers were into playing chess, but I wasn't much good at that so I spent my spare time reading or taking part in card games with the others. On sunny days when we couldn't do surveys for one reason or another, we could sunbathe or go for a walk or a swim.

We got Saturdays off, and we got to go on trips to nearby places. I visited a local school, some nice villages, and of course the zoo in the capital. One town has a park where you can hold out bananas for monkeys and they'd jump on your shoulders to get them – another great experience.

Some of the volunteers kept video recordings of their time there; they said they were going to upload them, but I haven't seen any of them yet. Others updated their blogs. I kept a record the old fashioned way – every night I'd update my diary with the events of the day. I got some copies made and you can buy one for a pound after this talk if you're interested. I might get round to turning it into a website one day!

UNIT 9 Being positive

VOCABULARY

1 1 f 2 g 3 h/j 4 h/j 5 b 6 a/i/k 7 a/i/k 8 a/i/k 9 l
10 d/e 11 d/e 12 c

2 1 looks bright 2 achieve your goals
3 take every opportunity 4 went wrong
5 made the best of 6 make a difference 7 had a go
8 see the best in 9 has strengths and weaknesses
10 make the most of 11 put an end to 12 sees the worst in

READING

1 optimist
2 1 D 2 C
3 3 A 4 B 5 A 6 D
4 Students should underline:
3 I had expected to be given some intensive training for this sales role, but the only guidance I received followed immediately after the interview, lasting all of five minutes.
4 I was only halfway through the script ... After practising my script for ten more minutes ...
5 I was making a small fortune in bonuses!
6 I'll never get tired of the thrill I get when I make a successful sale. That feeling will stay with me until the day I finally retire – why would I ever stop doing something I love doing?

Word profile

1 e 2 f 3 a 4 d 5 b 6 c 7 g

GRAMMAR

1 1 you'll have spent 2 I'll be sleeping
 3 will have been going 4 I'll have finished
 5 she'll be working 6 will have been living
 7 we'll have travelled 8 he'll be studying
2 1 'll have been writing 2 wont' have finished
 3 'll have been 4 will have read 5 'll have been building
 6 will have cooked 7 'll have been waiting
 8 'll have arrived
3 1 I'll have finished my examinations in a couple of days and then I'm going to a small island.
 2 When the concert has finished you can interview the conductor of the orchestra.
 3 I will continue for four days and finish on Saturday.
 4 ✓

VOCABULARY

1

Nouns	
-ity	majority personality responsibility
-ment	encouragement enjoyment
-ship	friendship relationship
-tion	competition satisfaction

Adjectives	
-able	remarkable valuable
-al	beneficial emotional practical
-ive	active effective

2 1 emotional 2 encouragement 3 competition 4 valuable
 5 responsibility 6 majority 7 effective 8 enjoyment
 9 friendship / relationship 10 active

WRITING

1 *Students' own answers*
2 Yes. / *Students' own answers*
3 Suggested answers:
 B It might give information about the campus, or sports facilities.
 C It might give information about classrooms.
 D It might give information about accommodation for students.
4 1 B 2 A 3 D 4 C
5 1 D 2 B 3 A 4 C
6 1 cool, great, awesome, fantastic
 2 Wouldn't that be great? / I'd definitely go there. Would you?
7 *Students' own answers*

UNIT 10 Surprise!
VOCABULARY

1 1 by 2 in 3 out of 4 in 5 in 6 in 7 by 8 at 9 at
 10 out of
2 1 d 2 c 3 a 4 e 5 b 6 f
3 1 in touch by text (messaging)
 2 (on my screen) out of nowhere 3 a lot in common
 4 in detail tomorrow 5 at the gym by accident
4 *Students' own answers*

READING

1 *Students' own answers*
2 1 D 2 B 3 A 4 F 5 C 6 E
3 a
4 1 King Umberto was surprised to find the restaurant owner had been married to a woman with the same name as his wife.
 2 The restaurant owner died before King Umberto.
 3 Joseph Figlock was not injured by the baby.
 4 ✓
 5 John Alan Paulos is not surprised that coincidences happen.
5 1 survived 2 revealed 3 consider 4 absence

GRAMMAR

1 1 shouldn't 2 should have 3 didn't need to take 4 should
 5 needn't 6 would 7 needn't
 8 shouldn't have
2 1 shouldn't have eaten 2 should have remembered
 3 shouldn't have bought 4 should have studied
 5 shouldn't have played
3 1 should have asked, wouldn't have let, shouldn't have taken, needn't have worried
 2 shouldn't have eaten, should have told, would have cooked, didn't need to ask
 3 didn't need to go, wouldn't have been, needn't have attended
 4 shouldn't/needn't have spent, wouldn't have got, needn't have asked, would have employed
4 1 It would have been better to stay in bed.
 2 I wondered how it would have been without you.
 3 It would have been OK if he really wanted to understand.
 4 I shouldn't have done this, because I failed the test.
 5 ✓
 6 We had mountain bikes, so we thought that it would be a great idea to visit the forest.

VOCABULARY

1 1 d 2 g 3 a 4 f 5 c 6 e 7 b 8 h
2 1 angel 2 foggy 3 grilled 4 boiling 5 flooded 6 hit
 7 bright 8 froze

LISTENING

1 *Students' own answers*
2 1 A
3 Students should underline: *I certainly like doing it* and *There's a lot of work and a lot of worry involved.*
4 2 B 3 C 4 C 5 C 6 B

▶6 Audioscript

Interviewer: This evening in our series on Dream Jobs, our guest is Rob Mitchell, who is a professional party planner, someone who arranges big parties and celebrations for other people. Hi Rob.

Rob: Hi.

Int: Is your job as much fun as it sounds?

Rob: Well, I certainly like doing it – but that's not to say it's one big party. It's a business, obviously, and you have to please the client. Just because you're throwing a party doesn't mean it's party time for you. There's a lot of work and a lot of worry involved, and you really can't relax until the last guest has left, and the venue is cleaned up. But if you don't mind working long hours, then yes – it's a fun job, and even better if you enjoy the social aspects.

Int: How did you get into the party planning business?

Rob: My mum is an interior designer and my dad is an architect, and what I do is kind of related to that. But to be honest, I almost fell into the business by accident. I'd just finished an art degree and – like a lot of art graduates – I hadn't been very successful in finding a related job. Then a friend of mine invited me to an art event which was arranged by her brother's party planning company. I got talking to him and we found we had a lot in common, and I ended up being offered a job there and then. That was three years ago. I have my own events company now, of course.

Int: And a very successful one, too. You arrange events for a lot of celebrities, don't you? What's that like?

Rob: You might expect celebrities to be hard work, but in fact it's the non-celebrity clients that can give you the biggest headaches. The non-celebrities have the money, but not the fame, and they tend to try to knock my fees down. I find the famous ones are much more relaxed about things, and let me run with my own ideas. Some of them have become good friends, I'm happy to say.

Int: Have you had any strange requests for party themes?

Rob: Every party planner has their favourite story about unusual parties they've hosted. For me, it was when a client insisted that they wanted live monkeys to hand out gifts to the guests as they arrived.

Int: Monkeys? I don't believe it!

Rob: Yes, monkeys. I tried to talk them out of it: the expense alone was huge, and of course there were health and safety issues, but the clients didn't care how much they cost, and were insistent. On the day, it wasn't quite the disaster it could have been. The monkeys started throwing food around, and some of the guests complained – but at least nobody was injured!

Int: Ha ha! What advice would you give to anyone throwing a party?

Rob: No monkeys! But seriously – don't be afraid to be creative. It helps if your room is the right size – not too big, or the place will look empty; not too small or it will be too crowded. But above all, and this is true no matter where the party is, make sure you invite the right guests. They can make or break a party – with the right crowd you could have fun at a bus stop!

Int: What do you like most about your job?

Rob: The fact that when I go into the office in the morning, I never know for sure what the day is going to bring. Some days will be quiet, other days I'll have an email from a rock star wanting me to arrange a party with a budget of half a million pounds! Sure, it's nice to meet celebrities, and with big clients the money is always pretty good, but on a day to day basis, that's really what gets me out of bed in the morning. And something that I'm quite excited about is …

Word profile

1 1 unexpected **2** expected **3** expectations **4** unexpectedly
5 expecting **6** expect

UNIT 11   The family unit
VOCABULARY
1 Across
  4 down **5** off **8** let **9** hit **10** take
Down
  1 look **2** finish **3** count **6** fall **7** stick
2 1 stick together **2** look up to **3** take after **4** count on
  5 let (you) down **6** look down on **7** fall out **8** hit (it) off
  9 go off

READING
1

	noun	verb	adjective	adverb
1	accident	xxxx	accidental	accidentally
2	assistant/ assistance	assist	xxxx	xxxx
3	bravery	xxxx	brave	bravely
4	belief	believe	believable	believably
5	confidence	xxxx	confident	confidently
6	doubt	doubt	doubtful	doubtfully
7	practice	practise*	practical	practically
8	proof	prove	xxxx	xxxx

practise is the British English spelling of the verb. The US English spelling is *practice*.

2 1 adj, practical **2** n, assistance **3** adv, accidentally
  4 v, prove **5** adv, bravely **6** adj, doubtful
  7 n, confidence **8** v, believe
3 1 impolite **2** unlikely **3** disagree **4** incorrect **5** dishonest
  6 impossible **7** unhappy **8** misunderstand
4 1 unlikely **2** Scientists **3** findings **4** beneficial
  5 competition **6** ability **7** behaviour **8** observation

Word profile

1 b **2** c **3** b **4** a **5** c **6** a

GRAMMAR
1 1 none **2** that **3** none **4** that **5** none **6** none
2 1 who **2** which **3** (which) **4** who **5** (who) **6** which
3 2 a Moscow is the city which is famous for the Kremlin.
  3 a I'll never forget that time (when) we went to the seaside in the rain.
  4 d This is the house where my grandfather was born / (which) my grandfather was born in.
  5 f There aren't many taxi drivers who have never had an accident.
  6 c There's that boy whose father teaches at my college.
4 1 You are lucky because I've got the information that/which you need about the new art class.
  2 You will go to Protagona 7, which has a little supermarket.
  3 One morning we went to the beach, which was about 30 minutes from our campsite.
  4 Tina had dreamed of winning a ballet contest since she was five years old, which was when she started her lessons.
  5 It was a book by Shakespeare, so it is Shakespeare who is to blame, not me!

VOCABULARY
1 1 behaved **2** organised **3** tech **4** balanced **5** grown
  6 confident
2 1 well-built **2** long-distance **3** last-minute
  4 middle-aged **5** well-paid **6** short-term

WRITING

1

Adding a new point	Furthermore Moreover In addition
Comparing/ contrasting	whereas compared to/with In contrast On the one/other hand
Concluding	In my view On balance To sum up

2 Students' own answers

3 **1** In contrast   **2** On the one hand
  3 Furthermore/Moreover/In addition   **4** On the other hand
  5 In addition   **6** To sum up   **7** On balance

4 **1** Yes.
  2 friendship in later life, holidays
  3 Students' own answers

5/6 Students' own answers

UNIT 12   Making a difference

VOCABULARY

1 **1** d **2** c **3** g **4** e **5** b **6** h **7** f **8** a

2 **1** amused   **2** promote   **3** cheer (her) up   **4** stimulate
  5 persuade   **6** express   **7** congratulate
  8 inspires / inspired

3 Students' own answers

READING

1 Suggested answer:
  not very happy, embarrassed

2 **1** c **2** e **3** f **4** b **5** a

3 **1** lonely   **2** nervous but optimistic
  3 it gives him a sense of achievement
  4 he hopes nothing will change
  5 to put the focus on his actions   **6** warm

Word profile

1 **1** as a result of   **2** As a matter of fact
  3 as far as I'm concerned   **4** as far as I know   **5** as far as

GRAMMAR

1 **1** Flour is used to make bread.
  2 People under 15 are not allowed to watch this film.
  3 The power in this house is provided by sunlight.
  4 Portuguese is spoken in Brazil.
  5 I was bitten on the leg by the neighbour's cat.
  6 Everything will be arranged by my brother.
  7 You will be given instructions on arrival.
  8 More is being spent on smartphones than ever before.

2 **1** Dad had been moved to an office in a different town.
  2 I have often been described as shy.
  3 I was being shown into the building.
  4 'I've been given the job of making you feel welcome here.'
  5 I was really impressed by her kindness that day.

3 **1** I like to wear clothes which <u>are made from</u> cotton.
  2 My bicycle <u>was stolen</u> on the 10th of September.
  3 I have a lot of friends, but my best friend <u>is called</u> Maria.
  4 They eat special cakes which <u>are made</u> for the wedding.
  5 ✓
  6 The first restaurant <u>specialises</u> in seafood.

4 **1** having/getting, painted
  2 get, to look
  3 have/get, taken
  4 got, to cut
  5 have/get, cleaned
  6 had, taken out (*had* is better here – slightly more formal)
  7 had/got, delivered
  8 are having/getting, built

5 Suggested answers:
  I'd have all my food delivered.
  I'd get an assistant to check my texts.
  I'd get all my clothes made.
  I'd have fresh flowers delivered and arranged every day.
  I'd get someone to check my homework for me before I hand it in.

VOCABULARY

1 **1** You can have either a cake or a biscuit.
  2 I don't like either cats or dogs. / I like neither cats nor dogs.
  3 The film was both funny and frightening.
  4 Neither Maria nor Donna has any time.
  5 Either Greg or Dave is lying.
  6 He speaks neither French nor Spanish. / He doesn't speak either French or Spanish.

2 Students' own answers

LISTENING

1 main topic: 2, 6
  speaker's purpose: 5
  speaker's feeling: 1
  speaker's opinion: 4
  a detail in the situation: 3, 8
  a reason for something: 7

3/4 **1** A **2** C **3** B **4** B **5** A **6** B **7** A **8** C

▶**7 Audioscript**

1 *You hear a girl talking about her summer job.*
My parents couldn't afford to pay the full cost of my university fees, so I took a summer job in a clothes shop. I'd never worked in a shop before, but my parents were keen for me to earn some money even though they thought I'd probably get bored. They couldn't have been more wrong. There was a lot to learn, and I had to ask for a lot of help at the beginning. But I really wanted to do well, so I threw myself into it. They've asked me to come back next summer, and I'm thinking about it. I made a fair bit of money, too, which has come in very handy.

2 *You hear a radio announcement about a youth circus.*
Belleview Youth Circus has been giving daily shows in the Memorial Park all summer, entertaining young and old with their amazing acts. They have just celebrated their 10th anniversary and to mark the occasion they're taking a break from performing to invite would-be circus acts and anyone else interested to come and learn about the company. Circus manager Bill Mayhew will be explaining the history of the group, and several of the performers will also be there. So here's your chance to meet and chat with the professionals. Come along to the big tent at the Memorial Park at 7.30 – refreshments will be provided!

3 *You hear a girl talking about a cycle race she's just won.*
It was a great feeling, but we'd driven for four hours to get to it, and then I had classes the next day So almost as soon as I got my trophy we jumped in the car, I flopped down exhausted into the front seat and we started the journey back home. Of course, I was thrilled by the whole thing, winning was just amazing, but there was no opportunity to enjoy my success afterwards with friends, which was a shame. I had to be up early for school the next day!

4 *You hear a TV producer talking about his favourite TV show.*

Hmm ... I guess my favourite TV show would have to be *The Family*. It's a classic, in my opinion. The cast is amazing – the characters are so brilliantly developed and the actors seem to fit the parts so well, and the situations they get themselves into really are out of the ordinary. I'm just in awe of it. I can't wait for Friday evenings. I never miss an episode. I'm frequently in tears of laughter. You know, it's completely ridiculous, but at the same time very human. The relationships they have with each other – even when they're fighting the affection shines through.

5 *You hear a journalist talking about his early career.*

To be honest with you, I came to journalism by chance. That's not a career path I'd recommend, even if it were open to young people nowadays. Competition is fiercer now than ever before, and it's essential that you graduate with a good degree and a portfolio of work on student publications. For me, I got a summer job at my local newspaper – making tea and posting letters, mostly. I got on well with the editor, and when I left school I asked him about working on the paper– and he said why not? It seemed that I was good at it, which is just as well I suppose!

6 *You hear two friends talking about a school event.*

Boy: Are you coming to the school art show on Saturday, Jenny? I heard you were annoyed that your painting wasn't in the final selection, but it's up to the judges really, isn't it?

Girl: That didn't bother me, I was just a bit angry that I found out about it by chance. They should have told me personally.

Boy: Well yes, that was a mistake, human error, but apart from that, they've got things right. Anyway, look, I'd really like you to come along. It'll be fun!

Girl: Aren't you just worried you won't have enough people helping?

Boy: No, honestly, there's no problem with numbers. I just think you'd enjoy the event.

7 *You hear a young woman talking about rock-climbing.*

I love rock-climbing. I've done it since I was in my early teens, and now I try to go on a climb at least four times a year. I learnt on a course with a group of about twenty, but nowadays I climb alone. There's no feeling like it when you finally get to the top of a mountain and you stand there, looking at the view all around and thinking 'I made it!' You really have to dig deep sometimes – but you get a real sense of having beaten a mountain. The really hard bit is getting up and going to classes at college again the next day!

8 *You hear a girl telling a friend about a problem she has with her phone.*

Girl: This phone isn't working properly. Photos don't come through at all well.

Boy: Which one is it – the B72? Yes, I think there's a problem with that. The B90s are much better. Why don't you get one of those?

Girl: Well, I'd like one, but they're expensive, aren't they?

Boy: Yeah, but good value. It's your birthday soon – maybe you could ask your parents for one?

Girl: No, they think I spent too much on the B72. Perhaps I could take it back to the shop.

Boy: Well, yes. If it doesn't work, they should change it or repair it really.

Girl: Of course, that's it. I'll ask the man in the shop tomorrow.

UNIT 13   Leading the way

VOCABULARY

1

Noun	Adjective	Verb	Adverb
appreciation	adventurous	doubt	fairly
criticism	cautious	stand out	
doubt	motivated	target	
influence	strict		
target	sympathetic		

2 1 adventurous **2** target **3** fairly **4** influence **5** cautious **6** criticism **7** doubt **8** stand out **9** strict **10** motivated **11** sympathetic **12** appreciation

3 1 doubt **2** motivated **3** cautious **4** target **5** criticism **6** adventurous **7** appreciation **8** sympathetic

4 *Students' own answers*

READING

1 Students should underline:
  2 'I am a leadership realist,' explains Prof. Spicer. ... To take one example ...
  3 the right personality to join the military, ... this attitude
  4 different styles of leadership for different situations. ... So, for example, there is no point in being a 'friend' in a situation which requires a 'commander'.
  5 addressing the needs of the group
  6 the idea they can, and should, be important leaders. ... this

2 1 G **2** F **3** A **4** B **5** E **6** C

3 1 aware (of) **2** inspire **3** factor **4** essentially

Word profile

1 1 a **2** c **3** b **4** f **5** d **6** e

GRAMMAR

1 1 always being made to do
  2 of being offered
  3 must be handed in
  4 are generally thought to be
  5 was the first to be
  6 might not be allowed to

2 1 be rewarded **2** being given **3** to be punished
  4 being helped **5** to be told **6** being handed

3 1 It will save a lot of electricity as solar energy <u>will be</u> used.
  2 As <u>can be</u> seen, bikes are really very good: cheap, fast and healthy.
  3 ✓
  4 It will be <u>prepared</u> by our school cook.

VOCABULARY

1 1 set **2** keep **3** make **4** came **5** lived **6** Speak **7** turned

2 1 ... he made up the whole thing / made the whole thing up!
  2 It lived up to all my expectations.
  3 ... it is hard to keep up with him.
  4 The policeman came up to me ...
  5 You'll have to speak up ...
  6 ... they eventually turned up an hour late.

WRITING

1 Three

2 Yes

3 **1** motivated **2** strictly **3** clear **4** fluently **5** essential
6 regular **7** extremely **8** hard-working **9** enthusiastically
10 relevant

4 **a** 2 **b** 4 **c** 1 **d** 3

5 **1** Last but not least **2** For instance **3** Besides that
4 what's more

6 *Students' own answers*

UNIT 14 Getting there

VOCABULARY

1 **Across**
  4 cool **6** drive **8** out **9** keep **11** run
Down
  1 Slow **2** hold **3** break **5** make **7** into **8** over **10** pull

2 **1** pull up **2** break down **3** cool down **4** run over
  5 make out **6** keep up **7** pull over **8** pull into
  9 drive off **10** pull out of **11** slow down **12** hold up

3 **1** pull over **2** held up **3** make out **4** Slow down
  5 pulled up **6** run over **7** keep up **8** pulled into
  9 drove off **10** cool down **11** breaks down **12** pulling out

READING

1 b

2 **1** D **2** C **3** E **4** B **5** F **6** A **7** G

3 **1** environmental damage **2** tourists and residents nearby
  3 conservation projects and local communities
  4 communities with no experience of foreigners
  5 very difficult

4 **1** welfare **2** remote **3** waste **4** donations **5** interacting

GRAMMAR

1 **1** couldn't **2** is, 's tried **3** were going **4** is, is served
  5 hadn't been

2 **1** (that) he won't be going on holiday this year.
  2 (had) wanted to come/go to Kenya with them.
  3 (that) she has always supported the idea of responsible
    tourism.
  4 (that) she was organising a trip to Tibet.
  5 (that) he could arrange the whole thing for us.
  6 (that) 50 million tourist will be visiting Africa this year.

3 **1** a **2** a **3** b **4** a

4 **1** Air travel is going to get much more expensive.
  2 I enjoyed my holiday in Nepal very much.
  3 I've been trying to reduce my carbon footprint.
  4 The best holidays aren't always the most expensive.
  5 I'll never forget the week I spent in India.
  6 You'll never have a better opportunity to study abroad.

VOCABULARY

1 **1** h **2** b **3** a **4** g **5** c **6** d **7** e **8** f

2 **1** persuaded **2** pointed out **3** confessed **4** agreed
  5 insisted **6** enquire

LISTENING

1 Suggested answers:
  entertainers, cleaners, waiters and waitresses, photographers,
  office staff

2 Probably Speaker 2

3 Speaker 1 – D

4 Students should underline:
  A major part of my job is to mix with the guests, and everyone
  knows me by the end of the week.

5 Speaker 2 – E Speaker 3 – B Speaker 4 – G Speaker 5 – C
  A, F and H aren't needed.

▶8 Audioscript

1

I help with the entertainment in the resort, the nightly stage shows, daily talks, talent contests. I'm the person who makes sure that everything runs smoothly, whether this means finding extra bottles of water for the bands or helping a guest to choose a costume for the talent show. Every day is different – I never get bored! And I seldom get a moment to myself. A major part of my job is to mix with the guests, and everyone knows me by the end of the week. If I'm not actually making announcements on stage, I'm chatting or dancing in the audience. It's all part of what I do.

2

I play a lot of sport at school, which is why I'm working in the fitness centre at the resort. I explain the facilities to new arrivals and invite them to join one of our programmes. Not all of them take up the offer, of course – some just want to relax. I give tennis lessons to the kids, as well, which is good fun. And, as I hope to train as a sports instructor, it also means I'm getting useful experience for the future. Sometimes I wish I only worked during the day, but as the centre stays open until 11 at night, I stay late two or three times a week.

3

I work in the office, doing everything from taking phone bookings and answering emails to helping out with the resort brochure for the following year. Some days it's a bit dull, especially when there's no one else around to chat to. But at the same time, I'm lucky because I never have to work at the weekend or in the evenings, unlike most of the others who have summer jobs here. It's the first time I've ever had a real job, too. I have no idea at this point what career I'm going to end up with, but I guess this is all good experience!

4

I have a great job here – I'm a photographer. There are three of us, and we take photos of the guests in various places: at the swimming pool, in the gym, dancing at the parties, or just walking around. People usually love having their picture taken, and are quite willing to buy prints from us. By evening my memory card has hundreds of photos on it, so I have to transfer them to the computer and prepare them to display on the big screen in our office the next day. Some of the others get bored by that part of the job, but I like it as I'm keen on photography.

5

This is my second summer working as a waitress at the resort. I'm enjoying it much more this year, as it's less of a challenge. I know quite a few of the staff working here now and we're quite a sociable bunch of people, who see each other outside work. The hours are long, but they move us around the different restaurants from week to week, so there's plenty of variety. My favourite is the Japanese restaurant because I love the sushi there. We're able to eat whatever we like after the guests have left, and we get breakfast if we're working early, too.

Word profile

1 **1** in two **2** the record **3** an agreement **4** the law **5** heart
6 the ice **7** off

UNIT 15   The bigger picture

VOCABULARY

1

	Noun	Verb
1	ban	ban
2	collection	collect
3	cooperation	cooperate
4	criticism	criticise
5	election	elect
6	supporter/ support	support

2 **1** criticise **2** collect **3** elect **4** ban **5** cooperate **6** support
3 **1** collecting **2** supporters **3** is banned **4** election
5 cooperate **6** criticism

READING

1 c
2 **1** C **2** B **3** D **4** A **5** B **6** C **7** D **8** C
3 Suggested answers:
   1 …they are more concerned with their own lives.
   2 … smaller issues that affect them directly, often using social media to comment and express their thoughts.
   3 … they can express their support through 'likes' and 'retweets'.
   4 … it makes people less likely to donate financially.
4 **1** have an unfortunate effect on **2** contribute **3** declare
4 generate

Word profile

1 f **2** b **3** e **4** c **5** a **6** d

GRAMMAR

1 **1** must have trained **2** can't be **3** could/might/may snow
4 must be **5** must have hurt **6** can't have waited
7 must have been **8** can't have seen, must have been
2 **1** might not have known about the party.
   2 could have forgotten to tell you about it.
   3 can't be your bag.
   4 may have met when they were on holiday.
   5 must have seen this film before.
   6 might have missed the early train.
   7 can't have been the first time he has played tennis.
   8 might still be in class.
3 **1** ✓
   2 It <u>might</u> go wrong, but it <u>might</u> go right too, and if it does it was worth the effort.
   3 We wouldn't be able to do 80 km on Saturday because in the mountains it is very difficult and we <u>could</u> get lost.
   4 ✓
   5 Obviously, it's wonderful to go to a zoo and see the animals from different countries all together, but it <u>can't</u> be very nice to be disturbed all day and to have no freedom.
   6 There are great views throughout the ride, and there's an astonishing castle and also a butterfly farm that <u>might</u> turn out to be very interesting.

VOCABULARY

1 **1** general **2** progress **3** secret **4** turn **5** all **6** public
2 **1** in public **2** in progress **3** in turn **4** in general
5 in all **6** in secret

WRITING

1 **1** a recent film
   2 on a website
   3 readers of the website all over the world
   4 what the film was about, its good points, its bad points, and whether you'd recommend it
2 positive
3 C   B   D   A
4 Yes
5 The phrases should appear in this order: highly original, really hilarious, quite witty, absolutely determined, totally crazy
6 *Students' own answers*

UNIT 16   New and improved!

VOCABULARY

1 **1** b **2** d **3** e **4** a **5** h **6** c **7** g **8** f
2 **1** sponsor **2** logo **3** aimed at **4** commercial breaks
5 samples **6** launched
3 **1** logo **2** sample **3** on offer **4** consumers **5** sponsor
6 launching, aimed at
4 *Students' own answers*

READING

1/2 *Students' own answers*
3 generally positive
4 **1** b **2** e **3** c **4** a **5** d
5 **1** Marketing is about finding information to inform the making of products; advertising is about selling them.
   2 No, because you have to have selling in your soul.
   3 You have to work hard, the hours are long and there's a lot of competition for jobs.
   4 You need to have talent and a little luck.
   5 Because it's illegal to make false statements and there are severe penalties for doing so.

Word profile

1 need, b **2** good, d **3** matter, a **4** wonder, c

GRAMMAR

1 **1** hear **2** watch **3** 'll save **4** formed **5** melts **6** won
7 'll have **8** hadn't played **9** banned **10** 'd have made
2 **1** … I hadn't loved the campaign, I wouldn't have bought the product.
   2 … the skirt had been on offer, she would have bought it.
   3 … have watched the film if I hadn't read a great review.
   4 … have sponsored you if you had asked me.
   5 … she hadn't asked all the right questions, she wouldn't have got the job.
   6 … have sold their products if they had advertised.
   7 … I hadn't needed to go shopping, I'd have gone to the library.
   8 … have met you at the cinema if we'd known you were going.
3 **1** You can go to the beach if the weather <u>is</u> good.
   2 ✓
   3 I would be very pleased if you came and <u>visited</u> me.
   4 Probably, if nothing <u>had happened</u>, I would have lost anyway.

VOCABULARY

1 1 conveniently 2 finely 3 warmly 4 nicely 5 naturally
6 well 7 automatically 8 actively

2 1 scientifically proven 2 automatically updated
3 globally recognised 4 ecologically sound
5 financially independent 6 incredibly economical
7 constantly updated

LISTENING

1 *Students' own answers*

2 Students should underline:
2 enjoy most about her work 3 does not enjoy her job
4 use a computer 5 gets her ideas
6 look for in a new employee 7 spare-time activity

3 1 A

4 Students should underline:
I had a low opinion of the advertising industry at that time – you know, it's the business of lying to people to persuade them to buy things they don't need.

5 for B: I'd just graduated with a degree in psychology
for C: there aren't that many opportunities around in that field

6 2 C 3 B 4 A 5 B 6 A 7 B

▶9 **Audioscript**

Interviewer: Today in our series on careers, we're talking to Tina Jakes, who works in advertising. Good morning Tina.

Tina: Good morning.

Int: So, Tina, how did you get started in your career in advertising?

Tina: By chance, really. Um I'd just graduated with a degree in psychology. As you can imagine, there aren't that many opportunities available in that field. And to be honest, I had a low opinion of the advertising industry at that time – you know: it's the business of lying to people to persuade them to buy things they don't need. But a friend of mine told me about a job available at the agency he was working at. I needed the money, so I applied – and soon grew to love it.

Int: What do you like most about your job?

Tina: We work with an interesting bunch of people – some of them very talented – so there's never a dull moment. And I appreciate the chance to be creative. But I suppose the main thing for me is just taking part in the process that makes a business become a success. You know, when a campaign goes well you get a real sense of achievement, that you've made a difference to your client.

Int: Are there any down sides?

Tina: Some people think it's a bit intense. I often take my work home with me – it's expected, especially if there's a deadline coming up. But I really don't mind that. Occasionally you'll get a difficult client who doesn't really know what they want from a campaign, you know, they have nothing to offer, and expect you do to it all. That can be annoying sometimes. I appreciate working for someone who knows what they want!

Int: Are computer skills important in your job?

Tina: Well, I use a computer quite a lot, but not as much as some others in my office. When I have to make a presentation, I usually pull a few images off the internet, or go out and take some digital photos which I'll download and edit. But then I transfer everything onto paper for the final stages, and that's what I show to the client and bosses. I don't use the computer or projector for that – I'm a bit old-fashioned that way. Nobody seems to mind, as long as the ideas are good.

Int: How do you come up with ideas for campaigns?

Tina: Everyone you talk to will give you a different answer to that question. I have colleagues that spend a lot of time on the internet, which is an amazing source of inspiration. Others like to get together and bounce ideas off each other until something comes up. I prefer to concentrate on my own; have a good look at exactly what the aims of the campaign are. And usually there's a clue there as to what direction you should take. I always come up with something eventually, and it's generally well received, I'm happy to say.

Int: You are involved in employing new people for the company. What sort of things do you look for in a candidate?

Tina: We employ a lot of people from a lot of different backgrounds at our agency. This summer we took on graduates in English, history, business – and even physics! The industry is very people-focused so, while we do value things like IT skills, maths and English, we're really looking for team workers. They need to be able to work well in a social environment, and to deal diplomatically with awkward clients occasionally.

Int: And what do you do when you're not working on a campaign, Tina. How do you get away from it all?

Tina: Sometimes it's really hard to switch off, but the thing that works best for me is music. I play the saxophone in a five-piece jazz band most weekends. We get paid very little, but we don't do it for the money. As well as helping me forget the office, I think it actually helps me to recharge, and go back in on Monday with fresh ideas. To me, it's really valuable, professionally.

UNIT 17 Making headlines

VOCABULARY

1 1 c/g 2 c/g 3 i 4 a 5 b 6 h 7 d 8 e 9 f

2 1 amused 2 reviews 3 comment 4 celebrate 5 date
6 gossip 7 make 8 highlight

3 *Students' own answers*

READING

1 Suggested answers:
Good journalists are curious; they have to be honest; they have to be accurate.

2 1 C 2 E 3 A 4 B 5 E 6 C 7 D 8 A 9 B 10 D

3 Students should underline:
1 (C) Using fewer words is often more powerful ...
2 (E) Trying different things lets you find out what you're good at and discover how different topics are covered.
3 (A) The most important thing I'm doing for my career is connecting with suitable people. ... If you don't find the right group to work with, you'll never be happy.
4 (B) ... say 'yes' to everything. Every job, however dull, gives you the chance to meet people.
5 (E) ... don't be afraid to say you don't understand. ... Better to ask a question at the time than feel foolish in print later on.
6 (C) Good journalism is all about honesty, even if it means being honest about being wrong.
7 (D) The most important thing I did for my career was to get relevant work experience at the start ... on your CV it shows you were interested and determined enough to get yourself there.
8 (A) It leaves the reader in a better or worse place than she or she started, but never in the same place.
9 (B) Triple check sources and tips, and make sure you're always 100% sure before you hit the 'submit' button.
10 (D) Be informed: read news, watch news, and don't just limit yourself to the ones you agree with.

4 1 compromise 2 commitment 3 meaningful 4 relevant
5 foolish

Word profile

1 1 back 2 out of 3 from 4 up to

GRAMMAR

1 1 c 2 e 3 b 4 h 5 f 6 a 7 g 8 d

2 1 If he had brought his mobile phone, he could call for help.

  2 I could have applied for the teaching job if I had a degree.

  3 would have come to the cinema with us if she enjoyed horror films.

  4 If we hadn't lost the match, we wouldn't be unhappy now.

  5 John might be married now if he had met the right person.

  6 If I was/were good at cooking, I would/might have become a chef.

  7 They would have gone on holiday in the summer if they didn't have a new baby.

  8 You would/might have some pocket money left if you hadn't broken the living room window.

3 1 I thought if I had failed, I <u>couldn't</u> show my face to my family.

  2 I think that our way of life would be very different if the telephone <u>hadn't been</u> invented.

  3 ✓ (Could also be if I asked my parents first – depending on whether the person had or not)

  4 I'd <u>really like to know</u> what would have happened if you hadn't been there.

  5 ✓

VOCABULARY

1 1 c 2 f 3 a 4 d 5 g 6 h 7 e 8 b

2 1 getting (ideas) across 2 clear up 3 followed up 4 backed (me) up 5 looks into 6 left out 7 catch up on 8 brought up

WRITING

1 1 D 2 C 3 A 4 B

2 1 However 2 once 3 now 4 Provided 5 considering

3 a

4 Paragraph 1: introduces the topic, refers back to the title

Paragraph 2: reacts to the idea in the title, gives details of arguments for

Paragraph 3: presents the other side of the argument, gives details of arguments against

Paragraph 4: summarises the two sides, possibly with a personal opinion

5/6 *Students' own answers*

UNIT 18   Start-up
VOCABULARY

1 1 being your own boss 2 creative

  3 flexible working hours 4 manual work

  5 opportunities for foreign travel 6 personally rewarding

  7 professional job 8 take time off 9 well-paid

  10 working shifts

2 1 manual work 2 being my own boss

  3 flexible working hours 4 well paid

  5 personally rewarding 6 opportunities for foreign travel

  7 working shifts 8 professional job 9 take time off

  10 creative

3 1 personally rewarding 2 being your own boss

  3 flexible working hours 4 opportunities for foreign travel

  5 manual work 6 creative

READING

1 *Students' own answers*

2 b

3 1 D 2 A 3 E 4 C 5 F 6 B

4 1 internships/work experience 2 youth camps

  3 office work 4 festivals 5 manual work 6 shop work

Word profile

1 a 2 c 3 d 4 b 5 e

GRAMMAR

1 1 writing 2 forgetting 3 using 4 correct 5 studying

  6 planning 7 correct 8 being

2 1 working 2 Applying 3 playing 4 trying 5 arriving

  6 watching 7 moving 8 feeling 9 Waiting 10 doing

3 *Students' own answers*

4 1 I <u>am writing</u> this letter to say thank you for your hospitality.

  2 ✓

  3 I don't mind <u>working</u> hard and I feel good when I use my time efficiently.

  4 I would prefer <u>to work</u> with animals instead of helping in an office.

VOCABULARY

1 1 more or less / more and more 2 round and round

  3 more and more / more or less 4 sooner or later

  5 now and then 6 one or two 7 up and down

  8 over and over

2 1 now and then 2 more or less 3 more and more

  4 up and down 5 sooner or later 6 one or two

  7 over and over 8 round and round

LISTENING

1 her job at a travel company

2		
an event	7	
a job	2, 9	
a topic	5	
a kind of text	6	
a subject of study	1	
a personal quality	10	
a person/organisation	3, 8	
a number	4	

3		
number	4	
singular noun	2, 3, 7, 9	
plural noun	6, 8	
uncountable noun	1, 5, 10	

4 1 French 2 youth leader 3 (best) friend 4 three

  5 green tourism 6 news reports 7 conference 8 charities

  9 presenter 10 determination

▶10 Audioscript

Good evening, and thank you for asking me to talk to you about my job at the travel and tourism website, HappyPlanetdotnet.

What's important for my work? Well, I think it helps that I speak several languages. I've recently learned Portuguese and my degree at university was in Spanish and French. I've always loved travelling, and I was very fortunate to be able to do a lot of it while I was a student. But I think it was my experience in journalism that actually got me the job at Happy Planet. I wrote a regular column for the college newspaper.

When I left university I worked as a teacher of English in Spain for a year, followed by a nine-month contract as a youth leader on a camp in Portugal. After such a long time abroad I began to feel homesick, so I went back to London and started to look for a full-time job.

My dad has been in journalism for most of his life – and he was very supportive – but it was my best friend who told me that HappyPlanet were looking for an assistant. Not exactly the most glamorous job in the world, but as an entry point into the world of travel writing it was ideal. I applied, was accepted, and started the following week.

It was pretty dull stuff – lots of paperwork, dealing with email enquiries – that sort of thing. Then the director's assistant left after working there for only six months, and I applied for her position. The company likes to recruit internally if they can and sure enough, after only three months in my first job, I was promoted.

That's when life really started to get interesting. My boss is quite a high-flyer in the travel industry. He's got a weekly TV show about holiday destinations, and does a regular weekly column on green tourism in a Sunday newspaper. So I was accompanying him around TV studios, making sure he knew his deadlines, and dealing with his travel arrangements for the first year of that job – quite exciting, really.

He's a real inspiration to work for. It was my boss who encouraged me to start writing up news reports for the website, which went down very well with other managers and led to me becoming one of the main writers for the company. Now I get sent to all sorts of destinations around the world!

But it's not just one holiday after another, although it might sound like it. You have to constantly be assessing your travel experience, and translating it into words, which can spoil a week on a beautiful island! I actually look forward to assignments that I don't have to write about, like attending trade fairs and exhibitions – I was in New York last month at a conference, for example, which I really enjoyed. I still do my assistant's duties for my boss when I'm not out and about. That consists mainly of doing interviews with other journalists, or responding to requests from various charities. HappyPlanet is a generous company, and we generally do make a donation. That's quite satisfying.

But that's not the end of my story. The company is expanding its media outlets and soon won't be restricted to written reviews on the website. We're also producing internet video content now, and my boss has encouraged me to have a go at being a presenter – something which I'm very keen to do. It's a new direction for me, and I'm very excited.

So, what advice would I give to anyone wanting to get into the travel writing business? Obviously, not everyone can follow the same path – some might start at journalism school, others might start with their own blogs and move on from there. But I'd say the most important thing is to have determination. There's a lot of competition for posts and the obvious attractions make it hard to break into. There's no room in it for the half-hearted – so if you want it, you've got to really go for it!

UNIT 19   Points of view

VOCABULARY

1 1 b **2** f **3** k **4** c **5** g **6** d **7** l **8** a **9** e **10** i
11 h **12** j
2 1 convinced **2** to my mind **3** isn't (totally) against **4** view on
5 go along with **6** is no doubt **7** As far as I'm **8** in favour

Word profile

1 two **2** bear **3** put **4** have **5** crossed **6** to

READING

1 1 C **2** A **3** C **4** B **5** A **6** D
2 1 approach **2** temptation **3** characteristic **4** individual
5 the latter

GRAMMAR

1 1 have asked **2** is **3** are **4** contributes / is contributing
5 understands **6** is **7** plans / plan / is planning / are planning
8 is **9** is taking **10** look
2 1 has **2** have **3** has **4** are **5** frightens **6** isn't/aren't
7 hasn't/haven't **8** arrives
3 1 I do not have <u>much</u> news to tell you.
2 The food at both of the <u>restaurants is</u> different.
3 ✓
4 If you visit some friends everybody <u>has</u> a computer at home.

VOCABULARY

1 1 lyrics **2** belongings **3** surroundings **4** contents
5 graphics **6** refreshments **7** savings
Word down: clothes
2 1 graphics **2** refreshments **3** lyrics **4** contents
5 surroundings **6** clothes **7** belongings **8** savings

WRITING

1 1 on an international students' website
2 students all over the world
3 informal
2 No, he/she doesn't say who it's aimed at.
3 (Students should include a couple from these)
1 you're, you've, there's, can't, don't, isn't, you're
2 … when you build the car of your dreams!, I still can't do better than third place on Track 10!, Keep an eye out for it!
3 came out, lets … down, be into something
4 loads of, if you're into, keep an eye out
4 1 C b **2** A a **3** B a **4** D a

UNIT 20   Speak up

VOCABULARY

1 1 c/f **2** c/f **3** g **4** d/h **5** d/h **6** e **7** b **8** a
2 1 being a pain **2** was a piece of cake **3** crossed my mind
4 break the ice **5** has an eye for **6** breaks my heart
7 took my/our breath away **8** 've lost track of
3 1 broke my heart **2** was a piece of cake
3 it ever crossed your mind **4** took my breath away
5 to break/of breaking the ice

READING

1 b
2 1 G **2** B **3** D **4** C **5** F **6** A
3 1 had varying success **2** it lacks cultural depth
3 caused social problems
4 it has achieved a lot in a short time
4 1 gather **2** curriculum **3** resisted **4** promoted **5** literary

Word profile

1 b **2** a **3** c

GRAMMAR

1 1 the, – 2 –, the, the 3 –, an 4 the, a, the 5 an, the
6 a, a 7 The, a 8 a, –, –

2 1 Plenty of 2 a bit of 3 number 4 many
5 amount, little 6 a lot of 7 Several 8 a few 9 a lot of
10 Some

3 1 little 2 few 3 a few 4 a little 5 few 6 little
7 a little 8 a few

4 1 I hope you will have <u>great fun/a lot of fun</u>.
2 Can you imagine <u>a</u> school where you can study only the subjects you enjoy?
3 ✓
4 However, not <u>many</u> people like to read a book.
5 I was really happy to spend <u>a</u> few days with you.

VOCABULARY

1 1 a 2 c 3 c 4 b 5 a 6 a 7 c 8 b 9 c 10 a 11 c
12 b

2 *Students' own answers*

LISTENING

2 A

3 Students should underline: Oh, I wouldn't have missed it for the world.

4 1 b 2 f 3 d 4 c 5 h 6 e 7 a 8 g

5 2 B 3 A 4 B 5 C 6 A 7 C 8 B

▶ 11 **Audioscript**

1 *You hear two people talking about a rugby match they've just seen.*

Girl: So, what did you think of your first rugby match? Impressed?

Boy: It was a bit confusing, actually. I still don't understand the rules.

Girl: So you didn't enjoy it? That's a shame.

Boy: Oh, I wouldn't have missed it for the world! I just didn't follow what was going on, that's all. But the players are obviously very good at what they do.

Girl: So, would you come again?

Boy: Yes, but I'll be sure to eat before we go next time. I was starving for most of the game. It was hard to concentrate.

Girl: OK, next time we'll have lunch at the clubhouse restaurant. It's very good.

2 *You overhear two friends talking about a new cafe.*

Girl: Sue was right. It's a great place. It was definitely worth a visit, wasn't it?

Boy: Yeah, the coffee was top quality, they used fresh bread for the sandwiches and the staff were really friendly!

Girl: Good value, too, I must say.

Boy: Indeed. You don't often get much change out of ten pounds from a place like that, do you?

Girl: No. It seemed like a nice crowd there, too, didn't it?

Boy: Mmm – it was a bit noisy though. I didn't like having to raise my voice to be heard.

Girl: Well, I didn't mind that.

3 *You hear a girl talking about a jacket she bought online.*

Girl: Well, that's definitely the last time I'm buying anything from that online store. I needed a new jacket for my holiday next week, and I saw what looked like the perfect one for me. So I ordered it, medium size, and paid extra for next day delivery. Their prices are pretty reasonable, I'll give them that, and it arrived when they said it would. But when I tried it on, the sleeves came down to my fingertips. Now I've sent it back and I have to wait another two days for the right one – it had better get here on time!

4 *You hear a dancer talking about his life and work.*

Man: I'd always been fascinated with movement, as far back as I can remember. My mother was a dance teacher – she owned her own school, in fact – but she never made it in the theatre and that was something she always regretted, I think. She used to take me to lots of shows, both classical and modern. I was hooked on both forms from a very early age. Of course, my mother's name opened a lot of doors for me when it came to getting parts, but I like to think my talent and enthusiasm has contributed more to my success.

5 *You hear two friends talking about going on holiday.*

Boy: So, Jen. Have you decided whether you're coming to France with my family next month? It won't cost you much.

Girl: Oh, I don't know, Tom. It's very generous of your parents and money's not a problem, but two weeks is a long time to be away from the drama club.

Boy: You said the director of the play thinks you're great, so you can't be worried about that.

Girl: No, it's not that. I don't think she'd mind either. I'm just not sure what they'll do without me. We all need to practise, and I don't think they'll be able to do it very well while I'm away.

Boy: Jen, let go sometimes!

6 *You hear an interview with a young businessman.*

Woman: Have you always wanted to get into this business?

Man: No, not really. It kind of grew naturally from what I used to do as a hobby – which was racing motorbikes.

Woman: How long have you been in business?

Man: About five years. Dad helped me buy the garage first, then we got the bikes to rent out. It's a holiday resort, and we do quite well.

Woman: What do you have to spend money on now?

Man: Well, there's the repair and maintenance costs – they're quite high. And we pay for advertising space in the local and national press in the summer, but that's worth every penny.

7 *You overhear a boy telling a friend about his summer job at a sports camp for kids.*

Girl: So, you survived your first week as a sports coach. How was it?

Boy: Nothing like I expected. I mean, I knew it'd be exhausting, but I was amazed how quickly the week passed. It was over in a flash!

Girl: What were the kids like?

Boy: Fine. I mean, not half as bad as I'd been led to expect. I'd been warned to stamp on any disruptive behaviour, but I didn't come up against any of that. I guess I was quite strict from the start. I wasn't sure how they'd take that – but fortunately, they all did as they were told, so I just got on with it!

8 *You hear a review of a TV documentary which is based on a book.*

Woman: Having read Mr Horgan's book on the natural history of South Africa, I was really looking forward to the documentary based on it. Now that part one has been broadcast, I can report that it's as good as I'd hoped. In fact, in many ways it's an improvement on the written format because the rich possibilities of sight and sound really bring the work to life. The book was full of information, and the TV show seems to have lost some of that in favour of entertainment, but it's no worse for that. Give it a go – you won't be disappointed.

Video extra

Unit	Title	Duration
Unit 1	Creative minds	00:52
Unit 2	Fashion	01:16
Unit 7	Stories	01:10
Unit 8	Where we live	01:44
Unit 10	Surprises!	01:37
Unit 11	Families	01:07
Unit 14	Travelling	01:34
Unit 15	The big picture	01:13
Unit 17	The news	00:56
Unit 18	Jobs	01:17

SPEAKING TESTS

Speaking Test 1	Duration
Part 1	01:55
Part 2	04:13
Part 3	03:52
Part 4	03:05

Speaking Test 2	Duration
Part 1	01:59
Part 2	04:32
Part 3	04:06
Part 4	04:11

Acknowledgements

Development of this publication has made use of the Cambridge English Corpus, a multi-billion word collection of spoken and written English. It includes the Cambridge Learner Corpus, a unique collection of candidate exam answers. Cambridge University Press has built up the Cambridge English Corpus to provide evidence about language use that helps to produce better language teaching materials.

This product is informed by English Profile, a Council of Europe-endorsed research programme that is providing detailed information about the language that learners of English know and use at each level of the Common European Framework of Reference (CEFR). For more information, please visit www. englishprofile.org

The publishers are grateful to the following contributors: text design and layouts: emc design Ltd; cover design: Andrew Ward; edited by Hazel Bosworth, Jane Coates and Edward Street.